Bristol Studies in I:

This series provides a platform for theoretically innovative scholarship that advances our understanding of the world and formulates new visions of, and solutions for, world politics.

Guided by an open mind about what innovation entails, and against the backdrop of various intellectual turns, interrogations of established paradigms, and a world facing complex political challenges, books in the series provoke and deepen theoretical conversations in the field of International Relations.

Also available

Broken Solidarities
How Open Global Governance Divides and Rules
By **Felix Anderl**

Care and the Pluriverse
Rethinking Global Ethics
By **Maggie FitzGerald**

Praxis as a Perspective on International Politics
Edited by **Gunther Hellmann** and **Jens Steffek**

The Civil Condition in World Politics
Beyond Tragedy and Utopianism
Edited by **Vassilios Paipais**

Snapshots from Home
Mind, Action and Strategy in an Uncertain World
By **Karin M. Fierke**

Find out more

bristoluniversitypress.co.uk/
bristol-studies-in-international-theory

Also available

What in the World?
Understanding Global Social Change
Edited by **Mathias Albert** and **Tobias Werron**

The Idea of Civilization and the Making of the Global Order
By **Andrew Linklater**

International advisory board

Find out more

bristoluniversitypress.co.uk/
bristol-studies-in-international-theory

INTERNATIONAL THEORY AT THE MARGINS

Neglected Essays, Recurring Themes

Nicholas Greenwood Onuf

BRISTOL
UNIVERSITY
PRESS

First published in Great Britain in 2024 by

Bristol University Press
University of Bristol
1-9 Old Park Hill
Bristol
BS2 8BB
UK
t: +44 (0)117 374 6645
e: bup-info@bristol.ac.uk

Details of international sales and distribution partners are available at bristoluniversitypress.co.uk

© Bristol University Press 2024

British Library Cataloguing in Publication Data
A catalogue record for this book is available from the British Library

ISBN 978-1-5292-2981-3 hardcover
ISBN 978-1-5292-2982-0 paperback
ISBN 978-1-5292-2983-7 ePub
ISBN 978-1-5292-2984-4 ePdf

Cover design: blu inc, Bristol
Front cover image: Alamy/Tamara Kulikova

Bristol University Press uses environmentally responsible print partners.

For Sandra—again, always

Contents

Acknowledgements

I am grateful to Will Bain, Jens Bartelson, Kurt Burch, Charlotte Epstein, Andreas Gofas, Harry Gould, Inanna Hamati-Ataya, Patrick Jackson, Pat James, Frank Klink, Paul Kowert, Jorg Kustermans, Victor Coutinho Lage, Hannes Peltonen, Nik Rajkovic, Chris Rossi and Jens Steffek for comments and encouragement on the Introduction and the project as a whole. As editors of Bristol Studies in International Theory, Felix Berenskoetter, Neta Crawford and Stefano Guzzini made a number of helpful suggestions, and so did three referees for the Press. I am also grateful to Zoë Forbes and Kelly Winter for their attention to so many details in the publication process, to Carolyn Fox for painstaking copy-editing, and to Stephen Wenham, the Press's Publisher and Deputy Editorial Director, for his interest and support.

Copyright acknowledgements

(Routledge, 2008), pp. 25–38. © Nicholas Onuf. Reproduced by permission of Taylor & Francis Group.

- 'The ambiguous modernism of Seyla Benhabib', *Journal of International Political Theory* 5, 2 (2009), pp. 125–37. SAGE Publishing granted permission to republish.
- 'Relative strangers: Reflections on hospitality, social distance, and diplomacy', in Gideon Baker, ed., *On Hospitality and World Politics* (Palgrave Macmillan, 2013), pp. 173–96. © Nicholas Onuf. Reproduced with permission of the Springer Nature BV through PLSclear.
- 'Many worlds, many theories, many rules: Formulating an ethical system for the world to come', *Revista Brasileira de Política Internacional* 59, 2 (2016), published online. The Editor-in-Chief has granted permission to reprint.
- 'Writing large: Habit, skill and grandiose theory', in Heidi H. Hobbs, ed., *Pondering Postinternationalism: A Paradigm for the 21st Century?* (State University of New York Press, 2000), pp. 99–115. The Press confirmed that formal permission is not needed.
- 'International/Intertextual Relations (1989), in "The nines: International Relations classics reappraised"', *Tidsskriftet Politik* 12, 4 (2009), pp. 48–54. Permission to reprint granted by the Department of Political Science, University of Copenhagen.
- 'World-making, state-building', in Nicolas Lemay-Hébert, Nicholas Onuf, Vojin Rakić and Petar Bojanić, eds, *The Semantics of State-Building* (Routledge, 2014), pp. 19–36. © Nicholas Onuf. Reproduced by permission of Taylor & Francis Group.
- 'What we do: IR as craft', in Andreas Gofas, Inanna Hamati-Ataya and Nicholas Onuf, eds, *SAGE Handbook of the History, Philosophy and Sociology of International Relations* (SAGE Publications, 2018), pp. 513–25. SAGE Publishing granted permission to republish.
- 'The dinosaur speaks!' in Mariano Bertucci, Jarrod Hayes and Patrick James, eds, *Constructivism Reconsidered: Past, Present and Future* (University of Michigan Press, 2018), pp. xiii–xix. © Nicholas Onuf. Republished with permission from the Press's Director.

Introduction

Ce texte-ci peut-il devenir la marge d'une marge? / Can this text
become the margin of a margin?

—Jacques Derrida[1]

In 1960, Martin Wight published a learned essay provocatively entitled 'Why
is there no international theory'?[2] 1960 was also the year I began my studies
of international relations and took adolescent delight in Hans Morgenthau's
realist theory of international politics.[3] Wight was spared the need to indicate
what assumptions international theory might be predicated upon, what it
would or could be about, what form (or forms) it might take, what value
it might have. One might suspect, as I did when I read Wight's essay a few
years later,[4] that he was rejecting the onslaught of realist theory from across
the Atlantic and, even more, claims on behalf of a science of international
politics, but that he was doing so indirectly, with characteristic English
circumspection and perhaps a whiff of snobbery.

What Wight *did* say about international theory bears recalling: political
theory, international law, and diplomatic history leave no space for
'speculation about the society of states, or the family or nations, or the
international community' and, by implication, obviate any need for it.[5]
I would say instead:

- As informed speculation, international theory long flourished at the
margins of political theory, international law and diplomatic history.

---

[1] Jacques Derrida, *Marges de la philosophie* (Paris: Les Éditions de Minuit, 1972), p. xix;
Jacques Derrida, *Margins of Philosophy*, trans. Alan Bass (Chicago: University of Chicago
Press, 1982), p. xxiii.

[2] Martin Wight, 'Why is there no international theory?', *International Relations* 2, 1 (1960),
pp. 35–48.

[3] Hans J. Morgenthau, *Politics among Nations: The Struggle for Power and Peace*, 3rd edn
(New York: Alfred Knopf, 1960).

[4] Reprinted in Herbert Butterfield and Martin Wight, eds, *Diplomatic Investigations: Essays in the
Theory of International Politics* (Cambridge, MA: Harvard University Press, 1968), pp. 17–34.

[5] Ibid., p. 18.

- Elevated to paradigms, liberalism and realism persist on the margins of law and history.
- A loose confederation of critical, feminist, constructivist, poststructuralist and postcolonial scholars has migrated from the margins of liberalism and realism to the margins of social and political theory, which already occupy the margins of philosophy.
- The prestige of science and the demands of the scientific method position quite a few students of international relations in the margins of economics and the so-called natural sciences.
- A great many people discuss policy issues, global developments, regional concerns, and preferred futures with little concern for fields of study and their theories.

In short, there is no theory to orient the study of international relations; 'the international' is a sentimental allusion to an undisciplined subject matter. There is, however, an abundance of theorizing at the margins. Theories are linked propositions about the world and its workings; theorizing is linguistically mediated activity falling somewhere, *anywhere*, between informed speculation and formal stipulation. Theorizing at the margins makes the best of being fixated on a subject matter to which scholars in better-defined disciplines are generally indifferent. It does so by selectively appropriating and adapting theories that those other scholars have proposed for matters they claim as theirs alone to study.

Consider this judicious formulation, taken from Bristol University Press's website:

> Bristol Studies in International Theory aims to provoke and deepen theoretical conversations in the field of International Relations and demonstrate their relevance.

Theorists in most fields of study feel no need to demonstrate their relevance because they do not see their fields and themselves as having been marginalized.

> Specifically, the series seeks to showcase work that (i) engages in conceptual analysis and the creation of new concepts, ...

Conceptual clarification is the first order of business in most fields of study and, for many theorists, a task already completed in the field's theoretical centring.

> (ii) harnesses empirical research to build theory, ...

Mentioning empirical research genuflects to science while leaving the content of 'the international', and the method and form of research, unspecified.

(iii) decentres existing paradigms and explores non-Western perspectives and approaches, ...

Decentring existing paradigms and their central claims denies the field its embodied centre and validates marginal theorizing, wherever it takes place, as long as such theorizing does not make paradigmatic claims for itself.

(iv) revisits the ideas and arguments of canonical thinkers and/or the evolution of theorizing world politics, ...

Revisiting canonical thinkers documents the emergence of 'the international' at the margins of theorizing in other fields of study; studying the evolution of the field points up the failed effort to build any paradigm centred on the political history of the modern world.

and (v) foregrounds ethical questions in world affairs and the ethics and politics of the practice of theorizing.

Theorists are always socially situated; theorizing always has ethical and political implications, whatever theorists say about themselves and their practices.

In my opinion, this programmatic statement is well aimed and ably developed for a field of study with no theory to centre it. Obviously, it does not exalt marginality, as I do, for the good reason that *margin*, as a concept, is negatively valenced. The proto-Indo-European root *merg- (edge, border) gave rise to the Latin *margō* and then a host of cognates: margin, mark, march, marches. Together they connote distance rather more than limit. Margins are remote places, distance is measured and marked, marching goes the distance, marches are borderlands, not borders. Movement takes energy; distance comes at a price. Remoteness is not just a 'spatial construct'. As Christopher Rossi has said, it also 'harbors psychological, social, and cultural constructs', often enough condescending, hostile, exoticizing or exploitive.[6]

Deserts are remote places, almost by definition. International theorists have almost nothing to say about them—unless, of course, they happen to sit upon resources suitable for extraction. Rossi is an international legal scholar well practised in theory. As he observed, the Atacama Desert is routinely taken to 'be *barren, bleak, lifeless,* and *empty*'. It is 'a metaphoric wasteland';

---

[6]   Christopher R. Rossi, *Remoteness Reconsidered: The Atacama Desert and International Law* (Ann Arbor: University of Michigan Press, 2021), p. 9; see generally pp. 1–11.

its remoteness has made it 'an almost completely marginalized depiction of earthly landscape'.[7]

Marginalization is a relatively recent extension of *margin*'s conceptual reach, one that turns a somewhat negative spatial construct into a psycho-cultural construct with actively, acutely negative connotations. There is, however, an earlier conceptual adjustment, less negative in its association: margins describe the space enclosing a text written or printed upon a blank sheet of paper or functionally similar material. This sense of the term prompted Jacques Derrida to declare that margins are 'virgin, homogeneous, and negative space'.[8] Virgin space offers possibility that barren space does not, homogeneous space is preferable to bleak and lifeless space, but empty space is still negatively charged. Text, margins: these are supple metaphors standing in for another metaphorical complex—social life in all its variety.

Derrida's textual margins are not entirely empty. They are populated with front matter, epigraphs, chapter titles, glosses and footnotes, all of them 'a negative working in the service of meaning'.[9] My first teacher of international relations esteemed footnotes because, he claimed, there were only marginal gains to be had after Niccolò Machiavelli and Thomas Hobbes set the terms of the realist paradigm. I read footnotes assiduously; often enough, they form a parallel counter-text. I tell students never to neglect an author's acknowledgements. I also write in the margins of almost any text, and I read the running commentaries of other readers. In this volume, this collection of texts, I massage the texts of many diverse writers: giants in Western philosophy (from Aristotle to Derrida), scholars of my own time and field of study (from Johan Galtung to Joseph Nye). I can only hope that my textual marginalia, assembled as a body, induce others to inscribe their own texts in the beckoning margins.

As Derrida indicates in the epigraph to this *text*, even the margins have margins, constituting 'an empty outside' and thus 'a negative without effect'. In short, margins are an 'inexhaustible reserve'; as the body of any text absorbs marginalia, it produces new margins, new opportunities to challenge old certitudes.[10] *This* text is situated in the near-margins because that is where I situate myself as a theorist (so proclaimed, earnestly, innocently, to one of my teachers). In the 1960s, realism and liberal institutionalism contended for my loyalty; I chose the latter. As a junior scholar and teacher, I found myself migrating to the margins of liberalism. Experiencing a scholar's

---

[7] Ibid., p. 10, emphasis in original.
[8] Derrida, *Margins of Philosophy*, p. xxvii.
[9] Ibid., p. xxiv.
[10] Ibid., pp. xxiv, xxiii.

version of a mid-life crisis in the early 1980s, I escaped to the margins of social and political theory.

Context always matters. At the beginning of my career, scholars based in my homeland, the United States—many of them émigrés—dominated International Relations as a field of study. That dominance was materially manifested in the post-war expansion of higher education and support from a government intent on making the world over. For scholarly purposes, that dominance radically favoured political realism and a commitment to science. In choosing neither at the time, I repudiated neither; there are intimations of both in several chapters of this volume. Throughout the 1970s, liberal institutionalism lost ground to realism as the paradigm of high politics, the simplifications of rational choice, and the manufacture and manipulation of data—all in the name of International Relations as 'an American social science'.[11] My disenchantment matched what was happening in the field, and I came to appreciate the critical implications of Marxist theorizing.

In the 1960s, the humanities had experienced a radical upheaval. Induced by the discontents of the time, summed up as the language turn, exemplified by the force and novelty of Derrida's textual strategies, and labelled post-this and post-that, this noisy, subversive movement infiltrated social theory in the 1970s and finally reached International Relations in the 1980s. Generally styled an attack on foundations (or universal truths, about which I will say more in just a few pages), it prompted a thoroughgoing reassessment of realism and liberalism as ideologies in theoretical guise. Even more, it legitimated scepticism about science as the only way forward. The 'post'-movement, as I came to think of it, encouraged daylight raids in distant fields and discouraged unification campaigns. Shifting metaphors (and honouring Derrida's conception of world as text), it focused attention on the margins of prevailing paradigms without presuming to construct a new centre for any field.

The 'post'-movement suited me perfectly. Jumping aboard cost me little enough in status. I had already secured a modest perch in the margins of the field and long since given up dreams of working at a top-tier university in my own country. Ensconced in the second tier, I had room to manoeuvre in the margins. I also had a few good friends and excellent doctoral students, many of them feminists, for support. I went about constructing something new to the field and called it constructivism.

This is not the place to document how the field changed as it globalized, how it glorified constructivism and benefitted me—far more, away from home. Insofar as International Relations remains 'an American social

---

[11] Stanley Hoffmann, 'An American social science: International Relations', *Daedalus* 106, 3 (1977), pp. 41–60.

science', I am still a marginal figure. Elsewhere in the world, I can pretend no such thing. If status defines the terms of reference, I have no claim to marginality in the now-globalized field of International Relations, and I am grateful to be able to say so.

If, however, the terms of reference are the field as it is today, then its multiple centres offer a panoply of intersecting margins. Despite my role in bringing constructivism to the field, I think I can fairly claim to work at the margins of constructivism as it has evolved. I have periodically affirmed my position at the margins of the 'post'-movement (as I do here). I can talk to realists and liberals alike; I would be a fool to deny the power and possibilities of science in practice. Claiming marginality, as I do, is not false modesty. It is an assertion of pride, a declaration of independence, a theorist's distinctive signature.

Theorizing requires space, which the margins would seem to provide. As I have already said, the margins are never as empty as they seem, as we declare them to be. There is rubble to be cleared, foundations exposed, legacies acknowledged and ownership asserted—all this before theories can be housed, landscaping completed. In due course, the field is *topo*graphically remapped, *typo*graphically reset with new chapters, new headings, new margins. Where theories dwell, theorizing meets resistance, texts are deployed in defence of the status quo, margins are romanticized as frontiers, and the messy process repeats itself.

Space at the margins always comes at a price. I find myself marginalized; I have marginalized myself. Once occupied, the margins are at first negatively valenced and then—at least some of the time—grudgingly granted content and acceptance. The reward for marginality is a relative lack of constraints on what one can say in the name of theory. The potential rewards are far greater. The margins await the marks of anyone who would venture there.

Neglected essays

Embraced by margins, this text is a volume—it has volume and other material properties such that we experience it as whole in itself. Its inscribed margins tell us that it consists of a series of parts, also wholes, called chapters and further identified as essays. There are 13 in all. The term *essay* calls attention to the form that each chapter takes, though not a form materially fixed by the margins of the text. Ever since Michel de Montaigne wrote his *Essais* (more than a hundred), published in three volumes (1580, 1588, 1592), the essay has been a preferred format for informed speculation at the margins of established disciplines.

Essayists address variously familiar topics as scaled-down wholes. They draw on available material eclectically and trespass with relative impunity. They identify recurrent themes, pass judgement on what other have to say, indicate more or less openly that they have something more, something new, to say themselves, yet rarely claim to have the last word on any topic. Their essays are brief but not gnomically so, carefully constructed if weakly substantiated. Essays may reflect authorial ambivalence, although they are not often deliberately ambiguous. They are splendid vehicles for sceptical voices, such as Montaigne's own voice. Or David Hume's, whose *Essays: Moral, Political, Literary* (1741–2) have earned my attention ever since my student days.

While I and my colleagues often use the term *piece* interchangeably with *essay* for any text appearing in a scholarly medium (as I do here, though marginally, in footnotes), I want my readers to bear in mind that this volume consists of brief, lightly documented, sometimes tendentious pieces of my work written over several decades. They are *not* research reports, literature reviews, or exercises in formal reasoning. They have no immediate implications for policy. They disclose a point of view. Like Hume, I am given to speculating about a variety of topics on which I take myself to be sufficiently informed to say something pertinent. Again like Hume, I am also given to systematizing a range of materials in scaled-up conceptual frameworks—*not* theories—and have sought to make them accessible to a puzzled audience.[12] In this volume, readers will encounter traces of these undertakings, duly indicated in the margins of the text.

The essays collected here are well-rounded wholes. At least I wrote them with considerable care to achieve this effect. Each one I deemed sufficiently complete to end where and when it does—in most cases after six to seven thousand words. Some of them were written by invitation, for an occasion; none did I consider an occasional piece of writing, to be written on the plane, tossed off in a few hours. Over the decades, the writing became less formal, more personal, as I became surer of my voice. Even when these essays began as talks (several did), I gave them a writer's cadences, not a speaker's, all the while breaking up long sentences and paragraphs. Upon rereading them (several times) in preparing this volume, I am satisfied that they still meet my own standards for an essay: each, a concise, compelling foray into an unsettled topic; together, a sketchy, necessarily partial (in both senses) roadmap for the margins of international theory.

I suspect that most scholars trained like me (in PhD programmes with German antecedents, at modern universities, in English) unthinkingly

---

[12] I am referring to Hume's *A Treatise of Human Nature* (1739–1740) and *An Enquiry concerning Human Understanding* (1748), and to several of my books. Frames and margins are *not* interchangeable metaphors; among many differences, the former is better suited to marking the passage of time. On frames and framing, see Nicholas Greenwood Onuf, *The Mightie Frame: Epochal Change and the Modern World* (New York: Oxford University Press, 2018), pp. 5–11.

marginalize essays in assessing their peers' work and the state of their fields of study. I do not doubt that I do, and for obvious reasons. Scholars generally direct major statements to important journals, where they are thoroughly vetted, revised to correct inadvertent errors and appease the field's gatekeepers, and cited as authoritative. By design, essays are *not* major statements.

In so-called Latin cultures, essays garner more attention and respect from scholars than they do in my world. I would guess this is the case in the rest of the world. Here, in my world, a centre absent a centre yet full of itself, essays betray limited intentions. They tend to be previews of work in progress, retrospective summaries of earlier work, celebrations of others' work, gratuitous suggestions about the work that others should be doing, one-sided quarrels with rivals, reflections on missteps and slippery slopes, lamentations on the state of the field, guided tours of other fields, sententious meditations on what it all means. They are written for symposium volumes, *Festschriften*, obscure journals and yearbooks— publications for which peer review is perfunctory or beside the point. Too often, essays come off as casual asides. As such, they are readily neglected, rarely cited.

The essays in this volume are rarely cited. If my peers even knew of their existence, they neglected them because I published them in just the sort of places that essays routinely get published. For all the work that I put into them, I neglected them once they were published—I failed to revise or expand them for publication in major journals. While I put a few snippets to use in a recent book project (just cited), I never thought to bring them in from the margins of the margins and bring them together in a volume extolling theory at the margins. Until now.

Recurrent themes

Assembling these essays, I was quickly reminded that certain themes pop up repeatedly. These themes are intrinsic to theory as a project and theorizing as a vocation. They raise problems that never get solved, issues that never get resolved. They transcend fields of study, such as mine, in which they find particular expression. They precede and constrain my field's working paradigms, and they work at the margins of international theory to constitutive effect.

It would help if, first, I list these themes before showing how they weave through the 13 essays making up this volume.

- In the first instance, my world consists of the sensations that I experience as I move about. Feeling resistance, moving objects—including myself— in space and time, I grant the world its apparent materiality and causal coherence, just as I grant other beings sundry powers, such as I recognize in myself.

- For beings with the power of speech—human beings—language mediates sensory experience and gives it meaning; it does so invisibly, intrusively, inescapably. Speaking to each other, agreeing more or less on semantic content, we make the world what it is to us.
- As figures of speech and prime conveyors of semantic content, metaphors stand in for—represent—mediated sensory experience, lose specificity through use, and become concepts. When we combine and manipulate concepts, we build models—elaborated representations—of the ways we think the world works.
- Language enables us to assign value to concepts and models, translate needs and wishes into goals, formulate intentions (however ineptly), deceive ourselves and others, imagine futures, evaluate alternative courses of action, and adjust our actions to achieve those goals. We devise models for how the world could or should work.
- Language depends on and gives rise to rules, which fix meanings, constitutes societies while holding them apart, and gives some people the means to rule over others, whether for their own good or for the common good as they define it.
- I profess to live in the modern world—a world that has a distinctive, well-documented history and global reach, a world that works differently from any other world. A signal difference is the multiplicity of ruled societies, allegedly autonomous and nominally equal, engaged in ruled relations with each other.
- Like everyone else, we in the modern world tend to universalize what we think we know. Claims that we make about the world as a whole, the human condition, or the common good are semantic traps. Carefully deployed, these claims can serve as margin-markers.

The first theme on this list stipulates an I, me, with sensorimotor powers, situated in and experiencing the world. It further stipulates a world of others like me. The very words *stipulate, situate, I, me* and *world* tell a story. An unannounced authorial voice, I, empathically asserts that I am, myself, a self, like other selves aware of what is going on around ourselves. Subject and object, I and me, I and the world, are linked by two verbs. The first joins me and the world through speech; the second conveys my sense of being positioned in what I can only describe as *my* world. This is, of course, the familiar Cartesian *ego* professing self-knowledge, but with a twist: I can only *know* anything because I can talk with you about my world, and your world, as *the* world—a world of apparent truths. The story has three elements: the sensory experience of beings in motion; selves who register where they are; the power to translate motion and place into space, time and cause. The third element depends on speech and thus society to make beings into selves—and selves into beings.

Such a stance would seem so basic, so marginal to most theoretical concerns, that few scholars would even trouble to comment on it. Yet it points to a philosophical issue to which I have given ever more attention over the years: Is the world *out there* what I take it to be, more or less? Or is the world *I know* what I have made it to be, albeit with others' help? If I answer the first question affirmatively, I am a philosophical realist, as are most scientists, most international theorists (many of whom are also political realists), and most people in my world.

Among realists, one important branch starts with sensations or impressions as the link between empowered selves and the world beyond—as I would. John Locke and Hume are notable cases in point. So is Ernst Mach, 19th-century physicist and philosopher:

> Colors, sounds, temperatures, pressures, spaces, times, and so forth, are connected with one another in manifold ways; and with them are associated dispositions of mind, feelings, and volitions. Out of this fabric, that which is relatively more fixed and permanent stands prominently forth, engraves itself on the memory, and expresses itself in language. Relatively greater permanency is exhibited, first, by certain complexes of colors, sounds, pressures, and so forth, functionally connected in time and space, which therefore receive special names, and are called bodies. Absolutely permanent such complexes are not.[13]

If, however, I answer the second question affirmatively, I am an anti-realist, or idealist in the manner of Immanuel Kant, who, like Mach, started with sensations in order to talk about bodies, objects, things. 'Objects are *given* to us by means of *sensibility* [sensory experience]; and it alone yields us *intuitions*'—more specifically, empirical intuitions. 'The undetermined object of an empirical intuition is entitled *appearance*.'[14]

> What objects may be in themselves, and apart from all this receptivity of our sensibility, remains completely unknown to us. We know nothing but our mode of perceiving them—a mode which is peculiar to us, and not necessarily shared in by every being, though certainly every human being.[15]

---

[13] Ernst Mach, *The Analysis of Sensations and the Relation of the Physical to the Psychical*, rev. Sydney Waterlow, trans. C. M. Williams (Chicago: Open Court, 1914), p. 2.
[14] Immanuel Kant, *Critique of Pure Reason*, trans. Norman Kemp Smith (New York: St Martin's, 1965), p. 65, emphases in translation.
[15] Ibid., p. 82.

For Kant, our powers give us objects that only appear to have objective properties; space and time are pure intuitions of the mind. For Mach, the senses reveal a manifold or fabric with objective properties, including space, time and 'associated dispositions'. Both add something else. For Kant, it is apperception—a power shared by us all. This is 'consciousness of self' or an 'inner sense' unifying and centring the self in a 'manifold of appearance'.[16] For Mach it is language, which mediates sensory experience among many selves and enables its functional assessment and manipulation. The result is a world of metastasizing metaphors, empowering predicates, working models, ruled practices and familiar artefacts. It is a world of our making, a world made up of 'storied matter'.[17]

With Mach and Kant, I grant myself and others a panoply of powers, both sensorimotor and cognitive. With Kant, I know what I cannot know. With Mach, I know what the world feels like—to me. I make plausible inferences about the way it feels to others, the way it seems to us all. I situate myself as a post-Kantian idealist. Yet I considered myself a materialist before I came to this stance, as the first two chapters in the volume strongly suggest, and I remain one—see Chapter 4. We get along in the world, whatever it 'really' is. We would not if we had not evolved, and survived, as a species. I am content to invoke evolutionary psychology and cognitive science in support of this inference. It is all we need to *know*—in the most provisional sense of the term.[18]

Let me say again: we always experience the world materially. This is an ontological stance, but one dovetailing with my resistance to realism's epistemological stance that we can know what the world *really* is like. What I know about the world is its *thereness*, which I experience as the world's resistance to my place in it, to my *being*—and that is *all* I know. In this volume, I use the term *empirical* and its cognates casually for the stuff of experience, as Kant did with 'empirical intuition', and most scholars do most of the time. Casual use merely sidesteps having to be clear, at that moment, about one's epistemological stance.

My epistemological commitments disallow such terms as *naturalism*, *physicalism* and *phenomenalism*, all of which point up ontological claims grounded in realism. Naturalism and physicalism too readily suggest an autonomous nature, or universe, reducible to necessary truths or physical

---

[16] Ibid., pp. 137, 66.

[17] Serenella Iovino, *Ecocriticism and Italy: Ecology, Resistance, and Liberation* (London: Bloomsbury, 2017), p. 4, scare marks in original. Iovino's route to this elegant formulation is quite unlike my own.

[18] Here see Donald D. Hoffman, *The Case against Reality: How Evolution Hid the Truth from Our Eyes* (London: Penguin Books, 2020). Hoffmann's subtitle is misleading; chapter 4's title is 'Sensory: Fitness beats truth'.

laws. Phenomenalism is trickier. I applaud phenomenalist attention to sensory experience—the world as it *appears* to us individually. Yet phenomenalists tend to *see* the world as passively experienced. The self disappears, so does the world actively experienced as friction, or resistance to which the self must respond.[19]

Few of my colleagues in the field of International Relations construe materiality as I do here. Philosophical realists of one sort or another, they tend to associate materialism with tangible stuff and idealism with what goes on in our heads. Even this is a crude division, used mainly to support realist and liberal paradigms as a valenced binary. Constructivists in pursuit of a middle way have argued that material conditions and widely circulated ideas 'interact' to constitute social meaning.[20] Interact, yes, if we define terms narrowly: bombs as a material capability, weapons as an idea. I take them to be both. Materiality is a pervasive feature of human life—we *feel* its presence here and now—and not just a factor variably affecting what happens in the world.

Nor do I think the term *idea* is an adequate description of what happens in our heads as we move about, experience sensations, learn from our experiences, speak to each other, learn even more, and live together. What then are we doing in our heads when we talk? Continuously and collectively, we are making models of the world 'as we see it'—we make what we think, and say, we see. We attribute materiality to those models we think we have made into objects. We constantly update our models of the many features of the world that impinge on our awareness, confident that these models work the way they do, and as well as they do, because the world we cannot know works that way too. As Mach might have said, they are instruments for making sense of our sensations.

Often enough our models do not seem to work. We disagree on what models to deploy or revise. To adopt a familiar expression, models 'go all the

---

[19] Nor should realist phenomenalism be confused with idealist phenomenology. For an attempt to enliven phenomenalism with a dose of phenomenology, see Patrick Thaddeus Jackson, *The Conduct of Inquiry in International Relations: Philosophy of Science and Its Implications for the Study of World Politics* (Abingdon: Routledge, 2011), chs 2–3. Jackson takes Mach's stance on sense and sensation to have been less realist than monist (mind–body dualism being a false conundrum) and intimates that this is my (and his) stance too (personal communication). I suspect that the very act of predication alienates self as subject from the world embodied in predicates (also see Chapter 7); speech thwarts any possible escape from dualism. Mach is another matter. Resisting metaphysics in favour of instrumental science, he complicated latter-day efforts to label him philosophically; see John Preston, ed., *Interpreting Mach: Critical Essays* (Cambridge: Cambridge University Press, 2021).

[20] See Alexander Wendt, *Social Theory of International Politics* (Cambridge: Cambridge University Press, 1999), pp. 110–12, for an influential example.

way down'. This is so because many others have already modelled a world that goes down level by level. Such a model works for me—for my purposes in making sense of the world we have made for ourselves. In Chapters 3, 12 and 13, I use the expression 'all the way down'; Chapter 12 is largely devoted to my model of a modelled world.

The full expression is 'turtles all the way down'. I did not bother to add the noun because any number of objects could substitute for turtles, and the expression is ontological in thrust, not epistemological.[21] The world consists of objects, such as turtles, in a specified set of relations. Ideas, factors, forces, levels, models, things-in-relation, and mental dispositions all count as honorary objects, but only when we honour them as such. We honour these things as *things* by speaking of them *as* things. Language is dispositive—in my model of the world. The faculty of speech, the power of language: this is where my descending turtles always end up. In this volume, I make up stories, play with words, embrace metaphors, engage in informed speculation, write in the margins of this and many other weightier books.

Words, phrases, sentences are syntactical units functioning as models. Every model ultimately depends on some kind of symbolic representation— simplified images or impressions, standardized by virtue of common use. Language serves this function (but not just this function). When I see an → on a signpost, point my finger at the sign, tell you 'the arrow points this way', and point my finger the same way, you will feel reasonably confident you know what I mean and act accordingly. When I see → in a diagram or text, I assume, more or less safely, that it substitutes for phrases or sentences indicating a causal sequence. Such an arrow is a stylized image of a model itself representing an activity sufficiently familiar to most of us that it brings forth an image—we imagine the arrow in flight and talk about what happens when it strikes its target. That image is already 'flattened and enclosed'.[22] The mind's eye has deleted detail, re-formed content, supplied margins.

Figures of speech are further flattened and enclosed—as figures, when spoken. Repetition flattens them even further and codifies their distance from other symbolic representations. The arrow-as-image becomes an →; the → becomes a symbol for direction; direction abstractly represents cause

---

[21] Thanks to Chris Brown, international theorists are well versed in the imagery of stacked turtles and its philosophical implications. '"Turtles all the way down": Anti-foundationalism, critical theory and international relations', *Millennium* 23, 1 (1994), pp. 213–36. As for 'levels', see my essay, so named, in *European Journal of International Relations* 1, 1 (1995), pp. 35–58.

[22] This is Arjun Appadurai's arresting description of statistics and maps, no less applicable to words, symbols and models of all sorts. *Modernity at Large: Cultural Dimensions of Globalization* (Minneapolis: University of Minnesota Press, 1996), p. 133.

as a concept; the concept of cause is indispensable to the way we model the world we think we live in. Chapter 4 considers cause and power as largely interchangeable metaphors (with due attention to Aristotle); Chapter 7 considers giving as a complex case of causing to move (with a focus on children and diplomats); Chapter 9 considers cause in relation to habit (foregrounding Hume). Other chapters have briefer discussions of cause. That I use the term *because* over a hundred times in this volume illustrates how causal assumptions, mostly unexamined and often indefensible, suffuse ordinary speech.

It is the same with such words as *may, could, would, should* and *must.* We use these modal auxiliaries with verbs indicating or implying causation to conceptualize possibility, potentiality, obligation and necessity. There exist many alternative ways to modify the concept of cause but few non-verbal symbols. Without this conceptual apparatus, we would not have rules. Without rules human society would not be possible.

When I, you, almost anyone sees an → on a road sign, we know whether we could, should or must go that way only *because* we know the rules of the road, normally articulated as such in natural language. We know what these rules say (propositional content), when and to whom they apply (scope), who made them (source, validity) and, often enough, why they got made (reasons). What we do not know, we know we can find out. We also know what might happen if we ignore them (more rules apply). In this volume, Chapters 5 and 6 deal with rules and their distinctive properties.

What some of us may not know, but should, is that the presence of rules, such as road signs, indicates a condition of rule, such as we typically associate with government and the state. As an international theorist, I would say more. International society is loaded with rules and these rules constitute a condition of rule—here see Chapter 3, reprising earlier work.[23] I concede that such a condition may not be obvious, if only because so many rules are themselves less than fully legible.

Such rules lack the formality of 'black letter law'—lexical specificity in content, scope, source, validity and rationale. To call them *norms* too often denies prescriptive force to habitual conduct. Sooner than later, repetition implies obligation, *is* becomes *ought,* because that is how most of us experience the world most of the time. Even worse, calling informal rules 'norms' instead of 'rules' mistakenly suggests that obligation follows from formality. On the contrary, a good many of the unspoken rules suffusing daily life are strictly observed. Deference patterns are an obvious case in point; ask any diplomat (and see Chapter 7).

---

[23] See especially Nicholas Greenwood Onuf, *World of Our Making: Rules and Rule in Social Theory and International Relations* (Columbia: University of South Carolina Press, 1989).

The range of modal qualifiers would suggest that rules are binding or obligatory in degree and that degrees of obligation and formality need not correlate. Modern systems of rule reside in normative frameworks melding principles (general statements of belief), a penumbra of informal rules, and the numerous individuated commands and demands we associate with ethical conduct (doing what is good, right or honourable in context). Chapter 8 explores these frameworks, inscribed as they are in the margins of rule and so necessary for its success.

Systems of rule need not be formal, any more than rules must be. When anthropologists used to talk about 'primitive law' and legal theorists asked if international law were a species of primitive law, they made formality, understood as legibility, a key consideration.[24] The very term *primitive* is of course negatively valenced (and *savage* perhaps even more); it marginalizes those to whom it is applied, not least by exoticizing them. I use the term in Chapter 1 in reproducing other international theorists' use, without comment or scare marks such as I would provide today. I also mention 'the Western state system' several times in that chapter; thereafter I use the term *West* and its cognates rarely. 'West' is perhaps less prejudicial than 'First World' or 'Developed World'; 'Global South' less offensive than 'Third World' or 'Developing World'. Yet all such terms increasingly challenge my sense of propriety. The subtle rules of scholarly discourse have changed in recent decades; evidence resides in the words we no longer use so freely and the ones we choose instead.

I have come to prefer the term *modern* for what I once called *Western*. I used this root a moment ago, and I use it hundreds of times in this volume—more often than I use the term *international*. I speak of 'modernity' and 'the modern world' more often than I pay notice to 'international relations'. Chapters 8 and 9 play with the binary of modernity and tradition, which is so integral to the way that we moderns talk about ourselves. Chapters 6, 7, 8 and 10 consider postmodern(ist) theorizing. In Chapter 2, I write as a late modern critic of 'late capitalism'; in Chapter 10, I identify my scholarly persona as 'late modern'. Chapter 11 breaks modernity into six epochs (Renaissance, c. 1500–1650; classical, c. 1650–1800; modern, c. 1800–1900; modernist, c. 1900–1970; late modern, c. 1970–) and speculates, as does Chapter 2, on what comes 'after modernity'.

At no point do I deny the conceptual imperialism embedded in the language of modernity and, more particularly, in speaking of the modern world and associating everything else with tradition. I hold the emergence of international society to have been a unique event in human history,

---

[24] See A. Campbell, 'International law and primitive law', *Oxford Journal of Legal Studies* 8, 2 (1988), pp. 169–96, for an overview.

modelled as it is on the principle of sovereign equality among member states. In describing international society as the mighty frame within which the modern world has unfolded over several centuries, I cannot but marginalize and thus trivialize everything that modernity is not. After all, the modern world is *my* world, a Husserlian *lifeworld*.[25] For me it is seemingly 'real'; its immediacy, contingency and apparent coherence are 'directly' available to my senses; it goes with me wherever I go; it brackets every other world and fills the void with scattered images and flattened language.

In acknowledging myself as the privileged object at the centre of my world, I admit to foreshortened perspective and ineradicable bias. Even as I forsake 'the view from nowhere' and, in Chapters 6, 7 and 8, dissociate myself from universalizing ethical systems, I do make any number of Olympian pronouncements about 'the world'—any world, every world. Inspired by Derrida's assault on structuralism, Charlotte Epstein has called this habit of mine a 'search for an absent centre', that is, an 'unconstructed universal posited beyond the social world that founds the possibility of theorizing it'.[26]

> Derrida draws out a persistent paradox running through structuralist thought, namely, that the centre tends to be sought simultaneously *within* the structure and *beyond* it; as an anchoring point that holds the whole together from without. This is the paradox of the absent centre, the hole at the heart of the whole.[27]

It is fair to say that I am a structuralist—of a sort. According to Derrida, 'within structure there is not only form, relation, and configuration. There is also interdependency and a totality which is always concrete.' I say, never concrete. Structure is a universal property of models, intrinsic to them by

---

[25] Husserlian only up to a point. For my reservations about Husserl's claims on behalf of intersubjectivity, see *The Mightie Frame*, pp. 137–43.

[26] Charlotte Epstein, 'Constructivism or the eternal return of universals in International Relations: Why returning to language is vital to prolonging the owl's flight', *European Journal of International Relations* 19, 3 (2013), pp. 499–519 (511).

[27] Ibid., p. 508, emphases in original, drawing on Jacques Derrida's 1966 lecture, 'Structure, sign and play in the discourse of the human sciences', reprinted in Derrida, *Writing and Difference*, trans. Richard Macksey and Alan Bass (Chicago: University of Chicago Press, 1978), ch. 10. 'Absent centre' never appears in that text. Elsewhere in *Writing and Difference* we find 'the duplicity of everything and nothing, of absent presence, of the black sun, of the open ring, of the eluded center, of the elliptical return': 'Ellipsis', p. 299. Also see Jacques Derrida, *Of Grammatology*, trans. Gayatri Chakravorty Spivak (Baltimore: Johns Hopkins University Press, 1974), p. 154: 'The sign, the image, the representation, which come to supplement the absent presence are the illusions that sidetrack us.' Note that 'centre' is a spatial metaphor, while 'presence' brings time into play—especially for Derrida; see Chapters 7 and 10.

definition, and not a property of any world (except as modelled).[28] Language broadly construed makes this so. Models have structure and function; we make place for them when we make them; we have our reasons for making them. These properties are universalized (for the model) by having been rendered in semantic, symbolic or graphic terms. Centres and margins, parts and wholes, are always notional, provisional—present (now, then) in their absence (here, anywhere). So it must be with any model, every theory.

A human universal, language itself has universalizing properties—'fixed structures' whose 'universality is founded in and guaranteed by human nature'.[29] Yes! More precisely, learning a language does not depend on a singular overarching, innate capacity, such as Noam Chomsky's universal grammar. It would seem that speaking is associated with other complex operations, such as counting, identifying geometric forms and making music. Variably developed and deployed, these capacities constitute what, in Chapter 7, I call 'natural dispositions' common to humanity. There are many such dispositions. When taken together, they give the human condition its distinctive features.

Taking speech by itself, however arbitrarily, six functionally defined, highly generalized, intricately braided processes, or cognitive powers, stand out. They are:

- representation (identifying objects and events);
- apperception (subjectivizing one's seemingly objective self);
- memory (recalling objects and events);
- abstraction (simplifying objects and events, giving them form);
- comparison and categorization (sorting objects and events by assigning them properties);
- predication (offering propositions about the world).

Qualifying predicates by tense, aspect and modality enables us to manipulate time and perspective; compounding predicates enables us to manipulate propositions, speak performatively, and make the world what it is to us. Mixed metaphors aside, I should point out that predication and associated operations are specific to speech and indispensable to judgement, normativity and narrative.

This is my list, constructed for the occasion. I do not pretend that it is definitive or exhaustive. While cognitivists, linguists and developmental

---

[28] 'Force and signification', in *Writing and Difference*, p. 5. I have more to say about structure in Chapters 5 and 12, and considerably more in *Making Sense, Making Worlds: Constructivism in Social Theory and International Relations* (Abingdon: Routledge, 2013), ch. 6.

[29] Epstein, 'Constructivism or the eternal return of universals', p. 502.

psychologists might quarrel over any such list, I hold that this one is compatible with a 'usage-based' approach to language acquisition. Evolution has seen to the necessary physiological equipment. Speaking in turn, at odds, in unison, across generations, telling stories, making things up: this is how we produce the patterns that we learn as children, that we find ourselves using ever after, that we teach our own children to find and use for themselves.[30] The result is language—at once materially grounded, arduously learned, socially imbricated, infinitely extendable and yet, in my native tongue at least, reduced to metaphor.

I have explored language acquisition on several occasions, always in the belief that humanity alone has 'the gift of speech', that we are, 'by nature', political animals, that speech is integral to social construction.[31] But this is so only if human nature is modelled as, and centred on, a bundle of powers defining what it means to be human. I fail to see how *any* of the universal properties *of* models can be missing from models *as* models. They give a given model its 'within' and 'beyond'; they anchor the model by establishing its margins; an → finds 'the heart of the whole'.

For example, status-ordering is a human universal in my working model of the world. Status figures among our goals; we use language to assign status and effectuate ordering. I would normally announce, and defend, this claim as an empirical generalization. You and I might quibble about 'exceptions to the rule'. You might say that one can seek to be free of status concerns, that stylized images can represent status, that a show of force can effectuate order. I would have to agree, and I would alter my model to make it work better at the margins. Notwithstanding all that talk, neither of us is likely to abandon our respective models of the world (another empirical generalization).

Derrida paid attention to models, for example, when he sorted 'examples' into 'samples' and 'models'.[32] I say, samples *are* models and they have centres— given by us. Indeed, they have no 'present-being', no 'natural site'. As we learn from the legendary lecture informing Epstein's critique, having centres gives them—whatever they are—'a function, a sort of nonlocus, in which an infinite number of sign-substitutions [come] into play'. Even the disruption of structuralism, which Derrida announced in that lecture, is nothing more

---

[30] I borrow the concept of 'pattern-finding' from Michael Tomasello, *Constructing a Language: A Usage-Based Theory of Language Acquisition* (Cambridge, MA: Harvard University Press, 2003), pp. 28–31. Tomasello's conventionally realist model takes the world to have patterns. I prefer to say that we experience the world as variably resistant and learn, largely through speech and with much help, to 'see' a resistant world as richly patterned.

[31] Quoting Aristotle, *Politics*, I, 1153a7–18, any translation. See Onuf, *World of Our Making*, ch. 3; Onuf, *Making Sense, Making Worlds*, ch. 5; Chapter 7 in this volume.

[32] Derrida, 'Cogito and the history of madness', in *Writing and Difference*, p. 42. For more on examples, see Chapter 12.

than a 'metaphorical displacement'—not an event, but an 'event' (his scare marks), the *model* of an event.[33]

To say that human beings have goals and engage in purposive behaviour, that they possess many powers, conspicuously including the power of speech, that language alienates self from world yet makes society possible, that traditional societies depend on status-ordering, that rules betray the presence of rule, that international society is one of a kind, that modernity never succeeded in banishing status, that the modern world cannot be sustained: these are unsupported declarations, not universal truths. As stated, every one of these claims contributes to a whole of many wholes, a model with unambiguous margins. That these claims are unqualified is a property of language in use, a textual artefact, a convenience of the moment; they function as placeholders, 'a sort of nonlocus', awaiting fuller articulation. Quick and dirty insertions routinely qualify such claims; I use the term *most* over a hundred times in this volume. With closer inspection and fuller articulation, the model's margins fill up with qualifications.

When, for example, I declare that language is a human universal, I do not trouble to say that some people cannot speak or hear others speak, and that many more cannot read or write. My unqualified declaration would seem to privilege speech over writing. Derrida saw in this writerly penchant a 'pious wish' for 'speech dreaming its full self-presence'.[34] I see myself as biased in favour of writing as a skill and literacy as an achievement—speech dissociated from dreaming. In my late modern model of the world beyond my world, it is language thus modelled—not some transcendental quest or human nature or 'material givens'—that functions as 'the outer limits to social construction'.[35]

While I make no claim to the effect that social construction is the unifying theme in this volume (or the defining theme of late modern theorizing), there are many hints coded in such terms as *make* and *making*: speaking is doing, doing is making. Social construction has been a significant concern of mine for many years. Many readers know this without my saying so here, or having to read Chapters 3 and 13, and they are likely to judge accordingly. The background can never be absent or empty, no deed undone.

Tall tales

In the foreground, I have arranged 13 essays into three Parts, respectively devoted to 'Politics: Deciding What Matters', 'Ethics: Doing What We

---

[33] Derrida, 'Structure, sign and play', pp. 280, 278.
[34] Derrida, *Of Grammatology*, p. 39.
[35] Epstein, 'Constructivism or the eternal return of universals', p. 508.

Should', 'Semantics: Saying What We See'. This is a rough and ready division; politics, ethics and semantics are elusive objects and inextricable concepts. Themes criss-cross Parts, whose margins overlap and disappear. Standing back, I see Part I in the margins of the realist paradigm in the field of International Relations, Part II in the margins of the liberal paradigm, and Part III swirling about in a decentred field of study.

I edited essays to conform with the Press's style requirements but otherwise left them largely unchanged. Even though I would no longer say 'real systems', for example, you will find these words stuck together in Chapter 1. Over the years, I have gradually shied away from using the term *real* and its cognates so casually, not to mention the term *epistemology*. For this volume, however, I did fix minor mistakes, rewrite a few puzzling passages for clarity, and delete some long, dated footnotes. Essays in each Part appear in the order of their publication. That I have arranged them in time makes them a narrative. I am telling a story in the usual sense.

Most stories exhibit a large causal sequence: from this to that, this causing that, albeit with various complications. Stories have plots going, or taking them, somewhere. Many such stories, like the story we moderns so often tell about our world, are tall tales of growth, achievement and progress—things get better over time. This is not the story I want to tell about the modern world. It just might be a self-vindicating story that I tell about myself.

The very short version of that story goes something like this: I spent the 1980s (a time under-represented in the essays collected here) writing *World of Our Making*. With that book, I naively hoped to erase the margins of the field, displace anarchy as the field's central assumption, and replace it with a pair of necessary relations: (1) Language and rules make each other, and society, possible; (2) rules constitute the conditions of rule in every society. I spent the 1990s thinking about republicanism. This involved steeping myself in Aristotle and clarifying the relation between rules and powers, institutions and agency. The net result was to complement the spatial, almost geometric sensibility informing my conception of world-making with a temporal dimension and historicist sensibility. I spent the two decades following the millennium writing about the modern world and how it got to be what it is. Throughout, I refined my foundational claims; at every moment, language matters; overall, it is a story Aristotle would have praised, a story of fulfilling one's potential.

There is, of course, far more to the story. I was born and raised in privileged circumstances. I can hardly claim to have been marginalized in life chances, educational opportunities, career choices, or occasions for my voice to be heard. I entered the field of International Relations before its margins were fixed. If I found myself marginalized, I did it to myself—as I have already admitted. In doing so, I helped to fence in the field, to impose margins on later generations.

The 13 chapters in this volume are strewn with bits and pieces of 'the whole story'—as if there were one.[36] Whether the volume as a whole, with its three Parts separately arranged in time, tells a story *by itself* is another question. I would like to think my work has got better over time. Deeper, richer, more compelling: I would like to think I am not just older but wiser.

Or not. Perhaps this volume tells the bleak story of one deluded, self-marginalizing scholar marching in place, going nowhere in a cloud of dust. Perhaps it tells three stories about international relations that hang together only loosely, or one story about modernity from three perspectives. Perhaps it is a pilgrim's tale, the quest for insignificant symmetries, an absent centre, a consoling presence. Patient readers can decide for themselves.

---

[36] For another, more elaborate version of this story, see 'Contradictions', in Naeem Inayatullah and Elizabeth Dauphinee, eds, *Narrative Global Politics: Theory, History and the Personal in International Relations* (Abingdon: Routledge, 2016), pp. 104–21.

PART I

Politics: Deciding What Matters

Each chapter in this volume tells a story, each chapter has a story. Chapter 1 has its origins in my first exposure, as a student, to Morton Kaplan's *System and Process in International Politics*. Kaplan's book enshrines the term *politics* in its title, and yet he described 'the international system' as a 'null political system' because it lacks centralized decision-making institutions.[1] At the time I found this apparent contradiction puzzling. In time, I came to realize that, for the most part, we students of international relations either ignore it or evade it with cheap talk about anarchy.

Chapter 1 also features the term *politics* in its title. The essay defines that term only parenthetically and in passing: it is a political act to participate in making 'crucial decisions' for one's society. Such a decision is likely to reflect a concern with the distribution of power and prestige in that society, which the essay also mentions in passing. A few years later, I worked out more fully a conception of politics along similar lines, and I stand by it still.[2]

Sometime in the mid- to late 1970s, the editors of *World Politics* decided to commemorate the 20th anniversary of the journal's special issue on the international system (and the first issue of any journal that I would add to my own library). Kaplan having contributed to the special issue, they asked me to contribute an assessment of his systems theorizing.[3] The editors ended up scrapping the project. They had nevertheless commended the several pages I had devoted to the 'rules' that Kaplan had proposed in modelling several 'types' of international systems. I had already steeped

---

[1] Morton A. Kaplan, *System and Process in International Politics* (New York: Wiley, 1957), pp. 13–14, 22–3.

[2] Nicholas Greenwood Onuf, *World of Our Making: Rules and Rule in Social Theory and International Relations* (Columbia: University of South Carolina Press, 1989), pp. 2–6.

[3] Morton A. Kaplan, 'Problems of theory building and theory confirmation in international politics', *World Politics* 14, 1 (1961), pp. 6–24.

myself in anthropological literature on 'primitive systems' and realized that defining culture by reference to rules points up the material conditions in which any system functions. I extended those few pages accordingly but found my peers little interested, I suspect because I was flirting with vulgar materialism when I used climate zones and population density, not system rules, for comparative purposes. Eventually the essay appeared in a yearbook mostly devoted to international law—a field in which I had already secured a modest reputation.

The second chapter in this Part shifts attention from politics generally considered to the production of valued things, or political economy, in the modern world. International relations fall out of the picture, and so do system types. This essay is a determined critique of liberal ideology and modern hubris from a broadly materialist perspective. In writing it, I was inspired particularly by the Club of Rome and its sensational first report on 'the predicament of mankind' titled *Limits to Growth* (1972).[4] The essay draws on discussions of long waves of expanding and declining growth in the world capitalist economy. Indebted to Ernest Mandel's work on revolutions in power technology, it foresees a shift from heavy work to cheap technologies of social control and sets forth a view of the future that would seem to be materializing roughly as, and when, I expected. I wanted the essay to be a major statement, reaching beyond disciplinary constraints, when I sent it to *Futures*, which published it unchanged in short order. I was naïve; its audience was too politically naïve to see what I was saying. Still is.

Chapter 3 picks up an early concern of mine—Johan Galtung's schematic yet powerful work on the structural properties of aggression, violence and imperialism. I realized that Galtung's model of radical inequality, which he applied so tellingly to centre–periphery relations in the modern world, could be generalized to almost any society. For many years, I had studied the pervasive presence of structural inequality and exploitation and came to see it as effectuated with rules, manifest in rule, yet marginalized by liberal thought. Much later, I honoured my debt to Galtung in a talk I gave in Ankara, in which I reconceptualized his structural model by reference to three primary kinds of rules and three generic forms of rule.

Soon after, I gave a talk in Sydney eventuating in Chapter 4. The prescribed topic of soft power allowed me to revisit an early interest in power. That the term *soft* metaphoricizes power helps to explain the enormous success of Joseph Nye's compelling formula; Nye himself joined many other scholars in discussing power in causal terms. Weight and balance as correlative metaphors point to the Scientific Revolution as the moment in which a proximate

---

[4] Also see Nicholas Greenwood Onuf, 'Reports to the Club of Rome', *World Politics* 36, 1 (1983), pp. 121–46.

sense of cause suffuses social thought and dominates relations of 'the great powers' after the Westphalian settlement in 1648. Lost is an Aristotelian sensibility linking cause to purpose. So is an appreciation of human powers, only now subject to revival, and finally an adequate accounting of agency and its metaphorical cognates.

1

Comparative International Politics (1982)

The era of systems thinking in political science dates from the mid-1950s. David Easton gave currency to the term *political system* in 1953, and major statements on how to study such systems appeared a short while thereafter.[1] Input-output analysis, general systems theory, equilibrium models all competed for attention. Even though students of foreign governments and relations among states were especially stimulated to abandon exclusively institutional and historical studies for brave new ways to comprehend political reality, there were signs even before the end of the decade that emergent fields of comparative politics and international politics were to part company in their preferred systemic formulations.

In comparative politics the structural-functional orientation popularized by Gabriel Almond prevailed as the convenient tool for investigating not just governments but anything political. In principle all political systems were subject to comparison because they all, regardless of form, share certain distinctively political functions. In practice this meant comparison of diverse systems nonetheless sharing important features qualifying them to be called states. The result was an ample but bounded universe of items for comparison.

Structural-functionalism inspired what has come to be called the comparative movement, penetrating most areas of political inquiry except, peculiarly enough, international relations.[2] The stated object of comparing systems is theory-building. While failing to create theories of any consequence, the effort was marked by a surge of conceptual clarification,

---

[1] David Easton, *The Political System* (New York: Alfred Knopf, 1953); G. A. Almond, 'Comparative political systems', *Journal of Politics* 18, 3 (1956), pp. 391–409; David Easton, 'An approach to the analysis of political systems', *World Politics* 9, 3 (1957), pp. 383–400. The term *system* has of course been used unsystematically for centuries.

[2] Gabriel A. Almond, *Political Development* (Boston: Little, Brown, 1970), p. 25.

taxonomic ordering and empirical enrichment. Substantial though these gains are over previous scholarship, they succeeded mostly in fuelling rising epistemological expectations that structural–functional comparison could never fulfil.

Opinion leaders in political science turned increasingly to neopositivist epistemology prevailing in philosophy of science, which provided damning critiques of anything functional and legitimated the quest for properly hypothetico-deductive theory.[3] Whether the rise of neopositivism and the quest for formally stated theory as the basis of 'real' science are benighted misadventure or passage to enlightenment cannot as yet be told. It can only be said that theory development in any form, or by any name, must be preceded by a period of conceptual and taxonomic growth. This would indeed seem to have been the pattern with all major advances in human understanding.

As much as its sister field of comparative politics, international politics initially celebrated the pursuit of theory in systemic terms. Yet there resemblance ends. Few of the gains associated with the comparative movement characterize current studies of international relations. Particularized research strategies by whatever epistemological warrant yield collective incoherence, while conceptual and taxonomic under-nourishment make the pursuit of theory an unimpressive and frequently maligned endeavour. The field dissolves from within, its makers increasingly unsure even that it exists. There are doubtless a number of factors contributing to such a remarkable parting of ways, with such untoward consequences for international politics as a field. Principal among them must be the appearance in 1957 of Morton Kaplan's exceptionally well-developed, apparently hypothetico-deductive models of six possible international systems.[4] Kaplan's formulations dwarfed all other claimants to favour. Their specificity and formality created the impression, it seems unduly, that Kaplan had avoided functionalist fallacies and complied with neopositivist strictures on the nature of the theory enterprise.

One burden of this essay is to show how and why Kaplan's success stifled systems thinking applied to international relations. A second burden is to sketch what might have been, had the comparative movement had a proper

---

[3] One of the more energetic attacks on structural-functional comparison from a neopositivist vantage point is Robert T. Holt and John E. Turner, 'Crises and sequences in collective theory development', *American Political Science Review* 69, 3 (1975), pp. 979–94. Almond, *Political Development*, retrospectively conceded the change in fashion by referring to his work, rather apologetically, as 'heuristic theory'.

[4] Morton A. Kaplan, *System and Process in International Politics* (New York: Wiley, 1957), Part I. 'Hypothetico-deductive' is not Kaplan's description. It is typical of commentaries on Kaplan's work and was used specifically by Oran R. Young, *A Systemic Approach to International Politics*, Research Monograph No. 33, Center of International Studies, Princeton University (1968), p. 10.

chance. In the absence of anything to compare, what came to be was an all too natural, almost narcissistic preoccupation with the international system, meaning of course the Western state system. George Modelski and Fred Riggs, in particular, early developed complementary structural-functional formulations to permit comparison of international systems.[5] Had these important but ignored initiatives been built upon, international politics might not have fallen so far behind its sister field. comparative politics might also have benefited, because the relatively unbounded nature of international political phenomena encourages recourse to the comparative literature of anthropology and sociology, where structural-functionalism arose and long flourished.[6] Multicultural international history, systemic in cast but conceptually impoverished, might even have lent its extraordinary descriptive range and contextual richness to the integration of two now entirely separate fields of political science in an openly interdisciplinary manner.[7]

The international system

To understand current partiality for one system and correlative disinterest in the comparative study of international politics, we must examine Kaplan's claims and contributions on behalf of systems thinking, thereby to establish the sources of his appeal. Kaplan presented his six models, which he later called 'theory sketches',[8] as particularly suitable for theory-building because they contain a small number of elements abstracted 'from a far richer historical context'.[9] Called variables, these elements are arranged in several classes, the principal ones being 'essential rules' and 'transformation rules'.[10]

5   George Modelski, 'Agraria and Industria: Two models of the international system', and Fred W. Riggs, 'International relations as a prismatic system', *World Politics* 14, 1 (1961), pp. 118–81.
6   See Marvin Harris, *The Rise of Anthropological Theory: A History of Theory of Cultures* (New York: Crowell, 1968), and Alvin W. Gouldner, *The Coming Crisis of Western Sociology* (New York: Basic Books, 1970), for major critical assessments.
7   The more so as multicultural international history gains in conceptual awareness and comparative intent. Contrast Adda B. Bozeman, *Politics and Culture International History* (Princeton: Princeton University Press, 1960), with Martin Wight, *Systems of States*, ed. Hedley Bull (Leicester: Leicester University Press, 1977) and Robert G. Wesson, *State Systems: International Pluralism, Politics, and Culture* (New York: Free Press, 1978).
8   'The six international systems ... are partial theory sketches that permit research programs of both comparative historical and analytical types.' See Morton A. Kaplan, *Towards Professionalism in International Theory: Macrosystem Analysis* (New York: Free Press, 1979), pp. 96–7.
9   Kaplan, *System and Process in International Politics*, p. 8.
10   Kaplan's terminology is confusing. While two classes of variables are called rules, the remaining classes are called variables—actor classificatory variables, capability variables and information variables. Yet the variables he specifically called variables he tended to

Collectively these rules provide for the identity and regulatory activity of hypothetical systems in equilibrium. Transformation rules are merely statements of failed essential rules. If any one essential rule fails, they all fail, and the system transforms.

Kaplan strengthened the impression that the rules represent a logical arrangement by insisting that fewer rules were impossible. While a larger number were possible, they would make his model less suitable as the basis of an eventual theory whose deductions would have generalized import. We surmise that no other rules would present themselves no matter who read the historical record. Furthermore, rules as a logical arrangement of postulates and deductions in hypothetical models would appear to function as hypotheses testable in terms of real systems.

In articulating his models Kaplan actually never talked about their deductive and hypothetical properties. He did enumerate a series of hypotheses about regulatory processes which on inspection turn out to be actor centred and not at all system related.[11] He also claimed that if a host of unspecified conditions were met, his models would be predictive. This is a trivial claim, however, because it is true of any model.

The language of variables, rules and system-states allows Kaplan to observe what certain systems look like at a dizzying level of abstraction. What he observed he stated as if it were being explained. John Weltman and Kenneth Waltz have each characterized Kaplan as a bad logician.[12] If the rules were not logically intended, however, then Kaplan can be no more than a bad historian. He made errors in culling the record, perhaps, and in reconstructing it so sparely. He may, as Waltz claimed, have lost the system as a distinctive reality in the process.[13] Certainly he befuddled his audience by not sounding like a historian.

Actually Kaplan's elaborate formulations are excess baggage. Four of the models were only imagined as possible systems in some future time, and their rules are whatever Kaplan chose them to be. The remaining models are the consequential ones for Kaplan, and for us, because they have historical

---

treat as parameters of stipulated, constant value for a given system state. Furthermore, the rules are not merely variables, but statements of variable relationships, containing or implying independent and dependent variables in each instance.

[11] Only in his separate discussion of regulatory processes, *System and Process in International Politics*, Part II, did Kaplan allude to 'systems hypotheses', and then only in passing, p. 87.

[12] John J. Weltman, *Systems Theory in International Relations* (Lexington, MA: Lexington Books, 1973), pp. 57–60; Kenneth N. Waltz, *Theory of International Politics* (Reading, MA: Addison-Wesley, 1979), pp. 52–8.

[13] But see Kaplan, *Towards Professionalism in International Theory*, pp. 12–13, 47–8, and Stanley Hoffmann, *Primacy or World Order: American Foreign Policy since the Cold War* (New York: McGraw Hill, 1978), pp. 146–7.

referents. Stripped of jargon, they are readily seen as distilled wisdom about balance of power and loose bipolar systems.[14] We need only turn to a book Kaplan co-authored on international law to find the Western state system historically treated, with little ado about essential rules and the rest. Balance of power and loose bipolar systems are temporal manifestations of a continuous historical experience and not the disembodied abstractions we find elsewhere.[15]

Both in its stated propositions and in its latent assumptions Kaplan's historical characterization follows in the liberal tradition of assuming the constancy of an economic order and the consequent primacy of interest defined politically—the pursuit of power—in the operation of the system in any of its possible states. Liberal theory depends on the autonomy of the principal actors and on their rationality, understood to mean their acceptance of interest as the governor of behaviour. Economic liberalism defines interests differently only substantively. Kaplan clearly stands in the liberal tradition as applied to politics and in that tradition tends to reflect the views particularly associated with Hans Morgenthau, whose Machiavellian posture supposes that political values, like power and prestige, definitionally constitute a fixed fund.[16] If one actor increases its share from the fund, other shares are diminished. Not to try to increase one's share is to run the risk of losing what one already has, making conflict inevitable. The attributes of conflict are decisively affected by such features of the system as the distribution of power, and this is the reason for engaging in systemic analysis.

Such is a liberal-evolutionary view of '*the* international system'. In content, it is as much Kaplan's as it is Morgenthau's. The differences between them are less epistemological than stylistic, and not at all substantive. It is also the substance of Stanley Hoffmann's view of the international system, which

---

[14] Note that one of Kaplan's imagined systems was called 'tight bipolar'. In common parlance the loose bipolar system is simply called bipolar. The degree of looseness is understood as being subject to considerable change and requiring empirical assessment at any point.

[15] Morton A. Kaplan and Nicholas de B. Katzenbach, *The Political Foundations of International Law* (New York: Wiley, 1961), ch. 2. Kaplan himself has held on to the view that his was a comparative analysis of different historical systems. *Towards Professionalism in International Theory*, p. 131. Nevertheless, specific studies undertaken by his students on the Renaissance Italian system and the 20th-century Chinese warlord system he characterized as 'local international systems embedded in the general international system but apparently sufficiently insulated for long periods to permit independent treatment'. Ibid., p. 162.

[16] As exemplars of the 'Realist' position, both Morgenthau and E. H. Carr excoriated liberals for believing in the likelihood of a 'harmony of interest'. This too limited construction of liberalism wrongly excludes the laissez-faire doctrine, which realism strongly resembles, from the liberal tradition, which, after all, has a 'dismal' or conservative as well as a progressive branch. See Hans J. Morgenthau, *Scientific Man vs. Power Politics* (Chicago: University of Chicago Press, 1946), chs 3, 4; Edward Hallett Carr, *The Twenty Years' Crisis 1919–1939*, 2nd edn (London: Macmillan, 1946), ch. 4.

he nonetheless held up as antipodal to Kaplan's.[17] Here again, differences, being procedural and stylistic, are less than meet the eye. Hoffmann simply sounded more like a historian.

Hoffmann perhaps even more than Kaplan insisted on partitioning the Western experience into discrete systems. As Waltz has shown, the result is a proliferation of systems with no clear criteria for distinguishing among them.[18] Enough change within a system, however much that is, means a change of system. The same tendency is more strikingly present in Richard Rosecrance's effort, published in 1963, to characterize no fewer than nine systems, one following on the other in Western international history after 1740.[19] Rosecrance combined Hoffmann's openly inductive method with Kaplan's substantive concern for systemic identity understood in terms of regulatory activity. Every major war, as an instance of regulatory failure, must spell the death of one system and the cessation of war therefore the birth of another.

Writing in 1965, Charles McClelland redefined the problem of repeated system transformations by reserving the term *transformation* for changes such that no international system would then exist.[20] The criterion for determining that transformation had indeed taken place is quite clear in such a case. The decentralized character of a system constituted of autonomous, 'sovereign' entities must give way to a centralized order. Inasmuch as there has been no such change over the last several centuries of the Western experience, we may freely speak of 'the international system' as one continuous, evolving experience. McClelland and virtually everyone else writing on the subject ever since have seen fit to view the system in just these terms.[21]

For all their talk of systems numberless in principle, Kaplan and Hoffmann came to the same conclusion. They identified two system

---

[17] See Stanley H. Hoffmann, 'International relations: The long road to theory', *World Politics* 11, 3 (1959), pp. 315–62. Hoffmann's most useful statements on the nature of the system are in Stanley H. Hoffmann, 'International systems and international law', *World Politics* 14, 1 (1961), pp. 205–37, and *Primacy or World Order*, ch. 3.

[18] Waltz, *Theory of International Politics*, p. 45.

[19] Richard N. Rosecrance, *Action and Reaction in World Politics: International Systems in Perspective* (Boston: Little, Brown, 1963).

[20] Charles A. McClelland, *Theory and the International System* (New York, Macmillan, 1965), ch. 2.

[21] The major exception would appear to be Michael Haas, 'International subsystems: Stability and polarity', *American Political Science Review* 64, 1 (1970), pp. 98–123. Reference to 'subsystem' sheds no light on the conceptual dilemma of one or many systems. It should also be noted that the study of analytical (sub-)systems—crisis systems, alliance systems, for example—is a vogue McClelland initiated. It takes for granted 'the international system' as a frame of reference. Charles A. McClelland, 'The acute international crisis', *World Politics* 14, 1 (1961), pp. 182–204.

types—Kaplan, balance of power and loose bipolar; for Hoffmann, stable and revolutionary—which together describe the history of the Western state system. The appearance of these two types in succession, in oscillation really, contributed to the now prevailing image of one system: two phases, frequent transitions, indefinite duration, and apparently infinite capacity to rebound from major disruptions such as world wars and absorb the impact of civilizational changes, such as industrialization, often described as revolutionary.

Recent monumental changes in the world are seen no differently. Unprecedented threats of destruction become a property of the system, namely its (in)stability. If there are but two states of the system, multipolar and bipolar, to use the now conventional labels for Kaplan's and Hoffmann's two system types, then one or the other may be the more stable and thus comport better with the structural reality of the balance of terror.[22] Note that answering the question of stability does nothing whatever to ensure the system's survival. On the contrary, it clearly supposes that changes in the distribution of state power, themselves autonomous and inevitable, change the system's polarity and with it our survival prospects.

The passivity of liberal-evolutionary systems thinking eventually provoked an equally evolutionary but actively illiberal view of the Western state system, or 'the modern world-system', as imperially created and dependency creating.[23] An adaptive capitalist economy supplants political relations of dominant powers as the system's explanatory nexus. Rejected is the liberal assumption that the system of competitive politics operates in the manner of a marketplace economy. In its place is the illiberal argument that the global economy is rigged to operate as a marketplace for the few, not just to the exclusion of the many, but at their expense. The point of what passes for international politics is to maintain and service this rigged economy. To the extent that contests among dominant powers are not merely illusory, they are an indulgence afforded the favoured few, again more at the many's expense than their own.

As competing constructions of Western international history, 'the international system' and 'the world-system' both fix on a single, continuous experience. To the extent that either construction is supported, as claimed,

---

[22] This is debated in a series of essays by Waltz, Karl W. Deutsch, J. David Singer, and Rosecrance, conveniently reprinted in James N. Rosenau, ed., *International Politics and Foreign Policy*, 2nd edn (New York: Free Press, 1969), pp. 304–55.

[23] Immanuel Wallerstein, *The Modern World-System: Capitalist Agriculture and the Origins of the European World-Economy in the Sixteenth Century* (New York: Academic Press, 1974); Immanuel Wallerstein, 'The rise and future demise of the world capitalist system: Concepts for comparative analysis', *Comparative Studies in Society and History* 16, 4 (1974), pp. 387–415.

by theory, it must be a theory derived from and applicable to an empirical universe with exactly one item in it. However grandly sketched and richly elaborated, theories of the case are the weakest kind of theory, if theory at all.

Types of international systems

The alternative to making theory for just one case is to delimit a universe of plausible cases, defined by an attribute common to those cases and only to them. The obvious candidate is decentralization. All social systems without centralized political institutions are therefore 'international systems'.[24] But this is not enough. The universe of such systems is potentially huge and inevitably heterogeneous. Such circumstances call for comparative analysis as a precondition of theory-making, and this in turn depends on the classification of cases within the relevant universe. The choice of attributes by which to organize cases is a matter of the analyst's judgement. What seems to work out best for comparative purposes? Differences of judgement may give way to settled opinion, in the manner of normal science, or they may persist at even higher levels of refinement. In any event, exhaustive classificatory schemes enable comparative analysis, and the theory enterprise as a whole, by pointing to the recurring relationships which demand a general form of explanation. Only by proceeding in this fashion can any writer speak of international systems as an object of inquiry.

Kaplan had a list of conceivable international systems. He and others were able to add to this list merely by applying their minds to it.[25] Never was it suggested that the list should be regarded as exhaustive. Nor were systematically comparative or general statements of any kind forthcoming. Modelski, by contrast, identified system types by the possible combination of two attributes ('system properties') characterizing decentralized social systems, which is what all conceivable international systems are, whatever else they may be. The two attributes are size and degree of homogeneity.[26] The former refers to population and the latter to the proportion of the population participating in public affairs. Modelski provided descriptive

---

[24] To call them *states-systems* would be misleading inasmuch as they need not be composed exclusively of states. Wight, *Systems of States*, used this term narrowly to include systems only of states and determined that history has known only three: Western, Greco-Roman and Chinese between 771 BC and 221 AD. Wight also noted the existence of systems including empires and systems of states as components. All such systems would come under the vaguer and more permissive term *international systems*.

[25] See, for example, material by Bruce M. Russett, Kaplan, and Young, also reprinted in Rosenau, *International Politics and Foreign Policy*, at pp. 119–30, 291–303 and 336–45 respectively.

[26] Modelski, 'Agraria and Industria', pp. 126–30.

labels for three of the four possible combinations: a small and homogeneous system is primitive, one that is small and heterogeneous he called agrarian, and one that is large and homogeneous an industrial system.

Modelski launched an important departure from the literature on international politics, and even more on international law, by not calling the Western state system essentially primitive, as the model case of a decentralized system. Instead he argued that the Western state system has features of both agrarian and industrial orders, as would any international system. Agraria and Industria are thus ideal types which occupy the end points of a continuum. Modelski also argued that this particular system was in transition from its largely agrarian origins to the industrial complexion of its dominant members.

Modelski accepted Kaplan's premise that the Western system is 'subsystem dominant', meaning that the system's characteristics are established by characteristics of its most prominent members.[27] One could argue that attributes such as size and degree of homogeneity inhere in the system itself, as well as in its members, and that a small system of big members, or a heterogeneous system of homogeneous members, is easily imagined. In fact, the Western state system would seem to be small, but rapidly growing and increasingly heterogeneous, thus moving from primitive towards agrarian and possibly on to the fourth type, which Modelski neither named nor discussed. Such a system, being both large and heterogeneous, might be called *feudal*, to use the term in its informal sense. It is altogether plausible to present the Western state system as increasingly feudal, yet having pockets (regional subsystems) of a more primitive, agrarian or industrial character. If the system is generally feudal, meaning large, stratified and decentralized, it would hardly be likely to function in the manner of the large, homogeneous industrial polities which appear to dominate it.

Modelski's typology, applied directly at the system level, rather than inferred from the character of its major members, can be supported by reference to an intellectual tradition quite alien to structural-functionalism. The clue is feudalism. This is Karl Marx's most prominent category of pre-capitalist socio-economic orders. There are others, namely primitive and ancient orders.[28] For Marx, primitive orders were indeed small and homogeneous, while ancient ones were small and heterogeneous, typically being urban slave economies. And an order that is both large and homogeneous would in

---

[27] Ibid., pp. 130–2. For Kaplan's argument on subsystem dominance, see *System and Process in International Politics*, pp. 16–18, and *Towards Professionalism in International Theory*, throughout ch. 1.

[28] See especially Karl Marx, *Pre-Capitalist Economic Formations*, trans. Jack Cohen (New York: International Publishers, 1965); K. P. Moseley and Immanuel Wallerstein, 'Precapitalist social structures', *Annual Review of Sociology* 4 (1978), pp. 261–8.

Marxian terms be capitalist, while an order that is large and heterogeneous would be feudal.

If Marx and Modelski used what is effectively the same typology, their concrete descriptions of system types diverge in one instance. What Modelski called agrarian, suggesting land-based, dispersed economic activity, was for Marx ancient, meaning city dominated (Athens, Rome). Modelski assigned several characteristics to an agrarian order which must be taken to represent the pervasiveness of tradition, kinship ties and ascription. These in considerable degree characterize both urban and rural life when the system is *small*. The term *agrarian* is clearly too inclusive and consequently imprecise.[29] Modelski's labels for his system types are less helpful than the typology itself, even though the latter is not fully articulated.

Riggs, from whom Modelski borrowed these labels in the first instance, characterized international system types in quite similar terms, but he avoided concrete descriptive labels altogether. Instead, he used ungainly conceptual labels, 'refracted' and 'fused', to represent Agraria and Industria as ideal types and 'prismatic' for the intermediate model approximated by the Western state system. Even if Riggs managed to avoid projecting the wrong concrete associations with his choice of labels, their lack of sensible references consigned the scheme to near oblivion.[30]

Scholars in the field of international politics have been loath to further Modelski's and Riggs' important efforts to organize comparative inquiry in a theoretically fruitful way. This has come in part, as we have seen, from the growing preoccupation with specific features of 'the international system'. It has come in part from a smug but unwarranted belief that their scholarship has escaped the epistemological weaknesses of structural-functionalism, not to mention its much advertised conservative bias.[31] It has also stemmed from a tendency among political scientists to invoke a narrow definition of politics and to relegate social orders lacking definite authoritative institutions to anthropology and sociology. Forgotten is the fact that a goodly proportion

---

[29] This is a general failing among those using the term *agrarian*. For an interesting attempt to establish all that the term includes, see Gerhard E. Lenski, *Power and Privilege: A Theory of Social Stratification* (Chapel Hill: University of North Carolina Press, 1966), pp. 190–210.

[30] Apparently the only work inspired by Riggs' essay is J. Martin Rochester, *International Institutions and World Order: The International System as a Prismatic Polity* (Beverly Hills, CA: Sage, 1974).

[31] Conservative bias better characterizes scholars choosing to work within the structural-functional tradition than structural-functionalism itself. Arthur L. Stinchcombe, *Constructing Social Theories* (New York: Harcourt, Brace & World, 1968), pp. 91–3; Oran R. Young, *Systems of Political Science* (Englewood Cliffs, NJ: Prentice-Hall, 1968), pp. 36–7. Deliberately comparative structural-functional analysis should lend itself to control over any such bias.

of all social orders, whether political by any given definition or not, happen to be decentralized in character and are therefore comparable as international systems.[32] A classificatory scheme for the comparison of international systems must therefore be appropriate for a universe of social arrangements dominating human history. Appropriate in this instance means sufficiently refined to make sense of the varieties of human experience definitionally encompassed, while simple enough to be of value in later stages of the theoretical enterprise.

We could begin by expanding and amplifying Modelski's typology, which uses a combination of physical and political attributes (size and homogeneity) to identify socio-economic types. There is a problem, however, with the implicit causality of this arrangement. It suggests, though it does not necessitate, that political organization (degree of participation in making crucial decisions for the order) determines the type of socio-economic order. While this may or may not be the case, it would seem to be a premature and avoidable judgement.[33]

It would be less problematic to use a pair of ecological attributes, one physical and one human, which then take the position of being provisionally antecedent to socio-economic and political organization. Modelski's size attribute is not clearly human or physical and is rather crude as a result. An obvious attribute of physical ecology germane to the human experience is climate. The three immediately distinguishable climatic zones of the earth subject to intensive human occupancy are temperate, semi-tropical and tropical. Distinctive socio-economic and political experiences seem to be associated with each, as we shall see later.[34] The most salient attributes of human ecology would seem to be density of population. Again we

---

[32] In this regard Oran Young is a striking exception: 'Over the bulk of recorded history man has organized himself for political purposes on bases other than those now subsumed under the concepts "state" and "nation-state."' 'The actors in world politics', in James N. Rosenau, Vincent Davis and Maurice A. East, eds, *The Analysis of International Politics: Essays in Honor of Harold and Margaret Sprout* (New York: Free Press, 1972), p. 127.

[33] A thorough treatment of this question in genetic terms, with an affirmative answer, is Elman R. Service, *Origins of the State and Civilization: The Process of Cultural Evolution* (New York: Norton, 1975). For the negative answer, see Marvin Harris, *Cultural Materialism: The Struggle for a Science of Culture* (New York: Random House, 1979), Part I.

[34] Speculation on the relation of politics and society to climate goes back to Montesquieu and, after a long period of disrepute, is being revived in the context of apparent global climatic change. [In the 1970s, a global dip in temperatures prompted talk of a coming ice age.] The nomenclature of North and South, now in high fashion, actively if not always explicitly refers to climatic zones, as economists especially seem to understand. See, for example. W. Arthur Lewis, *The Evolution of the International Economic Order* (Princeton: Princeton University Press, 1978). If North equals temperate and South tropical, current nomenclature fails to characterize semi-tropical for political purposes. Wallerstein's category, 'semi-periphery', though juxtaposed between the temperate core and mostly tropical periphery, is economically and politically but not geographically

Table 1.1: Types of International Systems

Climate	Population		
	Sparse	Moderate	Dense
Temperate	Feudal	Commercial-Imperial	Industrial
Semi-Tropical	Ancient	Bureaucratic-Imperial	Corporatist
Tropical	Chieftainly	Agricultural-Imperial	Involuted

commonly note three gradations—sparse, moderate and dense populations for a particular area—and impute distinguishable socio-economic and political consequences.[35]

Arranging the two sets of attributes in a matrix yields nine possible combinations, each of which represents a type of socio-economic and political system (see Table 1.1). Presumably all major instances of historical orders more or less fit into one or another of these typical systems. Labelling each type is bound to be influenced by what appear to be the appropriate historical examples and lends itself inevitably to counter-judgements by those with different readings of the historical record. Nevertheless, a brief rationale for each label is provided.

To begin, I should observe that the term *primitive* is reserved for those simple, egalitarian societies dependent on hunting, gathering and possibly rudimentary horticulture. Wherever found, they support extremely modest populations. The term *agrarian* refers to any land-based economy and probably fits as a general label most orders that are sparsely or moderately populated. Primitive orders are not agrarian because their use of land is not sufficiently systematic. Chieftaincies would appear to be close to the lower threshold of Agraria, while ancient orders, being urban and slave dependent, approach the upper threshold. Because of their reliance on hinterland agrarian activity, systems of the latter type nonetheless appear to be agrarian. Maritime societies, so typical of the temperate zone's moderately populated systems, are classed as agrarian on the basis of technological and social attributes.[36] In the tropics even the densest populations hew to the agrarian pattern.

determined. It tends to include semi-tropical regions but is not restricted to them. Wallerstein, 'Rise and future demise', pp. 403–4, 415.

[35] For a survey of anthropological speculation on the relation of population density to socio-economic and political organization, see Morton H. Fried, *The Evolution of Political Society: An Essay in Political Anthropology* (New York: McGraw Hill, 1967), pp. 196–204, and for a strongly stated argument of causal relation, see Marvin Harris, *Cannibals and Kings: The Origins of Cultures* (New York: Random House, 1977).

[36] On the general resemblance of maritime and agrarian orders, and on specific differences, see Lenski, *Power and Privilege*, pp. 191–2.

Turning now to specific labels, chieftainly systems involve simply organized hierarchies engaged in sporadic warfare and trading relations. Chieftaincies occur in all climates, but they persist in a stable form in the tropics because impenetrable vegetation deters the far-flung but loose organization of feudalism and the concentration of economic activity typical of urban, slave-based societies. While temperate zones do not lend themselves to economic concentration either, unless of course the population increases markedly, relative openness permits confederations of chieftaincies, all the variations of which may be loosely described as feudalism. Ancient systems are also generally capable of maintaining the order beyond the urban core, but doing so frequently involves an increase in population density sufficient to result in bureaucratic empires, which have been a well-known phenomenon throughout the semi-tropical world.

The relatively less hospitable physical circumstances of the temperate world, especially seasonal extremes and slow population growth, make the emergence of commercial empires less likely than in their semi-tropical cousins, bureaucratic empires. By contrast the severely constraining features of tropical life suggest that the imperial phase is likely to be externally fostered, prompting population growth suitable for more systematic exploitation of the tropical environment. Plantation economies seem rarely to evolve spontaneously. The pattern of over-intensive land use in the absence of colonial supervision, identified by Clifford Geertz as agricultural involution, would also seem to require external fostering.[37]

The emergence of Industria from commercial empires requires little comment. The emergence of corporatism from semi-tropical empires is another matter. It should be noted that such empires frequently collapse or are destroyed. Should they survive, they fall into the situation of having outstripped their ability to utilize new resources and provide sufficient growth to keep up with the needs of an expanding population. The result is a tendency for major interests to organize themselves to assure a continuing share of the steady or declining welfare available in that order. The same phenomenon of major sectors in a society squaring off and settling in also seems to characterize industrial systems which have reached the limit of their capacity to grow. In this light, the emergence of increasingly influential functional managers in states and in the industrial world as a whole may be understood as merely an emerging post-industrial form of corporatist order.[38]

---

[37] Clifford Geertz, *Agricultural Involution: The Processes of Ecological Change in Indonesia* (Berkeley: University of California Press, 1966).

[38] The best general statement on the nature of corporatist orders, their semi-tropical fluorescence and their increasing post-industrial incidence is Philippe C. Schmitter, 'Still the century of corporatism?' *Review of Politics* 36, 1 (1974), pp. 84–128.

The labels themselves connote socio-economic and, in some instances, political qualities. Ancient and industrial systems are not politically designated because no one form of political life is typically associated with them. In both instances the socio-economic type may be accompanied by highly centralized to less centralized, pluralistic polities. More generally the prime political variable of the degree of centralization in decision-making must be regarded as analytically separable from socio-economic organization. All socio-economic types admit to substantial variation in the degree of centralization, even if some system types, for example imperial systems, would generally display more centralization than would other system types, feudal systems being an example.

Although the tendency towards centralization within a system may be useful to know, it is not the same thing as centralization of the system. All of the system types identified here are decentralized. Rarely is there one empire, ancient city state, modern nation-state or whatever in the system. The rule is plural centralization: at least a couple, usually several, sometimes many more or less centralized entities coexisting in the system. The instance of singular or systemic centralization is so rare that the ideal, or prediction, of a world state-like order deserves the jaundiced reception it usually gets. In short, our system types are all multi-unit systems which, as a bonus, may do double duty in classifying variously centralized units, or subsystems, within international systems. Misplaced emphasis on the latter function follows from our myopic, unit-level view of social reality rather than what we might call a civilizational view.

It might be possible to provide a political label for each system type by noting the degree to which political roles are present at the system level.[39] This is another way of asking if a system, or type of system, is system or subsystem dominant. As such it is an empirical matter. While the degree of unit-level centralization obviously affects the way the system works, we need not stipulate, as Kaplan does, that a system of highly centralized units for that reason alone is subsystem dominant. Centralized units in an industrial order may choose to promote system-level political roles to manage their relations more efficiently, or they may insist on their autonomy at any cost. We need not assume that either choice is a norm for that system type, so that departures from the norm have to be explained away individually. Dominance is even harder to typify in feudal systems, for example, with their complicated and confining relationships between greater and lesser subsystemic centres.

---

[39] This procedure was suggested by David Easton for identifying the political in primitive systems. 'Political anthropology', in Bernard J. Siegel, ed., *Biennial Review of Anthropology, 1959* (Stanford: Stanford University Press, 1959), pp. 238–47. Easton expected a continuum of system types to emerge.

Systems of the corporatist type also defy conventional thinking about the dominance of territory-centred units because the functional division of labour at the system level is likely to be decisive. This is an important point made by scholars who contrast the state-centric paradigm, as they call it, with the emergence of large-scale transnational activity and attendant fragmentation of states' activity.[40]

Comparison using the nine-cell matrix of international systems presented in Table 1.1 also permits a more refined, or less arbitrary, view of systems transformation than currently found in the literature.[41] The transformation problem may be constructively understood as a change in type of system. Obviously transformation need not be progressive or linear, since movement from any particular cell may be in two, three or four directions (depending on its location in the matrix) to adjacent cells and could conceivably even jump to distant ones. The identification of transformations presupposes general, material causes, which, after all, define the conditions for the existence of a given system type, and encourages investigation of the specific, process-oriented features of each such transformation. Comparison of historical systems, not as transforming but as a sequence of types between transformations, may thus enable general statements about contextual pressures and systemic responses resulting in transformation.

Short of such overt theorizing, a comparison of types between transformations in a given historical system can help us read that system's history without taking for granted the liberal-evolutionary view fostered by those living inside the system's unfolding reality. Consider the several-hundred-year history of the Western state system, which reveals several transformations in system type.[42] If we look back to the system's origins in 15th-century Italy, the system was apparently well urbanized and on the threshold between temperate and semi-tropical. It would thus seem to fit the corporatist model with princes, merchants and prelates all consequential to the system's working. The Italian system also bore characteristics of a

[40] The starting place in the burgeoning literature on this point is Robert O. Keohane and Joseph S. Nye, Jr, eds, *Transnational Relations and World Politics* (Cambridge, MA: Harvard University Press, 1972).

[41] Recent treatments of the transformation problem include Rochester, *International Institutions and World Order*; Edward L. Morse, *Modernization and the Transformation of International Relations* (New York: Free Press, 1976); Dina A. Zinnes, 'Prerequisites to the study of system transformation', in Ole R. Holsti, Randolph M. Siverson, and Alexander L. George, eds, *Change in the International System* (Boulder, CO: Westview Press, 1980), pp. 3–21.

[42] For another, more recent view of international history as a succession of system types, but without any consideration of the transformation problem, and with a different construction of the temporal boundaries of the successive systems of Western international history than presented here, see Evan Luard, *Types of International Society* (New York: Free Press, 1976).

commercial-imperial system in the instance of Venice's role. And the system was quite plausibly flavoured by remembrance of the ancient systems of Greece and Rome.

Rapid northerly migration brought on an altogether feudal system. The classical balance of power is recognizable as a typical feudal institution in which the ascendant power (Spain and then France) is held in check by shifting alliances of somewhat lesser powers. After two centuries or more, population growth in the temperate core of the system transformed it slowly into the imperial order of the 19th century, with commercial rather than bureaucratic or agricultural tendencies except where colonization was involved. Bipolarity in our own time would appear to consummate the tendency towards empire—competing empires really—with all three imperial types manifest in different zones of the globe.

Where is our international system going now? If multinationals were to functionally supplant the territorially fixed (feudal-imperial) actors, as some suggest will happen, we would see an increasingly corporatist system, both in the temperate and semi-tropical zones. A largely corporatist system, populated with overly mature (post-industrial) and never maturing (Mediterranean) members, would have got there without going through an industrial phase, although the presumably interdependent industrial powers may well represent a transitional subordinate system at the present time. Meanwhile, the postcolonial tendency towards tropical involution would undoubtedly continue, pushing the system closer to the corporatist-involutional threshold of system types.

If, alternatively, the rise of the multinationals is overrated and the contemporary state system proves durable enough to contain political tensions and continues to support a healthy global capitalism, including rapid economic growth in the tropics, then we might see the gradual transformation of the global system from its imperial incarnation into something legitimately qualifying as industrial. Even then features of its feudal-imperial past would linger on.[43] Previous transformations were, after all, rarely quick and clean cut enough to present us with anything resembling pure types.

Neither this generalization nor any other we might devise with respect to the evolution of the Western state system necessarily fits the case of any other international system. Only comparative inquiry will tell. And only then are we prepared to venture into the realm of theory, not just theory of the case, but theory applicable to the universe of international systems.

---

[43] This assumes that at least in the short run a healthy capitalist order does not outgrow its need for the state system as a protective umbrella. In the longer run a healthy capitalist-industrial order could result in the transcendence of multinational functional actors. So must a stagnant corporatist, post-industrial order. See also Wallerstein, 'Rise and future demise'.

2

Prometheus Prostrate (1984)

The last decade has seen a fierce debate on the material prospects of industrial civilization. Spurred by the publication, in 1972, of *Limits to Growth*, controversial first report to the Club of Rome, this debate registers notes of anxiety and truculence not previously heard in discussions of the post-industrial future.[1] *Limits to Growth* attempts to identify the consequences of exponential growth in population, production and pollution, were high rates of growth to continue as they have in Western life for the last two centuries. Before the report few would have argued that such growth was possible indefinitely, but almost everyone conveniently assumed that material abundance produced by prior growth would permit deceleration of future growth and the solution of growth-induced problems. Underlying this assumption was a faith in instrumental knowledge, which has grown along with everything else and enabled the conquest of the most intractable problems by reducing them to manageable elements and subjecting them to specialized expertise, backed by mammoth societal resources as needed.

Limits to Growth also values analytic procedures. It reduces the characteristic products (and by-products) of industrial civilization—material advantages, capital (both human and physical), depletion and contamination—into several categories, the relations among which are represented as a model, subject to computer-facilitated simulation into the future. Upon reaching the scale and complexity we find today, the full range of productive activities results in an impenetrable tangle of difficulties and dilemmas having no historical parallel. The Club of Rome promoted a new and quite useful term for this phenomenon: the global *problematique*.

Limits to Growth further presumes that instrumental knowledge, problem-solving skills and technological advances can and do overcome obstacles to

---

[1] On the Club of Rome, *Limits to Growth*, and the other eight reports so far submitted to the Club, and their relation to the debate, see Nicholas Greenwood Onuf, 'Reports to the Club of Rome', *World Politics* 36, 1 (1983), pp. 121–46.

growth as they arise in each category of productive activity. Nevertheless, the *Limits* argument will not assign to technological problem-solving a redemptive role: technological success, and continued growth, cannot occur indefinitely in all categories because success in one is an additional problem for the others. New problems pyramid, compounding their effects and outstripping the capabilities of the problem-solving enterprise, itself increasingly cobbled by problems of scale and complexity. *Limits to Growth* follows this logic to its drastic conclusion that a collapse of the whole system within decades is a distinct possibility. Technological wizardry may buy time, but, by driving growth all the more certainly beyond sustainable limits, it also increases the likelihood of disaster. Even with a 'technological policy in every sector of the world model to circumvent in some way the various limits to growth', we nevertheless face 'an end to growth before the year 2100'.[2]

At no point do *Limits to Growth* authors actually and unequivocally forecast collapse. They hold out hope that recognition of the *problematique* will provoke an appropriately comprehensive response. They worry about learning lags under conditions of rapid change, and they leave it to our imagination how social awareness, political will and behavioural change will fuse in the right mould for a new world. For the most part readers drew different conclusions. Either they dismissed the report, alleging methodological or conceptual naivety, or damned it as alarmist, even seditious claptrap. Or they embraced its computer projections as dramatic warning of dire possibilities. *Limits to Growth* asked if the system of capitalist growth could be controlled; and provided an unconvincing answer. Readers asked if the costs and consequences of growth should be controlled. Their divergent answers—condemning or defending the system for the reason of its success—defined the terms of the ensuing debate.

Success means abundance. Rallying under *Limits'* banner are those concerned with environmental and distributive ailments accompanying abundance—for them quantity threatens quality. On the other side are technological enthusiasts and free marketeers, including defenders of trickle-down and devotees of the idea that scarcity is an artefact of price—quantity permits quality. Crudely, these two camps mirror left and right in the United States as little more than divergent attitudes on the meaning of responsibility and profligacy. They both also reject what Marxists would call the vulgar materialism of *Limits to Growth*, whether by advocating innovative learning, attitude shifts and institutional reform, or by extolling human inventiveness, responsiveness to market forces and institutional resilience. Finally both sides

---

2   Donella H. Meadows, Dennis L. Meadows, Jørgen Randers, and William W. Behrens III, *Limits to Growth: A Report for the Club of Rome's Project on the Predicament of Mankind* (New York: Universe Books, 1972), p. 141.

agree, at least implicitly, that abundance may present problems, but these will fall before public pressure for a more decent planet or the price mechanism, depending on one's position in the debate. Gone is the preoccupation with, and progressively even a recognition of, the global *problematique* as a distinctive condition of modernity. Even the Club of Rome, as reflected through the succession of reports it has accepted since *Limits to Growth*, has abandoned the *problematique*, with its nastily materialist and determinist connotations, not to mention its intimations of doom.

Limits to Growth came at a time of economic uncertainty and social stress. It linked historic processes of growth to a sense of unease and defensiveness about the fate of civilization 'as we know it'. A decade of abundance severed this link, so that the meaning of the economic downturn of the 1980s goes undebated as a systemic phenomenon. Apprehensions are linked instead to the deterioration of détente and discharged in the debate, important enough in its own right, about the nuclear arms race.

We might even suppose that the question of untrammelled growth in nuclear capabilities would be seen as a mutant form of the question posed by *Limits to Growth* about growth overall. Yet we find otherwise: discussion of nuclear limits, sadly mimicking that of material limits, uses the language of choice, margin of error, opportunity and control, as if it were a matter of management *versus* market for preferred regulation of the situation. Much less in evidence is any sense of material forces out of control, complexity rendering all choices illusory, limits long exceeded and disaster waiting, pent up, in crouching, explosive certainty. If publics fret and fear, soothe them with comforting messages about the future: things are not so bad, we can manage, freeze the situation, we're learning, let's just be careful for a while, we've made so much progress, the system does work in its way, we won't fail because we can't afford to, it's never too late.

Questions of growth

Behind the assertions and recommendations that constitute positions held in any debate stand theories—generally cast, usually rather simple causal statements held to account for the large and abiding features of the situation framed by debate. Parties to the debate may have their own theories or they may deploy the same theory to contrary effect. In *Limits to Growth* and the debate it inspired, growth is taken for granted; Prometheus bounds. Everyone seems to agree that technological gains cause material growth, but the two sides accompany this theory with significantly different definitions of the situation.

Those arguing the existence of objective limits to growth see technology as an engine of growth in an expansively defined situation, one in which there is room to grow. Run out of room and growth is impossible; yet pressure to grow continues, risking catastrophic down-growth. Those denying the existence of such limits see technology as coupled not only to growth but to the definition of the situation. With growth comes room in which to grow. Technology solves problems related to apparent resources scarcity, for example, when prices, reflecting scarcity, rise sufficiently to direct investment in such solutions. More or other resources become available, patterns of use are altered, efficiency increased, cost lowered, consumption encouraged, economies of scale achieved, and the rate of growth sustained.

That both sides take growth to be the consequence of gains in technology implies a shared anterior theory, to the effect that technology itself grows as a consequence of prior material growth. The system of growth is thus dominated by a powerful internal logic of growth fuelling itself in constant acceleration. Capitalism's distinctive and decisive trait—wealth breeding wealth—anchors the debate, making it intelligible to both sides and holding it close to the current, Keynesian centre of the liberal tradition. *Not* a part of the debate is recognition of the possibility, central to Marxism, that capitalism must fail from its own contradictions (this notwithstanding a striking resemblance in form between the *Limits to Growth* position and the Marxist one). Nor is it a part of the debate that contemporary liberalism may have betrayed the basic premise that wealth must be used in the first instance to generate more wealth and not rectify the social consequences of capitalist dynamics, since new wealth will result in amelioration anyway.

Contemporary liberalism, as well as Marxism, is bounded out of the debate. Important evidence of this is the uniform disregard by those discussing growth, and its limits, abundance and dangers, of regular, substantial fluctuations in the growth curve of capitalism. Economists and technologists operating within the dominant Keynesian tradition are disposed to see the curve of technological growth as relatively smooth and the rate of such growth rather constant, at least rather more constant than the rate of material growth.[3] Periodicity in the latter is said to be caused by intervening variables, susceptible to technical control, in the growth equation.

The alternative is, as a contemporary exponent, Gerhard Mensch, suggests, Schumpeterian in its general dimensions.[4] It is also familiar to Marxists. One overriding cause of growth is itself subject to a pattern of variation which, discounting lags and minor wobbles from intervening variables, matches the

---

[3] Confining such curves to particular industries aggravates the bias. For illustrations of what thus appear to be stable rates of technological growth, see Edwin Mansfield, *The Economics of Technological Change* (New York: Norton, 1968), ch. 2.

[4] Gerhard Mensch, *Stalemate in Technology: Innovations Overcome the Depression* (Cambridge, MA: Ballinger, 1979), pp. 212–14.

pattern of growth. In other words, technology may possess a periodicity which, when everything else is stripped away, explains the secular tendency for material growth to fall back suddenly between lurches forward. While the confluence of many factors may contribute to short-run, empirically well-established cycles of capitalist growth, 50-year fluctuations, which go by the name of Kondratiev, or long, waves, are also discernible.

Long discussed by Marxists and made famous by Joseph Schumpeter, long waves are currently enjoying a marked revival of interest, especially among European scholars.[5] Recent special issues on long waves in *Futures* (August and October 1981), with contributions from virtually every major student of the subject, represent an important step in focusing public attention on the technological spurs of cyclical growth. Certainly the sputtering world economy of recent years has readied the audience. Yet the long waves literature fails generally to place itself in the decade-long debate on growth. This is all the more perplexing because some of the principals figured in that debate's early days.[6]

Instead much energy is invested in demonstrating the existence of long waves in particular sectors of productive activity, presumably to appease sceptical economists, or refining the evidence of their relation to innovations of particular types. Despite protestations that most explanations for the occurrence of long waves complement each other at a certain level of generality, there appears to be no generalized, multi-factor construction of the long wave dynamic such that an informed public could see its relevance to the larger question of growth's prospects. It is not just that the long waves literature is remarkably reticent about the future, or the social and political implications of its message (although most of it is); rather, its authors fail to see their work as even having a message.

For purposes of debate, long waves must be endowed with the same paradigmatic significance that the report *Limits to Growth* granted to the idea of limits to growth. The writers who come closest to doing this are Mensch, the Schumpeterian liberal, and the great Trotskyite economist,

---

[5] Kondratiev's most fully developed statement, 'The long waves in economic life', and a number of essays reflecting the current revival, along with an annotated bibliography, comprise a special issue of *Review* 2, 4 (1979). On the liberal side, see Joseph Schumpeter, *Business Cycles*, 1 (New York: McGraw-Hill, 1939), chs 4–7; Mensch, *Stalemate in Technology*, ch. 2; Orio Giarini, *Dialogue on Wealth and Welfare: An Alternative View of World Capital Formation* (Elmsford: Pergamon Press, 1980), ch. 2.

[6] Specifically: Jay W. Forrester, who initiated work leading to *Limits to Growth*; Christopher Freeman, who contributed to the early and, for many, definitive critique of *Limits to Growth*, published in Britain as *Thinking about the Future*, in the United States as *Models of Doom* (1973); Jan Tinbergen, who coordinated work on the third report to the Club of Rome, *Reshaping the International Order* (1976).

Ernest Mandel.[7] Neither succeeds because of the other's effort; their central ideas stand in complementary opposition. What binds their views is an emphasis on the supply of whatever is needed for growth, rather than the demand for whatever growth might produce.[8] By doing undoubted violence to the subtleties of each, we can construct a relatively simple, though multicausal, historically situated account of the phenomenon of long waves.

Long waves—a generalized, multi-factor account

Fifty-year waves of material prosperity and decline follow on a progression of technological revolutions, which are themselves swells in the introduction and implementation of already available innovations. The first revolution (about 1775, triggering a long wave conventionally dated as beginning in 1787) was the Industrial Revolution itself. A second revolution (about 1825, long wave dating from the 1840s) resulted in 'railroadization'. A third (about 1886, long wave from 1890s) centred on innovations depending on electrical power and the combustion of petroleum derivatives. A fourth revolution (about 1935, long wave from 1940s) employed innovations initially satisfying military needs.[9]

All acknowledge that the innovative core of the Industrial Revolution was the steam engine's displacement of animal power. Liberal writers see innovations coming thereafter in clusters, the regular spacing of which is explained by diminishing returns on investment in the preceding cluster, economic depression and technological stagnation, and finally weakening resistance to entrepreneurial risk-taking. Mandel singles out innovations launching 'fundamental revolutions in power technology— the technology of the production of motive machines by machines'.[10] Mandel's focus on transformations in the means by which machines are made and used to

---

[7] Ernest Mandel, *Late Capitalism* (London: Verso, 1978), ch. 4; Ernest Mandel, *Long Waves of Capitalist Development* (Cambridge: Cambridge University Press, 1980); Ernest Mandel, 'Explaining long waves of capitalist development', *Futures* 13, 4 (1981), pp. 332–8.

[8] Long wave perspectives not centred on the conditions of supply are excluded from discussion here because they disavow the one assumption common to both sides in the public debate on the future—that technology governs growth. For convenient summaries and evaluation of the full range of long waves writings of the moment, see Jos Delbeke, 'Recent long-wave theories: A critical survey', *Futures* 13, 4 (1981), pp. 246–57.

[9] Fixing dates on cyclical phenomena like long waves and technological revolutions is inevitably arbitrary. Much depends on the indicators chosen; temporal lags and spatial variations are to be expected. It is difficult to know if what is said to be causally connected is even correlated.

[10] Mandel, *Late Capitalism*, p. 118.

perform work is evidently an empirical conclusion. His explanation for their occurrence at regular intervals covers all the innovations in a cluster and in no way requires a revolution specifically in power technology.[11]

In Mandel's scheme, each technological revolution rejuvenates capitalism by absorbing underemployed capital and rewarding its use with a high rate of profit. Gradually the rate of profit declines as technological gains are consolidated, markets saturate, the organic composition of capital rises until conditions are ripe again for capital to come out of 'hiding' and propel a new technological revolution. Mandel's analysis comports quite well with liberal, largely Schumpeterian accounts of the relation of long waves to clusters of technological innovation. Available capital, and entrepreneurial readiness to try unexploited innovations, together constitute a push–pull engine of exponential growth. No differently, diminishing returns on an entrenched technology, declining rates of profit, and entrepreneurial conservatism push and pull capitalism into a phase of exponential down-growth, thus creating conditions for underemployed capital and a new set of innovations to come forth.

According to this logic, a fifth technological revolution should be starting now, or have already started, its effects on the global capitalist economy becoming appreciable by the end of the decade. Mensch, for example, holds this view and projects an impending period of 'hyperindustrialization'.[12] Mandel seems to be unwilling to grant capitalism a fifth technological revolution and another 50 years. In recent work, he admits to the possibility, but believes that labour and liberation forces will not accept the costs in dislocation and repression.[13] Instead he expects a transition to socialism pre-empting technological rejuvenation which otherwise is due presently. Inasmuch as the last third of each wave—the decay phase—is likely to reveal stresses in capitalist dynamics, it would seem there is no greater reason to anticipate transition to socialism now than in the equally traumatic periods 1920–40, 1870–90 and 1820–40.

---

[11] Mandel specifically rejects the argument that infrastructural transformation, implying a particular set of innovations, is the dominant feature of each new wave. Ibid., pp. 51–3. It would appear, however, that power revolutions occasion infrastructural transformation and, in so doing, enforce a temporal regularity on the cycle. On infrastructural transformation, defended as a more integrally Marxist explanation for long waves, see David M. Gordon, 'Stages of accumulation and long economic cycles', in Terence K. Hopkins and Immanuel Wallerstein, eds, *Processes of the World System* (Beverly Hills, CA: Sage Publications, 1980), pp. 26–31. Among liberals, Forrester adopts an infrastructural orientation, but his does not assign technology a causally significant role; Jay W. Forrester, 'Innovation and economic change', *Futures* 13, 4 (1981), pp. 323–31.

[12] Mensch, *Stalemate in Technology*, ch. 9.

[13] Mandel, 'Explaining long waves', p. 338.

There is even a case that present circumstances are even less conducive to the overthrow of capitalism than were those previous periods of decay and discontent.

Necessary to this case is Mandel's empirically astute but, in terms of his explanation for long waves, peripheral observation that the heart of each technological revolution has been transformation in the means of powering the means for doing work. Mandel grouped nuclear and electronic motive forces in a single revolution beginning in the 1940s. The subsequent three decades of technological development strongly suggest that these simultaneously appearing and transforming sectors of technology should be decoupled. Quite plausibly, nuclear technology has followed the path dictated by long wave logic and is now reaching its point of decline. The recent troubled history of nuclear power would so indicate. Electronics technology has followed a markedly different course. Accelerating technological advances reveal that transformation was only intimated 30 years ago and has even yet to reach a crescendo.

Standing alone, the nuclear revolution looks like a weak transformation, the consolidating effects of which might take only 30 years, instead of the usual 50, to be played through. Perhaps we should see it as a failed revolution, not to be counted at all. By contrast, electronics looks like a fifth technological revolution not anticipated by Mandel. It departs from the norm by appearing to have begun before the previous, albeit weak revolution had completed its cycle, and its extraordinary dynamism over three decades suggests that it will be as strong as its predecessor is weak, taking who knows how much longer to reach its peak.

Inasmuch as a technological surge does not coincide with the availability of requisite inventions, but depends rather on social and economic conditions encouraging their coordinate development and use, circumstances may offer a choice of revolutions. In such cases, pressure will develop in favour of the cheapest among the candidates. Nuclear and electronic revolutions initially competed, but the former quickly and conclusively showed itself to be uncompetitive.

The fact that the electronic revolution is so much more cost-attractive than the nuclear revolution is directly related to a distinctive attribute of the former. The development of computers, microprocessors and correlative high-speed communications equipment cannot, after all, be called a transformation of power technology in the usual sense. It substitutes the digestion and manipulation of huge amounts of information for sheer physical power to do a given amount of work. If increments of power are more expensive than increments of information processing, per unit of work accomplished, cost drops. On the face of it, this condition is met. The electronic revolution has dissociated the movement of information from unwieldy vehicles within which it must be moved. Even more, information is organized to work in place of things that must be made and moved at costs determined by outmoded power technologies.

Technology—the guiding hand?

The fifth technological revolution is the first revolution to lower the need for power to drive growth, instead of augmenting the amount of power available. It can only have a decisive effect on industrial civilization and gives warrant to the much discussed notion of a service-oriented post-industrial world. But what of the next such revolution? The peculiar configuration of current technologies admits two possibilities here. One would proceed even further in the direction of substituting control over how work is done for gross capabilities to do work. In short, revolutions in control technologies would supersede revolutions in power technologies, and growth of information would supersede material growth. This means that the present is a turning point in capitalism's evolution, with probable changes in associated social and political practices. Control technologies strongly suggest that what one could call the social function of technology will surpass its material function in importance. Technologists will be preoccupied with managerial concerns, not the least of which is organizing work to cost less. Whether such technomanagerialism will in turn promote pluralist functionalism or friendly fascism remains to be seen.[14]

The alternative to a change of dynasty from power technologies to control technologies must be the arrival of an authentic revolution in power technology. The time for this is ripe, as evidenced by chronic energy-related problems in the global economy today. Probably some of the inventions needed have already been made. Also needed is imaginative entrepreneurial leadership (Schumpeter) and a superabundance of under-rewarded capital (Mandel). Observe, however, that costs of successive revolutions in power technology have risen enormously, no doubt exponentially at a rate

---

[14] The term 'friendly fascism' is borrowed from Bertram Gross, *Friendly Fascism: The New Face of American Power* (New York: M. Evans, 1980). Of writers represented in *Futures'* special issues on long waves, only Mandel, 'Explaining long waves', and Andre Piatier, 'Innovation, information and long-term growth', *Futures* 13, 5 (1981), pp. 371–82, see the next wave as dominated by control technologies. The former is repelled, the latter elated, by the idea. Forrester, 'Innovation and economic change', pp. 330–1, contents himself with recommending political innovation, especially to control population and food problems, without examining what such control implies. Some of his associates have expanded on the role of political and social innovation but have given even less attention to the implications of control. Alan K. Graham and Peter M. Senge, 'A long-wave hypothesis of innovation', *Technological Forecasting and Social Change* 17, 4 (1980), pp. 306–8.

comparable to or even greater than that of material growth generally. It is not simply that the innovative process is more expensive and riskier, although it is surely both. The process of consolidating and developing diverse inventions into a technological revolution is equally susceptible to exponentially increasing costs and risks.[15]

The capital generated by each maturing wave has also grown exponentially—obviously sufficiently to finance successive revolutions. It cannot be taken for granted, however, that the capital so generated will always suffice. If science and technology are by their nature, and after a point, subject to diseconomies of scale and diminishing returns on investment, the rate at which costs grow will eventually surpass the rate at which capital grows. Powerful grounds exist for viewing science and technology in these terms, but the point at which the curve of capital costs crosses the curve of capital growth may not yet have been reached. Even so, the proportion of capital available for frivolous use must be declining. At the same time, the organizational means for gathering and distributing capital must also keep pace with both the growing volume of capital and the growing share of that capital needed for a technological revolution.

Historically, each revolution has been accompanied by the emergence of a capital-mobilizing vehicle on a successively larger scale. The industrialist as capitalist was succeeded by financiers, who were in turn succeeded by state monopolies of capital. The next higher stage would likely be Kautsky's legendary 'ultraimperialist' consortium of 'internationally united finance capital', presumably involving public bureaucracies and private multinational enterprises.[16] It is altogether problematic whether the state system, which operated so efficiently to enable state monopoly capitalism in the context of the current nuclear and electronic revolutions, will bow out, blow up or blend into a mixed-actor, ultraimperialist combination of capital mobilizers.

Control technology or power technology?

Even if enough capital exists in principle to finance the next revolution in power technology—presumably a revolution in the provision of ample, cheap and inexhaustible energy—it is unlikely to happen spontaneously, meaning

---

[15] Orio Giarini and Henri Loubergé, *The Diminishing Returns of Technology: An Essay on the Crisis in Economic Growth* (Elmsford: Pergamon Press, 1978), pp. 92–6, illustrate this point with respect to risks. Nicholas Rescher, *Scientific Progress: A Philosophical Essay on the Economics of Research in Natural Science* (Pittsburgh: University of Pittsburgh Press, 1978), does so for costs.

[16] Quoted words are from a passage of Kautsky's, which Lenin reproduced for purposes of vituperative attack. V. I. Lenin, *Imperialism, The Highest Stage of Capitalism* (New York: International Publishers, 1939), p. 117.

as a matter of entrepreneurial good fortune and capital finding its way to the big payoff. It is a possible consequence of conscious policy. Such a policy could be described as 'modified global Lafferism'. The current vogue for 'supply-side' economics in the United States should not disguise the warrant for this view in a Schumpeterian orientation.

The now famous Laffer curve proposes that once a state absorbs a certain proportion of newly created wealth into the public sector, the private sector is sufficiently impoverished that classical growth mechanisms cease to operate.[17] In concrete terms, the diversion of profits into transfer payments precludes investment necessary for capitalist growth. No longer is it possible for privately held capital to be pooled on a scale sufficient to finance a new technological revolution. If public authorities were to continue to secure for their use the same or an even higher proportion of available new wealth but at the same time decrease distributive obligations, we might then have in one place the wealth needed to pay for a new revolution in power technology. What the modern state does now for military purposes it would do on the same or larger scale for the single purpose of fostering a revolution in power technology. Extrapolating from costs of contemporary revolutions, even this might not be sufficient.

Countries could have to pool their wealth in some global arrangement. Countries most experienced in mobilizing capital for designated purposes are those with centrally planned economies premised on a repudiation of capitalism. Apparently, saving capitalism, in the important sense of ensuring its capacity to deliver a sustained rate of growth, may prove inconsistent with capitalism's *laissez-faire* origins, and even more may require an embrace of uncongenial practices. Whether the consequences are called socially managed capitalism or capital-dependent socialism, Lafferism is stood upon its head.

There is obvious irony in combining Lafferesque logic with statism, not to mention ultrastatism. Since the usual justification for statism is redistribution, not growth, the characteristic political alignments of late capitalism are unsuited to the confounding requirements of a modified global Lafferism.[18] So unlikely is a sixth reign in the current dynasty of revolutions in power technology, with its hyperindustrial consequences, that any comment on its normative and political implications is superfluous.

The major possibilities, aside from an ever-present possibility of a thermonuclear *Endlösung*, are, first, collapse, not from too much growth, but

---

[17] For a simple presentation, see Jude Wanninski, 'Taxes, revenues and the "Laffer curve"', *Public Interest*, 50 (1978), pp. 3–16.

[18] For observations to similar effect but without reference to the particular policy discussed here, see Charles E. Lindblom, *Politics and Markets: The World's Political-Economic Systems* (New York: Basic Books, 1977), part V.

from too little in the twilight of a last technological revolution dragged out by institutionalizing imperialism and arms economies. The capitalist world order ends gasping and whimpering. Or, second, the overthrow of a dynasty of power technologies and their replacement with a post-capitalist dynasty of control technologies. Control over information leads duly to psychochemical control and thence to genetic engineering and eugenic control. Social need more than technological readiness will regulate their succession.

The liberal mind, which has enough difficulty with behaviourism and sociobiology, cannot countenance the second alternative in the disciplined terms of social science. It takes refuge instead in fictional treatments of the future and interprets the inversion of liberal values foretold therein as a nightmare to be avoided. The poverty of functionalism as a social and political philosophy is precisely its inability to assess the implications of technomanagerialism in circumstances of stagnant or declining wealth. Functionalism, in short, has never confronted the possibility of downward growth because it has never had to. If downward growth comes to characterize capitalism, it bears asking whether functionalism in such circumstances is actually a recipe for what are often called corporatist and fascist orders. The costs of control technologies are likely to be so much less than those incurred for another revolution in power technology that they are easily reconciled with functionalism as efficient, non-territorial authoritarianism, less personalized than fascism in either friendly or unfriendly versions and certainly more sanitized. And the people, some reduced in material circumstances, some gaining, will be supplied with new and different comforts.[19]

The changing debate

Perhaps the debate on the future will retrieve a focus on the overriding issue of growth, and capitalism's ability to sustain it, when Western economies undergo additional, even more jolting rounds of disruption—when the limp Prometheus convulses. Those with at least a glimmer of the malady's cause smugly assert that a little tax relief will cure the problem. Those who correctly sense the magnitude of the patient's symptoms seem to be so dumbfounded as to disregard even the possibility of a diagnosis. The intellectual climate of the early 1980s suggests that a compounding of the symptoms of distress is not enough. Something dire must happen—an energy crisis of vastly greater proportions than the last one, collapse of a major economy, breakdown of the system of international payments. Conceivably some such event and

---

[19] Also see Chapter 11, with particular reference to functionalism, social control, and the effects of weightless information on social arrangements.

its many untoward repercussions will conspire to raise the magnitude and quality of the debate to the level sustained in an earlier incarnation just prior to World War II.

The earlier version of the debate on the future was prompted by the great depression and the rise of fascism. It was closed off by the peremptory exigencies of a world war and was not renewed after the war's close because circumstances seemed to have changed fundamentally. Only with the hindsight of several post-war decades are we beginning to realize that the aberration in the evolution of Western civilization was not the period of the 1930s and 1940s but the distortedly prosperous and peculiarly stable 1950s and 1960s. As befits a debate on the future of industrial civilization, the nodes of concern were the health of capitalism and the relation of capitalism's alternatives—socialism and fascism—to the liberal political tradition of the West. If one theme can be said to have characterized the debate, it was posed as the choice between planning and freedom. If one assumption dominated discussion, it was that the rise of planning represented, at least potentially, a transition in the development of advanced economies comparable to the transition from feudalism to capitalism.[20]

There are several things about the pre-World War II debate worth noting. It raised the largest possible political questions, as well as the more obvious economic ones, in sizing up trends and their implications. Participants openly acknowledged their preferences; the debate was unambiguously ideological, and it was directed towards the public without the patronizing tone so often heard from experts. By and large the frame of reference was the future of one or a few countries, which provided audiences for individual salvos in the engagement, but all exchanges were pervaded with an awareness of what was at stake for the entire industrial world.

Compare features of this debate with the version initiated by the Club of Rome. The revived debate has routinely avoided large political questions. It has smothered genuine fears and suspicions about the future in a blanket

---

[20] Important contributions to the debate include Karl Mannheim, *Man and Society in an Age of Reconstruction: Studies in Modern Social Structure* (London: Kegan Paul, 1940); Joseph A. Schumpeter, *Capitalism, Socialism and Democracy* (New York: Harper, 1942); Karl Polanyi, *The Great Transformation: The Political and Economic Origins of Our Time* (New York: Farrar & Rinehart, 1944); Friedrich A. Hayek, *The Road to Serfdom* (Chicago: University of Chicago Press, 1944). Note that participants in the debate were typically driven by fascism to the English-speaking world, and their statements appeared first in German and then in English, achieving a final book form during the war. At least two other enduring works emerged from the debate but are thematically less central to it: Erich Fromm, *Escape from Freedom* (New York: Rinehart and Winston, 1941), and Karl A. Popper, *The Poverty of Historicism* (London: Routledge & Kegan Paul, 1957), the latter first appearing in journal form in 1944–45.

of technical chatter and lofty sentiments. Experts speak only to their own constituencies, ignoring the large audience gathered by *Limits to Growth*. The question of planning versus freedom is falsely assumed to have been answered by events. The triumph of planning in most advanced economies perhaps encourages economists not to resume their leading roles in the debate, but it also ignores one point that is presumably central to the debate. This is the widely accepted assertion that the future of industrial civilization entails meshing many more-or-less planned economies. If the rhetoric of interdependence is taken seriously, then we must conclude that the question of planning versus freedom on a global scale is more important than ever.[21]

In the liberal intellectual community, it is chiefly the late Herman Kahn and his associates at the Hudson Institute who have treated the renewed debate as central to the general public's concern for the future and worthy of repeated if unanswered broadsides.[22] Kahn's combative tone conveys a distinctive appreciation of the stakes involved. Economic issues and their relation to technology are paramount, especially in Kahn's last major work before his death, but the discussion is not technical, for Kahn and many of his associates are not economists. Arguably Kahn short-changed the political implications of his preferred and probable future, but other commentators on post-industrialism are less sanguine and more expansive on this question.[23] Of course these other forays into the future take the adaptive and innovative capabilities of capitalism for granted. Nevertheless, their focus on the texture of post-industrial life is commendably popular in tone and directs attention to the real possibility that civilization has reached one of the great turning points in its history.[24] Which way it turns is another matter—a matter of debate.

If the best qualities of the discussion on post-industrialism were grafted onto the debate on the prospects of industrial civilization, addressed most

---

[21] Writers in the United States are particularly remiss in this respect, with Lindblom's *Politics and Markets* a striking exception. Lindblom, however, deliberately eschews debate and 'the grand critiques', like Polanyi's, that debate entails. See pp. 76–77 and note a rather Olympian tone throughout.

[22] Herman Kahn, William Brown, and Leon Martel, *The Next Two Hundred Years: A Scenario for America and the World* (New York: William Morrow, 1976); Herman Kahn and John B. Phelps, 'The economic present and future', *The Futurist* 13, 3 (1979), pp. 202–22; Herman Kahn, *The Coming Boom: Economic, Social and Political* (New York: Simon and Schuster, 1982). See also Julian L. Simon, *The Ultimate Resource* (Princeton: Princeton University Press, 1981).

[23] See, foremost, Daniel Bell, *The Coming Post-Industrial Society: A Venture in Social Forecasting* (New York: Basic Books, 1973) and Daniel Bell, *The Cultural Contradictions of Capitalism* (New York: Basic Books, 1976).

[24] Kahn and Phelps, 'The economic present and future', Chart 2, p. 202, and p. 204, see the entire period of industrial growth as a great transition from stable agricultural communities to a stable post-industrial and, in due course, truly planetary economy.

plausibly in terms of growth, the debate could acquire the force and vitality of its earlier manifestation. Needed most are exponents of any alternative to the Hudson position with the same seriousness of purpose and sense of the proportion of the debate. Lacking proportion are those ever more numerous studies devoted to the relative decline of the United States. The resurgence of capitalism in new productive sectors and different places in the world is taken for granted.[25] Kahn's work aside, only Western Marxists are sustaining a major debate on the transition from capitalism.[26] While they have appropriated a term once central to liberal discourse, their debate on transition is as impenetrable as it is alien to those who have been awarded, or who have arrogated, responsibility for our future.[27] They—we—seem intent in wrapping the prostrate Prometheus in a shroud of silence, all the while industriously debating other, lesser matters.

All I'm saying is that knowledge brings a penalty with it of course, it was enterprising of him—what's his name, Jason, Prometheus, that fellow—in his place I might have done the same.

Doris Lessing, *Briefing for a Descent into Hell*

---

[25] While most such studies are concretely cast and country specific, at least one major theoretical treatment completely disregards the global *problematique* of growth: Mancur Olson, *The Rise and Decline of Nations: Economic Growth, Stagflation, and Social Rigidities* (New Haven: Yale University Press, 1982).

[26] See, for example, Paul M. Sweezy and Charles Bettelheim, *The Transition to Socialism* (New York: Monthly Review Press, 1971). For access to the much larger Marxist literature on crisis in capitalism, see John Bellamy Foster, 'Marxian economics and the state', *Science & Society* 46, 3 (1982), pp. 257–83.

[27] One of the few attempts from the left to use language intelligible to liberals is Michael Harrington, *The Twilight of Capitalism* (New York: Simon and Schuster, 1976).

3

Centre–Periphery Relations (2017)

One of the aims of *All Azimuth* [the Turkish journal in which this essay originally appeared] is to 'publish pieces bridging the theory-practice gap; dealing with under-represented conceptual approaches in the field; and making scholarly engagements in the dialogue between the "center" and the "periphery"'.[1] I cannot pretend to bridge the theory–practice gap in these pages. Instead I devote considerable attention to a legendary scholar who, early in his career, made a stunning contribution to peace research theory and has, since then, dedicated himself to bridging the gap between theory and conflict settlement. I do deal with an under-represented conceptual approach to the field of International Relations. In the field, this conceptual approach is a version of constructivism identified with me (hence under-represented); it emphasizes the importance of rules and conditions of rule in social relations generally.[2] Finally, I argue that rule always manifests itself as the domination by those whom we may style the 'centre' over those whom we may then style the 'periphery'. I have elsewhere expressed my reservations about speaking this way.[3] Nevertheless, I realize that many scholars see me in the centre and themselves in the periphery and that it is important (for me, at least) to engage them in dialogue.

The scholar in question is Johan Galtung. A Norwegian by birth, he was educated as a mathematician and sociologist. He was instrumental in founding the Peace Research Institute Oslo (PRIO) in 1959, which he directed for a decade, and the *Journal of Peace Research* in 1964. A few years

---

[1] {www.allazimuth.com/all-azimuth-a-journal-of-foreign-policy-and-peace/} accessed 11 February 2022.

[2] Nicholas Greenwood Onuf, *World of Our Making: Rules and Rule in Social Theory and International Relations* (Columbia: University of South Carolina Press, 1989); Nicholas Greenwood Onuf, *Making Sense, Making Worlds: Constructivism in Social Theory and International Relations* (Abingdon: Routledge, 2013), ch. 1.

[3] Onuf, *Making Sense, Making Worlds*, ch. 12.

later, Galtung published two pieces in that journal, together constituting the core of his contribution to peace research theory, here emphasizing the term *theory*. Judging from the thousands of times that these two pieces have been cited, I am not alone in reaching this conclusion.[4]

In the first, called 'Violence, Peace and Peace Research', Galtung argued for '*an extended concept of violence*'—one that included violence where there is no one actually engaged in violence, where violence is '*structural or indirect*'.[5] Galtung's incisive description of violence in this form lends itself to empirical assessment and thus leads directly to practical improvement in the welfare of vast numbers of people. In my view, this alone accounts for the extraordinary reception accorded the notion of structural violence. Yet Galtung meant for his readers to see the importance of the abstract term *structural* for theoretical purposes. Social orders have structures, and they range from relatively egalitarian to highly hierarchical.[6] Quoting Galtung at some length:

We can now mention six factors that serve to maintain inegalitarian distributions, and consequently can be seen as mechanisms of structural violence:

1. linear ranking order—the ranking is complete, leaving no doubt as to who is higher in any pair of actors;
2. a cyclical interaction pattern—all actors are connected, but only one way—there is only one 'correct' path of interaction;
3. correlation between rank and centrality—the higher the rank of the actor in the system, the more central his position in the interaction network;
4. congruence between the systems—the interaction networks are structurally similar;

---

[4] Two other pieces might be added to give a fuller picture of Galtung's theoretical concerns in this early period. 'A structural theory of aggression', *Journal of Peace Research* 1, 2 (1964), pp. 95–119, considers the social sources of personal aggression, understood as direct violence. 'Feudal systems, structural violence, and the structural theory of revolutions', *Proceedings of the International Peace Research Association Third General Conference*, 1 (Assen: Van Gorcum, 1970), pp. 110–88, develops many themes to be found in the two pieces under consideration in these pages. In view of its limited availability and influence (it has been cited only 27 times, once by me), I am ignoring it for present purposes.

[5] Johan Galtung, 'Violence, peace and peace research', *Journal of Peace Research* 6, 3 (1969), pp. 168, 170, emphases in original.

[6] Ibid., p. 172.

5. concordance between the ranks—if an actor is high in one system then he also tends to be high in another system where he participates and

6. high rank coupling between levels—so that the actors at level n-1 are represented at level n through the highest ranking actor at level n-1.[7]

Notice the brief mention of 'centrality' in the third mechanism. Rather than decoding and then commenting on this or the five other mechanisms, I turn now to the second piece, called 'A Structural Theory of Imperialism'.[8] In it, Galtung took the centre–periphery relation and made it central to his theoretical work. He later reported that he wrote the piece in the course of a weekend in August of 1970, when he was 40 years old and at the height of his extraordinary powers.[9] As the author or co-author of 1,700 papers and 170 books (not to mention mediator in 150 conflicts), he remains staggeringly productive.[10] Yet I do not have the slightest doubt that his 1971 piece is the most important thing that he has ever written.

In my own case, reading it was a decisive moment in my early development as a scholar in the fields of International Law and International Relations. Rereading the piece decades later, I can see this even more clearly than I could then. Consider the power and cogency of Galtung's opening words:

> This theory takes as its point of departure two of the most glaring facts about the world: the tremendous inequality, within and between nations, in almost all aspects of human living conditions, including the power to decide over those living conditions; *and* the resistance of this inequality to change. The world consists of Center and Periphery nations; each nation, in turn, has its centers and periphery.[11]

Galtung then declared his normative concern: he is committed to liberation from any 'dominance system'. Centre–periphery relations represent 'a sophisticated type of dominance relation which cuts across nations, basing itself on a bridgehead which the center in the Center nation establishes

---

[7] Ibid., p. 176.

[8] Johan Galtung, 'A structural theory of imperialism', *Journal of Peace Research* 8, 2 (1971), pp. 81–117.

[9] Johan Galtung (1980) ' "A structural theory of imperialism"—Ten years later', *Millennium: Journal of International Studies* 9, 3, pp. 181–96 (183).

[10] As reported on TRANSCEND International's website, available at: {www.transcend.org/galtung/#bio}. For a complete bibliography, see {www.transcend.org/galtung/#publications} both accessed 11 February 2022.

[11] Galtung, 'A structural theory of imperialism', p. 81, emphasis in original.

in the center of the Periphery nation, for the joint benefit of both'. This type of system he called *imperialism*. 'Briefly stated, imperialism is a system that splits up collectivities and relates some of the parts to each other in relations of *harmony of interest*, and relations of *disharmony of interest*, or *conflict of interest*.'[12] It should be obvious that privileged Centre academics speaking to privileged Periphery academics and publishing in their academic journals exemplify the very dominance relation that Galtung called imperialist. And I should also point out that virtually all of his illustrious career exemplifies the same relation. I return to the implications of this 'structural' condition later.

Galtung proceeded to identify two *mechanisms* and five *types* of imperialism. In his 1969 piece, he had identified six mechanisms together producing structural violence. Without expressly saying so, Galtung seems to have viewed structural violence as an effect of imperialism and mechanism as an analytic device—an observer's construction, a way of representing the proximate cause of structural violence. That he reduced the number of mechanisms from six to two simply records a shift in stance. In order to characterize imperialism fully, he needed to stand back from one of its empirically discernible effects (structural violence). Any such shift in stance or perspective confirms that structure is not inherent in objects (or systems of objects) under observation, but an observer's construct.[13] Galtung implicitly confirmed this conception of structure when he titled his 1971 piece 'A Structural Theory of Imperialism', and not 'A Theory of Structural Imperialism'.

One might suppose that Galtung's two mechanisms operate to produce five, and only five, types of imperialism. This turns out not to be so because the mechanisms are sketches of the two operating parts of *any* imperialist system, however many types one might go on to identify by reference to some list of relevant properties. The causes that matter most (from any given observer's point of view) are those that enable the system to function—to work towards the end, goal or purpose for which the system exists. In this way of thinking, function is a species of causation.[14] Mechanisms are functionally relevant structures. Any system depends on structures oriented to ends, whether those ends are a function of design or the cumulative effect of 'natural selection'. In an imperialist system, the defining end or goal is *domination* on the part of some few, whether a conscious strategy or

---

12 Ibid., emphasis in original.
13 See Onuf, *Making Sense, Making Worlds*, ch. 6, for more on this; then see Jonathan Joseph, 'Is Waltz a realist?' *International Relations* 24, 4 (2010), pp. 478–93.
14 See Arthur L. Stinchcombe, *Constructing Social Theories* (New York: Harcourt, Brace & World, 1968), pp. 80–101, on function as a 'complex causal structure'.

the unplanned result of many contingent interactions among system units (nations, corporate entities of any sort, human individuals).

Galtung called the two mechanisms a 'vertical interaction structure' and a 'feudal interaction structure'.[15] The first sketches the usual asymmetric relations of the few units with access to resources (centre) and those many without (periphery); it is conventionally represented as a pyramid. The feudal interaction structure is a linked series of symmetric relations among the few. Those few are rough equals with an interest in coordination at the expense of the many. The relations of the few constituting the centre can be represented as a circle. When the two mechanisms are combined, we visualize something resembling a flat-topped volcano.[16] Galtung used the metaphor of a wheel's hub, spokes and rim.[17]

In my view, Galtung's two mechanisms are not mechanisms at all, or at least not mechanisms in the usual sense, because they do not tell us *how* the system works. Evidently each of the five types of imperialist systems works differently; each must have its own type of mechanism. On Galtung's account, the five types are economic, political, military, communication and cultural. He acknowledged that the 'order of presentation is rather random: we have no theory that one is more basic than the others, or precedes the others'.[18]

With no type-specific mechanisms, there can be no way to order the list, or even to restrict it to the five possibilities that Galtung set forth. He might have argued, *à la* Talcott Parsons, that any social system must perform some small number of functions to survive as a system, but this would have complicated his exposition significantly. In any event, he abjured Parsons' structural-functionalism, perhaps because of its much discussed normative bias in favour of system survival. I should point out, however, that Galtung's claim, quoted earlier, that inequality is resistant to change implies that system survival is a functional imperative. Galtung's structuralism dispatches such functional considerations, not to mention institutional arrangements, in favour of a metaphorical language that conveys solidity and endurance. Structure, structures, structural features and conditions are just *there*.

Domination, rule

Given Galtung's distant perch, a dominance system has only one function, which is for the few to dominate the many. I should point out that he culled his five types from the historical record; they are inductive, conventionalized

---

[15] Galtung, 'A structural theory of imperialism', p. 85.
[16] My image, not Galtung's; Fig. 2, in ibid., p. 89, looks like a volcano viewed from above.
[17] For example, ibid., p. 97.
[18] Ibid., p. 91.

and descriptive—typical examples, and not ideal types. Indeed they are contingent modes or techniques of domination, whether discovered or designed, parading as abstract universals. All of them are present in greater or lesser degree in every example of an enduring dominance system.

Conspicuously missing from the list is law as a mode or technique of domination.[19] There are a number of possible reasons for this omission: unconscious resistance to the smug liberal equation of law and order, careless subordination of law to politics (as when he associated politics with decision and obedience[20]), cavalier dismissal of institutional arrangements in favour of structure as an all-purpose metaphor. Conceivably he thought that law results in any centre's direct domination of its periphery, while imperialism is indirect domination through a periphery's centre. If so, then he failed to see that a federal legal order law operating at two or more levels is an imperialist system. Designated agents drawn from the periphery's centre in some constitutional (emphatically legal) electoral process are said to represent the periphery's periphery in the centre's decision-making apparatus.[21]

From Galtung's point of view, electoral representation may be a fig leaf for a dominance system. Or it may open up possible alternatives. As a Norwegian, he might have an ingrained normative preference for social democracy. It seems unlikely, however, that he would consider law in general as a benign alternative to the modes of domination on his list. All too familiar is the positivist model of law as a coercive instrument and the state as a legal order potentially monopolizing the use of force in social relations.[22] Indeed it is quite fashionable these days to say that law is physical violence by another name.[23]

Not all theories or models of law make the use of force a central feature. All theories do share another feature, namely that law takes the form of

---

[19] 'As used in these investigations, the concept of law has no moral connotation whatsoever. It designates a specific technique of social organization. The problem of law ... is the problem of social technique, not a problem of morals.' Hans Kelsen, *General Theory of Law and State* (New York: Russell & Russell, 1961), p. 5. Galtung would surely say that law is *both* a problem of technique *and*, by its nature, a moral problem.

[20] Galtung, 'A structural theory of imperialism', Table 4, 92.

[21] Galtung has since concerned himself with (con)federal systems, although in terms too sketchy to contribute to his structural theory. Johan Galtung, *Peace by Peaceful Means: Peace and Conflict, Development and Civilization* (London: SAGE Publications, 1996), ch. 5.

[22] Kelsen's *General Theory of Law and State*, just quoted, is a systematic and highly influential explication of the positivist model. Among English speakers, H. L. A. Hart's *The Concept of Law* (Oxford: Clarendon Press, 1960) is no doubt even more influential.

[23] Nicholas Onuf, 'Old mistakes: Bourdieu, Derrida, and the "force of law"', *International Political Sociology* 3, 4 (2010), pp. 315–18.

rules.[24] Not all rules are legal. As a general matter, legal rules are formal, specified as to source and scope, and backed by sanctions—legal rules stipulating consequences for failing to follow other legal rules. Under the influence of sociologists, we in the field of International Relations often call informal rules of uncertain source and scope *norms*, while philosophers usually speak of rules generically. I follow the philosophers here: rules call for conduct consistent with their content. One ought to do what the rule says one should; if one chooses to follow the rule, or not, there are likely consequences assessed in advance.[25]

Equipped with this understanding of rules, we can now take up the issue of imperialist mechanisms and take it beyond Galtung's confused discussion. There may be other such mechanisms that I have yet to consider. For my purposes here, I will stipulate four.

- Domination takes place by means, or use, of force—threatening the use of force often suffices, but only if the threat is periodically carried out.
- Domination takes place by use of rules—including legal rules.
- Domination takes place through speech—as when we assign value to people or institutions and give reasons for doing so.
- Domination takes place through intimidation and incitement—through the manipulation of emotions.

As an observer, I offer these mechanisms tentatively, fully aware that other observers will see them overlapping. Thus the positivist model of law combines the first and second mechanisms. Any attempt to draw a firm distinction between reasoned speech and emotional manipulation is highly suspect. When Galtung introduced the concept of 'cultural violence' in 1990, his frame of reference included my fourth mechanism and elements of the third.[26] We can expect all four mechanisms to appear in various combinations in actual dominance systems—in those systems that some community of observers consistently describe as such, as indeed we do in repeating what those observers have to say.

---

[24] Not all theorists use the term *rule*—notably members of the so-called New Haven School of 'configurative jurisprudence' do not. See Myres S. McDougal and Harold Lasswell, 'The identification and appraisal of diverse systems of public order', *American Journal of International Law* 53, 1 (1959), where the authors use the term *prescription* in place of rule: '*Prescription* is the articulation of general requirements of conduct' (p. 9, emphasis in original). They slipped just once in this piece and fell back on the term *rule*.

[25] Onuf, *World of Our Making*, ch. 2.

[26] Johan Galtung, 'Cultural violence', *Journal of Peace Research* 27, 3 (1990), pp. 291–305. In this piece, he no longer spoke of mechanisms as he had earlier.

Before Galtung introduced the concept of structural violence, peace researchers tended to see the world primarily in terms of domination by use of force. Galtung's signal innovation was to dissociate violence from coercion. Nevertheless, most peace researchers, not to mention most scholars in the field of International Relations, equate peace with the absence of violence, and violence as the material manifestation of coercion. So do most people; ordinary language defeats any effort to dissociate force as a mechanism of social control from violence as the direct infliction of damage to the human body, the experience of pain and threat of immediate death. For anyone equating force and violence, other mechanisms merely serve to make violence tolerable. The threat of violence is always latent in social relations.

In my view (as a scholar seeking, like Galtung, to understand domination), the use of rules comes first. As speaking beings, we prefer to use rules to dominate one another because they do the job better than direct violence (or, as we often say, naked force) does. Reliance on rules allows us to rationalize asymmetric social relations—make them seem reasonable, even necessary—and then to keep these relations in place for an indefinite period of time. The use of force consumes resources; as its effects wear off, it is necessary to use force again and again, all the while replenishing the resources consumed. This is, of course, exactly how many people see imperialism—a dominance system in which the costs of domination are ruthlessly extracted from its victims.

The use of rules is domination on the cheap. Other mechanisms lend support to the use of rules, thereby making it even less expensive. The benefits of using rules are so great that rules are to be found everywhere in social relations. Arguably this mechanism is humanity's greatest, most distinctive invention. It is an invention that makes speech possible and an invention that speech makes possible. That it is a mechanism for domination is less obvious, precisely because it makes domination less visible than the naked use of force does.

I offer therefore a general rule, indeed an iron law, for social existence: Where there are rules, there is a condition of rule.[27] As I said earlier, our conduct, singly and together, is always, if not consciously or actively, a matter of choosing whether to follow rules, or not. We typically choose to follow rules, and effectuate rule, for all sorts of compelling reasons. When we do not, we anticipate adverse consequences. Since rules are everywhere, rule is everywhere, including, I should emphasize, the relations of nations. One might be tempted to say that rule is the natural condition of humanity. Better to say, those who make the rules benefit disproportionately, if not always

---

[27] Paraphrasing Onuf, *Making Sense, Making Worlds*, p. 7.

obviously, from the condition of rule. Ruler–ruled relations constitute a dominance system—the one that matters the most for humanity.

Elsewhere in my work, I have tried to develop this conception of rule and rules into a framework for the purpose of clarifying how rule works.[28] In doing so I have drawn on speech act theory to identify three primary kinds of rules, to which three generic forms of rule correspond. Let me summarize this framework, before going on to show how centre–periphery relations function as a system of rule.

First, the three basic kinds of rules: Instruction-rules, directive-rules and commitment-rules.

- *Instruction-rules* draw distinctions among members of any society and assign value to those distinctions, thus defining status and constituting status cohorts. These cohorts occupy ranks in a status-order, each rank valued more than the rank below but less than the rank above. Being valued roughly equally, rank members form a network and occupy a single plane in Euclidian space. Taken together, these networks constitute a stratified system. Rank members effectively assure the system's integrity by initiating and following instruction-rules that are specific to their rank in the status-order. Such rules accord deference to rank members by granting titles, honours, prizes, immunities and courtesies. At the bottom of the status-order, so much is disvalued that the rules grant few privileges of any kind.
- *Directive-rules* take the form of standing, enforceable orders, such as positivist legal theory stipulates. These rules need to be carried out, and for this purpose there will be rules (often but not always directive-rules) creating offices; officers exercise closely related powers and duties appropriate to their assigned task (such as enforcing legal rules). While a single office may seem to stand above, or over, those who have no office, we might better say that there will always exist at least two offices, one over the other. Members of the lower office—the 'rank and file'—may have few powers, but they have the general duty of following the rules, thereby carrying them out. Offices arranged by rank in descending order form an organization or chain of command. That the term *rank* is routinely applied to status-orders and organizations is a source of confusion, with consequences that I will address later.
- *Commitment-rules* are recognizable in rights that have correlative duties: for every right that I possess, others have the duty to allow me the exercise of that right, and I have those same duties when others exercise their rights. Many legal theorists put rights and rules in separate categories, in

---

[28] Onuf, *World of Our Making*, chs 2, 6; Onuf, *Making Sense, Making Worlds*, ch. 1.

order (I suspect) to give rights a more exalted status suiting their liberal sentiments (more on this later). Only when taken as a unit do any right and correlative duty function as a rule (technique, mechanism) by which to effectuate dominance. How such rules do so is not obvious—at least it was not obvious until Parsons linked norms (informal rules) and roles ('role-expectations') and assumed that expectations acquire normative weight.[29] Roles are voluntarily assumed, just as rights are voluntarily exercised. I may have the right to speak, but I may choose not to speak—to assume the role of speaker in designated institutional settings.

While roles differ in this respect from statuses and offices, they are also arranged on a horizontal plane. Thus actors, as role-holders, are members of a single status cohort, or status equals. Although their roles may differ greatly, they constitute an association. Insofar as rights and correlative duties make members partners of a sort, commitment-rules give rise to a generalized partnership. For Parsons, roles and associated expectations make social systems work, but only if expectations conform to rules, roles are stable, and partners acknowledge each as equals in respect to the relevant rules.

Now let me identify the three forms of rule that I believe follow from putting each of the three kinds of rule to use. In bringing the rules–rule relation to my colleagues' attention almost three decades ago, I named them *hegemony*, *hierarchy* and *heteronomy*.[30] Each of these names is variously problematic, but I have yet to come up with a better alternative.

• A term used frequently in the field of International Relations, *hegemony* 'draws attention to the ways that social conditions of production, coercion, consent and leadership must combine in specific strategies that project themselves across a range of social institutions and practices'.[31] I use the term more precisely than Jonathan Joseph does in the passage just quoted. In doing so, I draw attention to rules (Joseph calls them 'technologies') and thus to the *form* of rule. By my reckoning, hegemony is the form of rule in which instruction-rules are dominant, and this results in stratification and associated patterns of deference.

---

[29] Talcott Parsons, *The Social System* (New York: Free Press, 1951). For a critical discussion of loose talk about expectations and their normative status, see Nicholas Onuf, *International Legal Theory: Essays and Engagements, 1966–2006* (Abingdon: Routledge-Cavendish, 2008), pp. 443–8.

[30] Onuf, *World of Our Making*, ch. 5.

[31] Jonathan Joseph, 'The hegemony of governmentality: Towards a research agenda', *All Azimuth* 6, 2 (2017), pp. 5–18 (6). Simon Reich and Richard N. Lebow's 'Influence and hegemony: Shifting patterns of material and social power in world politics', *All Azimuth* 6, 1 (2017), pp. 17–47, exemplifies this highly generalized conception of hegemony.

Members of the top status rank (or ranks) are charged with the responsibility for leadership (in Greek, this is *hegemonia*). In the first instance, they lead by example or, more specifically, but exemplifying the personal qualities that identify them as holders of the highest ranks in society. Hegemonial rule (re)produces a status-order at every rank, and it is likely to produce resistance at lower ranks, most especially when a society's leaders prove themselves to be incompetent, corrupt and unworthy of their status. While so-called traditional societies are typically status-ordered in the first instance, it is naïve to think that self-styled modern societies have erased hegemony as a form of rule.[32]

• *Hierarchy* is the form of rule in which directive-rules are paramount. Rule depends on a rank-order of offices assuring that these rules are carried out. Orders or commands move down the chain and information moves up. This, of course, is the familiar Weberian model of the modern state or indeed any organization as a chain of command. When Galtung discussed 'linear ranking order' as the first of his six mechanisms of structural violence, he offered no clue as to whether ranking is a sign of hegemony or hierarchy at work. Trained as a sociologist, he was from the beginning attentive to status and its implications for personal conduct.[33] He has been less attentive to organizational imperatives and their relevance to conduct. Nor, as far as I know, has he ever clarified whether rank merely registers the allocation of values in any dominance system or functions as a distributive mechanism.

In my view, rule, not rank, is the relevant mechanism. There is, however, a significant difference between ranks in a status-order and ranks in a chain of command. While successively higher status ranks will generally have fewer and fewer members, the number is rarely fixed and has no functional relevance for adjacent positions. Rank by rank, offices are routinely fixed in size and function; if there is an increase in size at any rank, offices will tend to be divided on functional grounds while most officers will find their rank unchanged.

That the term *rank* is routinely used to describe status position and the place of an office in a chain of command is no accident. Status and office frequently reinforce each other—status justifies office, office protects status—and the term *hierarchy* is used indiscriminately for both status-orders and chains of command. Combining the Greek words for *sacred* (*hieros*) and *rule* (*archē*), the term found an important place in the celestial imagery and ecclesiastical arrangements of Western Christianity.

---

[32] Onuf, *Making Sense, Making Worlds*, ch. 11; Nicholas Onuf, 'Recognition and the constitution of epochal change', *International Relations* 27, 2 (2013), pp. 121–40.

[33] As Galtung, 'A structural theory of aggression', makes clear.

Priestly rule combines sacralized status and formalized office. In my view, the likelihood that hegemony and hierarchy will be mutually supportive does not excuse observers from distinguishing between the kinds of rules, and forms of rule, that work in demonstrably different ways even when they are working together. I count Galtung among those observers.

- *Heteronomy* is a term that I have taken from Immanuel Kant's moral philosophy. Kant distinguished between a 'supersensible world' to which belongs 'the *autonomy* of pure reason' and the 'sensible world' to which belongs 'the *heteronomy* of choice'.[34] The latter is the world we live in—a social world. In the field of International Relations, the term is frequently used to describe feudal arrangements.[35] I take the term to have a distinctively modern sense, given the preoccupation since Kant's time with individual autonomy and egalitarian social arrangements. Commitment-rules manifest in right and duties (whether belonging to autonomous individuals or sovereign states) constitute heteronomy as a form of rule, one that creates the appearance of a spontaneous order.[36]

Liberals call the exercise or rights and duties 'the rule of law', exchange among putative equals a 'self-regulating market', and the reciprocal commitments of a contract the constitutive basis for stable social arrangements. Joseph suggests that this condition is pretty much what Michel Foucault had come to call governmentality. 'The majority of Foucault's arguments about governmentality are concentrated on a specifically liberal form of rule that works, in particular, through the encouragement of free conduct, self-awareness and more generally, an appeal to the freedom of the governed.'[37] Foucault just as clearly understood that governmentality (or, as I would prefer to say, heteronomy) disguises a system of rules that disproportionately benefits some members of society. Because those few need not actively make the rules in question, they are given credit for their relative success. The result is a form of

---

[34] Immanuel Kant, *Critique of Practical Reason*, trans. Mary Gregor (Cambridge: Cambridge University Press, 1997), quoting 30, 38, emphasis in translation. See Onuf, *World of Our Making*, pp. 212–18, for pertinent discussion.

[35] For an influential example, see John Gerard Ruggie, 'Continuity and transformation in the world polity: Toward a neorealist synthesis', *World Politics* 35, 2 (1983), pp. 261–85 (274–5); John Gerard Ruggie, *Constructing the World Polity: Essays on International Institutionalization* (London: Routledge, 1998), pp. 179–80. Ruggie attributed this use of the term to Friedrich Meinecke.

[36] Onuf, *Making Sense, Making Worlds*, ch. 10.

[37] Joseph, 'The hegemony of governmentality', p. 10.

rule that liberals consider just or fair, whatever their rewards for living by the rules.

Hegemonial imperialism

Now we can ask what form or forms of rule lend themselves to the centre–periphery relation. Recall that Galtung concerned himself with the relations of nations, each of which has a centre dominating its own periphery. This is a direct centre–periphery relation, and not an imperialist system. The latter constitutes an indirect relation by linking the centres of centre nations to the centres of peripheral nations, thereby extending domination by the centre's centres to peripheral nations' peripheries in what we might properly call a global system. In such a system, the centre's centres reward the periphery's centres by allowing them to take what amounts to a service charge in effectuating domination 'all the way down' or 'all the way out' (depending on the imagery one prefers). As I have already argued, rule through the use of rules generally works better than other modes of domination, and we would expect this to be just as true of imperialist systems.

Extrapolating from a very wide range of societal experiences, I would further expect that an imperialist system of rule would be hegemonial in the first instance, but with significant support from a parallel hierarchy or chain of command. Insofar as we follow Galtung and speak of nations in a centre–periphery relation, this is a specifically modern instance of imperialist rule. Nations are very much a modern invention, even when their inventors claim tradition as their guide. Modernization theory holds that status-ordering gives way to rationalized administration and individual rights—that is to say, hierarchy and heteronomy take over from hegemony. They do not.[38] Hegemony may change its coloration and those who rule may claim that achievement trumps ascription, but status confers the capacity to rule much as it always has, falling back on the coercive mechanism of hierarchy when it needs to.

The key to hegemonial imperialism is the situation of the periphery's centres. Holders of high status in the centre reward their peripheral counterparts with status denominated in the currency of the centre's centres, effectively doubling up on the latter's status. Many of them will find themselves full members of the centre's centre. Collegial practices and egalitarian ideology (the promise of heteronomy) will reinforce the sense that one can be top dog in two worlds—centre and periphery. Even if status gradations remain in place in the centre's centre, and peripheral centre

---

[38] Again see Onuf, *Making Sense, Making Worlds*, ch. 11; Onuf, 'Recognition and constitution'.

members realize there is a 'glass ceiling' in the centre's centre, they still have a distinct status advantage over traditional elites in their own societies, not to mention members of the centre's peripheries. Their complicity in imperialist hegemony pays off for them *and* for modernity as a global status-order. Any Marxist would call this 'false consciousness'.[39]

I suggest that this global system of hegemonial imperialism is also segmented in functional terms. We may visualize it as a many-sided step-pyramid. Here Galtung's five types become relevant. The political sphere of nations-in-relation may still rely on occasional naked force. Yet hierarchical rule through so-called spheres of influence is more pervasive. Even here institutionalized threat, 'soft power' and ceaseless technical innovation mitigate the resort to overt coercion retroactively validated as lawful intervention and responsibility to protect. Status considerations have effectively delivered the economic sphere into the hands of superbly educated professionals drawn from multiple centres and committed to the centre's centre. Surveillance is omnipresent; advances in communication have combined with the diffusion of popular culture to pacify peripheries everywhere.

Earlier I alluded to the general tendency for organizations to divide on functional grounds as they grow in size and complexity. Functional differentiation has always been a large concern for sociologists; scholars in the field of International Relations have belatedly come to acknowledge the importance of this phenomenon.[40] Functional differentiation within and among organizations (governments, non-governmental organizations, multinational corporations, criminal syndicates) has sliced Galtung's five types repeatedly in recent decades. Hegemony and hierarchy operate in tandem yet again, sliver by technically defined sliver. Specialized, certified experts belonging to high-ranking status cohorts are positioned in numerous obscure offices, where they identify problems, launch investigations and issue detailed regulations—directive-rules disguised as instructions. By this means, they rule the modern world invisibly, unaccountably.

---

[39] Although Marx never used this formula and Engels did only once in a letter. But see Karl Marx and Friedrich Engels, *The German Ideology*, 3rd edn (Moscow: Progress Publishers, 1970) and Georg Lukács, *History and Class Consciousness: Studies in Marxist Dialectics* (Cambridge, MA: MIT Press, 1972).

[40] Mathias Albert, Barry Buzan, and Michael Zürn, eds, *Bringing Sociology to International Relations: World Politics as Differentiation Theory* (Cambridge: Cambridge University Press, 2013). Currently international lawyers are much interested in functional differentiation as manifest in global administrative law. For a critical assessment, see Friedrich Kratochwil, *The Status of Law in World Society: Meditations on the Role and Rule of Law* (Cambridge: Cambridge University Press, 2014): chs 4, 6. It should also be noted that the proliferation of technical international organizations in the 19th century prompted an earlier wave of functionalist theorizing, now mostly forgotten.

Politics disappears into public spectacle. Most people take for granted that the relations of autonomous nation-states continue to give the world a viable structure, the legitimacy of which stems from its apparently heteronomous character. Resistance to the effects of functionally differentiated status (re)ordering tends to be unfocussed, expressed as nostalgia for old ways, anger over obvious injustices and glaring inequities, and anxiety about the future. In the peripheries, the old status-order still holds sway over many of the people who benefited least from it. They see themselves denied any meaningful status—meaningful to them—in the modern world, and they have good reason to think so.

Whether this sort of resistance can well up and disrupt the global system of apparent heteronomy, imperialist hegemony and segmented hierarchies is an open question. I suspect the answer depends less on the properties of rule in today's world than it does on the continued capacity of the capitalist world economy to pay for such a system. Rule and rules may be cheaper than domination through the use of force. Nevertheless, hegemony on a global scale does have escalating costs since it must pay for an increasingly monetized status-order and the proliferation of organizations that do not directly produce wealth. And this is only one reason why inequality is increasing in today's world, Galtung's heroic efforts notwithstanding.

Let me conclude by taking a quick look at Galtung's career as a globe-trotting intellectual from the centre's centre. As I hinted earlier, his extraordinary career would seem to illustrate the extraordinary power of hegemonial rule adapted to modern circumstances. This phenomenon prompts a large question. Is hegemony, perhaps dressed up in heteronomous conceits, a better form of rule for the planet as a whole than any of the imaginable alternatives? When I gave a talk on centre–periphery relations at Bilkent University eventuating in this essay, was this another illustration of 'good' hegemony? After all, the event enhanced my status (in the centre), just as my presence enhanced my auditors' status (in two centres). Was the publication of this essay in *All Azimuth* another illustration? Or is it simply that we, as beneficiaries of hegemonial privilege, have a huge stake in believing that some sort of hegemony is best way to run a planet?

4

On Power (2017)

Power is a central concept in social theory and political discourse. Yet we use this word metaphorically all of the time. To speak of 'the power of metaphor' is to invoke a powerful metaphor. The same goes for *soft power*. Joseph Nye introduced this terminology more than a quarter of a century ago.[1] Since then we find it everywhere: in scholarly discussions of power, in policy pronouncements, in newspaper stories. Searching 'soft power' on Google yields half a million results. Even if power were not obviously a metaphor, the addition of an adjective like soft instantly metaphoricizes it.

After reading and writing about metaphors for many years,[2] I have come to the conclusion that *every* concept reveals itself to be a metaphor, but not the converse. Not every metaphor is a concept. Rather, I hold that every concept has its origin as a metaphor. I should say more about this general, perhaps surprising claim. The *Merriam-Webster Online Dictionary* says that a metaphor is a 'figure of speech in which a word or phrase literally denoting one kind of object or idea is used in place of another to suggest a likeness'. We use figures of speech to represent some state of the world in such a way as to persuade others to adopt our representations.

Most people are empirical realists. They think that, by speaking, and thus through mutual persuasion, they succeed in representing the world more or less as it is. As a philosophical idealist (or if you prefer, anti-realist), I think otherwise. A metaphor represents some state of the world already constituted

---

[1]   Joseph S. Nye, Jr, 'Soft power', *Foreign Policy*, 80 (1990), pp. 153–71; Joseph S. Nye, Jr, *Bound to Lead: The Changing Nature of American Power* (New York: Basic Books, 1990).

[2]   Nicholas Greenwood Onuf, *World of Our Making: Rules and Rule in Social Theory and International Relations* (Columbia: University of South Carolina Press, 1989), pp. 155–9; Nicholas Onuf, 'Fitting metaphors: The case of the European Union', *Perspectives: Review of International Affairs* 18, 1 (2010), pp. 63–76; Nicholas Greenwood Onuf, *Making Sense, Making Worlds: Constructivism in Social Theory and International Relations* (Abingdon: Routledge, 2013), ch. 3.

as such through the use of other, familiar metaphors. We collectively make the world what we individually say we see, what we take to be given. Merriam-Webster notwithstanding, no representation is ever 'literal'.

Aristotle had important things to say about metaphors. To work effectively for persuasive purposes, they must be both *fitting* and *fresh* (*Rhetoric* III, 1410b13, 1410b32-33). An ill-fitting metaphor persuades no one, inspires no one to use it again for persuasive purposes, and changes nothing. A fitting metaphor oft repeated affirms and supports the world as given. A fresh metaphor gives something new to the world. Obviously, fit and freshness are closely related. In speaking persuasively, people pick up fresh metaphors and repeat them endlessly. As these metaphors fit the world by making the world fit them, they lose their freshness.

In abstract terms, well-used metaphors become abstract terms. We call them concepts. Because they seem so fitting, we tend to see them as 'real' or 'natural'—as deep, necessary features of the world 'out there'. This is, of course, the kind of philosophical idealism associated with Plato, and a position wholly at odds with the anti-realist stance that I have already announced. In my view, concepts are nothing more than conventions, or metaphors with histories. Over time they prove themselves useful or salient, and they duly find their place among a large number of related concepts.

When we talk about concepts, we need to attend to their metaphorical histories to make sense of the way that we deploy them. We are likely to notice that some metaphors never become concepts, or better said, become concepts without losing the freshness that Aristotle associated with metaphors. I would say that, as metaphors, they are continuously *refreshed*. Such a process will affect their apparent status as concepts—they never achieve abstract fixity. Following W. B. Gallie, we often refer to them as 'essentially contested concepts' subject to 'rival descriptions'.[3] I prefer to call them endlessly conscripted metaphors.

Causation

To explore the metaphor of power, I take advantage of Joseph Nye's influential work. He is well versed in the relevant scholarship, and he renders it accessible to a large literate audience. For convenience, I confine my discussion to two of Nye's later books, both of them exceedingly influential: *Soft Power* (2004) and *The Future of Power* (2011).[4] I start with two assertions opening

---

[3] W. B. Gallie, 'Essentially contested concepts', *Proceedings of the Aristotelian Society*, new series, 56 (1955–6), pp. 167–98 (172).

[4] Joseph S. Nye, Jr, *Soft Power: The Means to Success in World Politics* (New York: Public Affairs, 2004); Joseph S. Nye, Jr, *The Future of Power* (New York: Public Affairs, 2011).

his 2004 book: 'Power is like the weather'; 'Power is also like love, easier to experience than to define or measure, but no less real for that.'[5]

To say that one thing is *like* another is to resort to a simile, and not a metaphor. As representations, similes are like metaphors; to employ a no longer fresh metaphor, they possess a family resemblance. Similes are less demanding as to fit, thereby allowing for greater freshness and persuasive effect than metaphors do. Nye's two similes emphatically tell us that power is an unsettled or ambiguous concept. Yet he backed away from an anti-realist stance that would construe power as nothing more than a contingent social construction. Power is 'real', whatever we say about it.

Several years later, in *The Future of Power*, Nye wrote that 'power is a contested concept. No one definition is accepted by all who use the word, and people's choice of definition reflects their interests and values.' Here he has given up the suggestive similes in favour of Gallie's familiar formula, followed by the obvious point that contestation reflects important differences in how people see the world and what they want. Nye went on to declare his 'interest in actions and policies', where 'power is the capacity to do things and in social situations to affect others to get the outcomes we want'.[6]

This formulation clearly conceptualizes power in causal terms. The note to this passage makes the relation between power and causation all the clearer:

> Power implies causation and is like the word 'cause'. When we speak of causation, we choose to pick out the relation between two items in a long and complex chain of events because we are interested in them more than the myriad other things that we might focus upon.[7]

Nye is hardly alone in this conception of power. Herbert Simon formulated it concisely in 1975: 'for the assertion "A has power over B," we can substitute the assertion, "A's behavior causes B's behavior"'.[8] I have myself held this view of power since I read Jack Nagel's *The Descriptive Analysis of Power* decades ago. Here I would further argue that power and cause are interchangeable metaphors. I should say: largely interchangeable. Many scholars take power to be a subset of cause; cause is the more capacious metaphor (and power a metaphor more readily refreshed). When Nye said that power is *like* cause, he chose the simile only because the term *influence* also implies causation.[9]

---

5   *Soft Power*, p. 1.
6   *The Future of Power*, pp. 5–6.
7   Ibid., n. 11, p. 239.
8   Herbert A. Simon, *Models of Man: Social and Rational* (New York: Wiley, 1957), p. 5.
9   Jack H. Nagel, *The Descriptive Analysis of Power* (New Haven: Yale University Press, 1975), p. 11; Nye, *The Future of Power*, p. 6.

There are quarrels and quibbles over causal conceptions of power; most definitions are qualified.[10] For example, Nye argued that we need to know people's preferences in order to measure power's effect on them, but we also need to know the context in which the exercise of power takes place.[11] By contrast, Nagel had earlier claimed that we need to know the preferences of whoever exercises power. Inasmuch as preferences already account for context, they are the proximate cause in any power relation.[12] In my view, preferences matter on both sides of the equation. Whether preferences constitute proximate causes is a matter of perspective. Where an observer stands, what she can see, and what she thinks she already knows causes her to assign the status of proximate cause to any given event.

Four causes

Such quibbles do not defeat the metaphorical pairing of power and causation or vitiate its power; metaphors are never exact. Nor do these quibbles help very much in sorting out what makes either metaphor so compelling—so fresh and still fitting—when we talk about the other. I believe that we can find the help we need by going back again to Aristotle. Consider his list of the four senses in which Greek speakers replied to the question *why*—why does an event take place? The term he used, *aitios*, pl. *aitia*, we generally translate as cause, but broadly, so as to include reason and even being responsible (*Physics* II, 194b16-195b30; *Metaphysics* V, 1013a24-1014a24; these two passages match very closely).

Aristotle's first sense of cause is material—that from which 'a thing comes into being' (1013a24-5). In this sense, the term *material (hulē)* is not just 'the bronze of the statue and the silver of the saucer' (1013a25). By (metaphorical) extension, it applies to letters as 'causes of syllables', parts as 'causes of the whole' and hypotheses as 'causes of the conclusion' (1013b18-21). The second sense is form or pattern (*eidos, paradeigma*). The third sense indicates change or 'the source of movement' (*archē kinēseos*, 1013b10). 'The semen, the physician, the man who has deliberated, and in general the agent, are all *sources of change* or of rest' (1013b24-5, emphasis in translation).[13] The fourth sense stipulates an ultimate end, the good of all things, for the sake of which all that happens indeed happens.

---

[10] Ruth Zimmerling, *Influence and Power: Variations on a Messy Theme* (Dordrecht: Springer, 2005), pp. 76–83.

[11] Nye, *Soft Power*, p. 2.

[12] Nagel, *The Descriptive Analysis of Power*, pp. 27–9.

[13] Quoting Jonathan Barnes, ed., *The Complete Works of Aristotle*, Revised Oxford Translation, 2 (Princeton: Princeton University Press, 1984), p. 1600.

Let me comment briefly on Aristotle's list. By convention, we treat the first and second senses as complementary properties of things held to occupy a causal relation. The third sense we think of as proximate or efficient cause, and this is the standard contemporary sense of a causal relation between two things. Thus the sculptor uses some material, call it marble or bronze, and gives that material the form or shape of a woman or a horse; the sculptor thereby causes the statue to be what it is. Every causal relation is connected *causally* to other such relations. Excising any one causal relation from the web of all such relations and subjecting it to inspection is an arbitrary act. In Aristotle's holistic, teleological way of thinking, the web of causal relations has an end in itself, and this is both first and final cause.

It is easy enough to see power in just these terms. We say that power in the first instance is material—a matter of capabilities or resources. Here is how Nye puts it: 'Power is conveyed through resources, whether tangible or intangible.' Nye went on to say that these resources are the 'raw materials or vehicles that underlie power relationships'. In other words, they are necessary but not sufficient. 'Converting resources into realized power in the sense of desired outcomes requires well-defined strategies and skillful leadership.'[14]

For Nye, the context is policymaking. Yet the same considerations hold for Aristotle's sculptor, who must take the relevant resource, be it bronze or marble, decide on how it can be 'realized' in the form of a horse or woman, and then apply relevant skills to the execution of the plan, altering that plan as circumstances require. By 'converting resources', the policymaker and the sculptor are both the proximate cause of the 'desired outcome'. We see them differently only because we take for granted a difference in context. The marble may resist the sculptor's skilled activities, but its resistance is passively contained in its material properties. The policymaker encounters resistance expressed in the skilled activities of other people as they seek to achieve their preferences.

An act of resistance to the exercise of power is no less an exercise of power. Recall that for Aristotle, the key to cause in the third sense is the source of motion. If social power takes the form of strategic interaction, this is a matter of motion inducing motion in a causal pattern that we typically metaphorize in the language of play and games (as did Nye in *The Future of Power*). What we typically do not do, and Nye certainly did not, is talk about power in the fourth sense of cause. In that sense, cause is harnessed to larger purpose; power is never passive.

Key to Aristotle's worldview is *dunamis*, which is motion directed to an end, thereby fulfilling the potential contained in whatever is set in motion. In Latin this is *potentia*; early modern translations call it *power*, as in the powers

---

[14] Nye, *The Future of Power*, pp. 8–9.

or faculties that living bodies possess. Power then is a disposition, a capacity available for use, and we still talk this way, typically in the plural: powers of mind, the separation of powers. When we do so, we hark back to an Aristotle shorn of his distinctive commitment to a whole of all wholes, in which every part, as a whole, seeks to fulfil its potential for the sake of ever larger wholes. In short, we have settled on a twofold conception of power as cause. Active power is proximate cause, and latent powers are potential causes, awaiting use. Aristotle's fourth sense of cause, or potential power implicit in the relations of parts in any whole, seems to have dropped out of sight.

Weight

Whatever happened to Aristotle's fourth sense of cause? The oft-told story assigns the cause of its disappearance to the Scientific Revolution of the 16th and 17th centuries, and more especially finds the (more or less) proximate cause in Galileo's demolition of Aristotelian physics and Isaac Newton's formal explication of the laws of motion and gravitation. In the relations of the European ruling houses, the sudden metaphorical ascendancy of *balance* and *power* as linked metaphors speaks to the impact of the Scientific Revolution. Hans Morgenthau told this story with his usual lucidity:

> The idea of a balance among a number of nations for the purpose of preventing any one of them from becoming strong enough to threaten the independence of the others is a metaphor taken from the field of mechanics. It was appropriate to the way of thinking of the sixteenth, seventeenth and eighteenth centuries. ... The metaphor of two scales kept in balance by an equal distribution of weights on either side, providing the mechanism for the maintenance of stability and order on the international scene, has its origin in this mechanistic philosophy. It was applied to the practical affairs of international politics in the spirit of that philosophy.[15]

As with most commentators, Morgenthau was more concerned with the metaphorical balance of the powers than with power as metaphor. Yet the metaphor of the balance relies on yet another metaphor, to the effect that there is some thing to place in the balance, something that can be weighed. What then is being weighed? The state as such, as a whole. Despite its irregular conformation and complex socio-political arrangements, the state is taken to be a homogenized mass with few discernible properties.

---

[15] Hans J. Morgenthau, *Politics among Nations: The Struggle for Power and Peace*, 4th edn (New York: Alfred Knopf, 1967), p. 197.

In 1687, Newton introduced the concept of mass when, in the opening pages of the *Principia Mathematica*, he defined his terms. *Massa*, or lump of dough, is a metaphorical appropriation. Let me quote:

> *The Quantity of Matter is the measure of the same, arising from its density and bulk conjunctly.* .... It is this quantity that I mean hereafter everywhere under the name of Body or Mass. And the same is known by the weight of each body, for it [mass] is proportional to the weight.[16]

Physicists are happy to tell us that mass translates to weight only when gravity is constant, as indeed it is for mundane purposes. Once we think of some thing as a homogenous substance, its paramount property is its mass, which, as weight, is susceptible to measurement. If the state is a lump of dough, metaphorically speaking, then throwing it on the scales and weighing it tells us its strength relative to any other state thus weighed. We still think this way, and we can only do so because the metaphor of power as cause underwent a transformative refreshment in a time of epochal change.

A trans*form*ative event is a causal nexus, the source of many enduring changes observed as a change in the form of subsequent causal chains. Such an event need not correspond to particular events, such as Newton sitting under an apple tree or the European 'policymakers' working out the terms of the Westphalian settlement in 1648, and usually does not. Judgements about proximate cause depend on observers' proximity to events.

Powers

Ever since the Scientific Revolution (this is a metaphor for a nexus of causal relations) effectively disavowed final cause, we tend to view the formal properties of any causal relation by reference to specific socio-cultural objects. These objects are either close at hand and tractable in scale or rescaled to make them manageable in size.[17] In any case, we give these objects a functional characterization—we decide what they do, what they are for. A gun is a weapon the formal properties of which describe the gun's functioning parts—barrel, chamber, trigger and so on. These formal properties take advantage of a variety of available materials, the description of which generally enters into any functional assessment. In the process, Aristotle's encompassing sense of matter—for example, letters as the cause

---

16 Isaac Newton, *The Mathematical Principles of Natural Philosophy*, trans. Andrew Motte, 1 (London: printed for Benjamin Motte, 1729), pp. 1–2, emphasis in translation.

17 Nicholas Onuf, 'Constructivism at the crossroads; or, the problem of moderate-sized dry goods', *International Political Sociology* 10, 1 (2016), pp. 115–32; Chapter 13.

of syllables—narrows to substances like bronze, but not agents like sculptors of physicians. When the latter act, they function as proximate causes.

We may argue about the observer's stance in relation to any chain of proximate causes: Is the bullet the cause of death, the gun, the decision of some agent to pull the trigger, or the interests and values of that agent? Yet we pretty much agree on the sequence of events constituting the causal chain. We talk much the same way when it comes to power: war, policymakers, taxes, research funding, manufacturing innovations, more effective bullets and guns, better equipped soldiers, war and so on. Power manifests itself differently at every point in every causal chain.

We do not always talk this way. Often we stand back and talk about kinds of power. For example, Nye devoted separate chapters to three 'types' of power—military power, economic power and soft power—in his 2011 book. For Walter Russell Mead, fresh metaphors are in order—military power is 'sharp' and economic power is 'sticky'[18]—but Nye's scheme remains. Of course, Nye might have added political power to his list, had he not assumed that power in international relations is always political by definition. He might also have called soft power 'social power' (as have other scholars[19]), but to have done so would trade a fresh metaphor for an overworked concept. Nye's scheme works as well as it does because his types of power correspond to the broad functional categories of social activity standardized in 20th-century sociology.

In other words, we talk this way a lot. When we do, power loses its immediate formal-materiality. We begin to speak of capabilities and open the door to explaining how kinds of power eventuate in kinds of outcomes. Stepping even farther back, we see power in Newtonian terms. At a distance, power is materially homogeneous; the specificities of form and matter no longer matter. Indicatively, we speak of capability or capacity in the singular, in principle subject to measurement and comparison.

We also talk about the distribution of power in a system of relations that has its own properties, about which we can generalize in functional terms. Nye alluded to a systems perspective by introducing the term 'structural power'. 'A structure is simply an arrangement of all the parts of a whole.'[20] Not so simple, after all: the parts are wholes functioning as structures in functioning wholes; every such whole is an observer's construction of apparent causal chains, loops and knots.

---

[18]   Walter Russell Mead, 'America's sticky power', *Foreign Policy* 141 (2004), pp. 46–53.

[19]   Peter van Ham, *Social Power in International Politics* (Abingdon: Routledge, 2010); Simon Reich and Richard N. Lebow, *Good-Bye Hegemony! Power and Influence in the Global System* (Princeton: Princeton University Press, 2014).

[20]   Nye, *The Future of Power*, p. 14.

Not a few social theorists detect a whiff of Aristotelian teleology whenever we use functional language. The latter permeates everyday speech. As Morgenthau implied, mechanistic philosophy gives power its strong sense of connection to proximate cause—to a universe of discernible events and their proximate causes. In the context of international relations, behaviour and preferences are the metaphors of choice in identifying these events, searching for proximate causes and generalizing about causal relations. Yet language betrays this undertaking. Metaphors of work, doings, deeds and needs constantly freshen our assessments of what goes on in the world. One wonders if the epochal transformation of the 16th and 17th centuries changed everything after all.[21]

Soft power

In what we might call the classic, Newtonian view, power is a function of weight, and weight is the best measure of the size of homogenous objects that otherwise vary in form. Nye saw this formula as 'truncated and impoverished': power thus conceived is 'something that can be dropped on your foot or on cities'.[22] Metaphorical consistency demands that less power be seen as less weighty—as lighter. We associate lightness and weakness; to be light is to be lacking in power. Yet we never speak of light power.

We also associate lightness and softness, and this implies that softness is weakness. 'No politician wants to appear "soft"'.[23] Obviously Nye did not make this association or draw this conclusion. Neither do most people. On the contrary, coupling the terms *soft* and *power* would seem to compound the metaphorical power of both.

Having introduced and developed soft power as a formula, Nye granted no attention to softness as a metaphorical property of power. He could have associated softness with springiness or resilience, then to be told that only the weak need to bounce back. He could have associated softness with femininity, but then to have many men tell him that women are weak. He could have associated softness with warmth or emotional openness, only to be told that displays of emotion are signs of weakness. Had Nye explored the metaphorical sense of being soft, it would have been even more difficult for him to explain that his concern is not just the power of the weak or the meek, but social power in any context and, most of all, the power of the world's most powerful state.

---

[21] Nicholas Onuf, 'Recognition and the constitution of epochal change', *International Relations* 27, 2 (2013), pp. 121–40.

[22] Nye, *The Future of Power*, p. 82.

[23] Ibid., p. 18.

Instead we find Nye contrasting soft power with hard power. Soft power 'is the ability to get what you want through attraction rather than coercion or payments'.[24] The latter is a concise definition of hard power.[25] Coercion refers to military power, negative sanctions, punishment; payment refers to economic power, positive sanctions, inducements. The metaphorical properties of hardness also go unremarked. To have paid them any attention would have sucked Nye into the black hole of dogmatic realism, where power is nothing if it is not ultimately coercive.

Attraction

Contrasting soft and hard power is not an invitation to pit weak-kneed liberals such as Nye against the tough realists who dominate the national security community in the United States. Nye's conception of power grants it a *single* metaphorical property: degrees or grades of hardness. 'The distinction between hard and soft power resources is one of degree, both in the nature of the behavior and in the tangibility of the resources.'[26] Hardness in some degree is, of course, a conspicuous property of the many physical objects we all encounter in our daily lives. Yet he introduces another metaphor, *attraction*, to characterize only some relations of power. When objects are soft, their relation is one of attraction. Hard objects are another matter. To imply that they do *not* attract (or sometimes repel) each other is clearly wrong-headed.

The causal relations of familiar objects vary as a matter of both their respective weight and hardness. To associate degrees of hardness with degrees of attraction seems like mixing metaphors—they do not fit together. Consider attraction. The word itself derives from the Latin verb *trahō* and ultimately from the proto-Indo-European root **tragh*, meaning to drag or pull, by implication something weighty. The very history of the word attests to its fitness in any talk about the (human) exercise of power. During the Scientific Revolution, the metaphor freshened so as to include natural phenomena, such as gravity and magnetism.

Ever since, we have freely used mechanical metaphors for social relations. We attribute mass and weight to states construed as homogeneous entities, call this attribute power, and assign it causal significance. In the classical, Newtonian view, agents use power to get what they want, and this is exactly what Nye said. Thanks to gravity, the large homogenous mass called the earth draws me to it, and I use the resources available to me to resist the effects of gravity.

---

[24] Nye, *Soft Power*, p. x.
[25] See, for example, Nye, *The Future of Power*, pp. xiii, 16.
[26] Nye, *Bound to Lead*, p. 267 n. 11.

As we saw, Nye affirmed the effects of gravity: any mass will drop to the earth unless it is caused not to. By mixing metaphors and restricting attraction to soft power, Nye was pointing to something else. Gravity may be a universal force, but it has no goals and makes no choices; it does not confer agency on objects by virtue of their mass. In effect, by denying agency to natural phenomena and disallowing mechanical metaphors, Nye ended up directing attention away from whatever object or agent that may be said to be using its power, whether the earth and its gravitational pull or the state as a weighty object.

Instead Nye drew attention to the objects or agents that we see as being subjected to that power. Recall his definition of soft power as 'the ability to get what you want through attraction'. The very next sentence reads: 'It arises from the attractiveness of a country's culture, political ideals, and policies.'[27] There is no denying that *attractiveness* is for most purposes a more enticing, more attractive metaphor than its cognate. One way or another, all of us would like to be attractive. There are costs, however, to using this metaphor as extensively as Nye has.

The passive voice effectively denies agency in the exercise of soft power. We can say that culture has agency only in the broadest metaphorical sense. When we say that culture *shapes* preferences, we choose a metaphorical construction indicating a loose relationship—indeed one so loose as to avoid any imputation of proximate cause. We may attribute causal efficacy to a nearly weightless, hence very soft event—metaphorically, the 'butterfly effect'—knowing full well that each event in any train of events multiplies the number of proximate causes contributing to an observed state of affairs, whether a hurricane or a policymaker's decision.[28] Political ideals shape preferences more directly perhaps, but this relation still stretches the usual meaning of agency. Only policies would seem to be directly related to agents and their preferences. Even here the assumed relation between policies and their makers is fraught with ambiguity.[29]

Agency

Nye is faced with a paradox. His preferred audience includes policymakers, and yet his conception of soft power effectively denies agency and thus power to those very policymakers. When he turned to the 'wielding' of soft

---

[27] Nye, *Soft Power*, p. x.
[28] But see Richard N. Lebow, *Forbidden Fruit: Counterfactuals and International Relations* (Princeton: Princeton University Press, 2010), p. 274.
[29] Onuf, *Making Sense, Making Worlds*, ch. 7.

power, it is no wonder that his large concern has been public diplomacy.[30] Whether Nye has had anything very penetrating to say about public diplomacy is not the point, although, in my view, he has not. More to the point, perhaps, nothing he has written about public diplomacy counters the widespread tendency to treat soft power and public diplomacy as 'conjoined twins'.[31]

Policymakers will argue that their agency—their power to bring about outcomes that *they* favour—can only be realized behind closed doors. Any such metaphor encompasses traditional diplomatic circuits, back channels, and whatever transpires behind the staged events at summit meetings. It acknowledges the way that governments are organized and the way they work or, indeed, do not work. In these circumstances, policymakers will put to use whatever resources that are available to them, soft or hard in whatever degree. Nye has called this 'smart power'.[32] For persuasive purposes, this is a smart metaphor because it appeals to policymakers' self-esteem, their sense of agency. It is, however, a weak metaphor insofar as it helps not at all in identifying who has agency in what circumstances.

Individuals act on preferences, as economists insist; states pursue their interests. States are institutions performing functions, thus constituting a functioning system. States are persons; as legal persons, they possess powers specified as such in legal practice. Living or not, agents are proximate causes, just as chemists, merchants, philosophers and social theorists take for granted. We find the same assumption in Nye's work, and not just his work on soft power. States are agents and they have agents: proximate cause depends on an observer's perspective.

Now familiar metaphors hark back to an ancient, Aristotelian metaphorical complex linking faculties to function. At the same time, there arose a novel metaphorical complex linking preferences or interests to choice, rational conduct and patterned social relations. As an ideology and in practice, liberalism depends on and advances the second of these metaphorical complexes. As a liberal institutionalist, Nye has always started with a state's policymakers, granted them preferences presumptively in line with political ideals, assigned them agency, and asked how their acts affect other agents' preferences, their choices and finally the institutionalized pattern of

---

[30] Nye, *Soft Power*, pp. 99–125; Joseph S. Nye, Jr, 'Public diplomacy and soft power', *Annals of the American Academy of Political and Social Science* 616, 1 (2008), pp. 94–109; Nye, *The Future of Power*, pp. 100–9.

[31] Naren Chitty, 'Introduction', in Naren Chitty, Li Ji, Gary D. Rawnsley, and Craig Hayden, eds, *The Routledge Handbook of Soft Power* (Abingdon: Routledge, 2017), p. 1.

[32] Introducing this concept in *Soft Power*, pp. 32, 147, Nye developed it in *The Future of Power*, pp. 22–4, 207–17.

inter-state relations. Rarely do we find the term *function* in his writings on soft power, and his somewhat more frequent allusions to systems do not shift discussion to the 'systems level of analysis'.

Ever since Émile Durkheim, functional language has enabled sociologists to talk about social relations without taking individuals out of society or stipulating preferences in the first instance. Nye was exposed early on to systems thinking and functional language, which had crested in the field of International Relations in the 1960s, and to which his teacher, the legendary Stanley Hoffmann, made significant contributions. Nye's first two books focused on functional integration in regional international systems.[33] Despite this legacy, Nye has long preferred to talk about—and, perhaps more importantly, talk *to*—policymakers as agents who know their preferences and would like to know how to get others to change theirs. As a result, he has nothing systematic to say about how their societies work. Indeed, he is hard-pressed to say what any society *is*—what agents may be said to constitute a society, or system, by virtue of their acts having effects on each other.

In recent years, sociology has experienced a surge of interest in systems and their functioning. The proximate cause of this development is globalization, in which sociologists see an acceleration of what they call functional differentiation. Increasing density of social relations brings complexity, which would lead to system overload, dysfunction and even breakdown if agents did not respond by constituting themselves in smaller systems, thus bringing agents' goals and system functions back into line. In short, functional differentiation saves the whole by partitioning it into functional wholes. Each part/whole has an identity that is functionally distinct only by reference to the greater whole. As I observed earlier, it is easy enough to see Aristotle's fourth sense of cause in this way of thinking.

Expertise

With globalization as a frame of reference, scholars in the field of International Relations have begun to talk about functional differentiation.[34] This kind of talk started earlier and has garnered far more attention among international lawyers. They noticed the rapid increase in what they called global

---

[33] Joseph S. Nye, Jr, *Pan-Africanism and East African Integration* (Cambridge, MA: Harvard University Press, 1965); Joseph S. Nye, Jr, *Peace in Parts: Integration and Conflict in Regional Organizations* (Boston: Little, Brown, 1971).

[34] Mathias Albert, Barry Buzan, and Michael Zürn, eds, *Bringing Sociology to International Relations: World Politics as Differentiation Theory* (Cambridge: Cambridge University Press, 2013).

administrative law and worried about the fragmentation of the international law as a 'universal' system.[35] If we were to talk instead about agency, then functional differentiation is the proliferation and professionalization of expertise as complementary processes.

The proliferation of experts has meant the narrowing of expertise; this phenomenon is just what functional differentiation points up. More important, in my opinion, is the professionalization of expertise, itself a subject of sustained interest among sociologists.[36] A member of a profession is someone who has specified powers, and thus power, in some narrowly construed slice of the world. Only someone with requisite powers can bestow such powers.

These powers assure an expert, as agent, a place in the profession's status-order, in organizations exercising hard power, and in a variety of institutional settings in which experts put their expertise to work. Sociologists have long held that role performance enables social systems to function. I would refine this formula to say that rules assigning statuses, offices and roles simultaneously constitute agency and the institutions through which (we say) systems do their work.[37] As a process, professionalization means that conditions for membership—the conferral of powers—become more formal, rigorous and exclusive. It also means that conferred powers are less likely to be contested. While ceremonial conferral of powers remains important, formality is buttressed through legal enactment.

At least in the books that I have relied on here, Nye had nothing to say about expertise and its professionalization, either in relation to globalization or in the context of policymaking. Yet the professionalization of expertise, and the concomitant narrowing of its substantive range, points to the functional differentiation of policy-relevant institutions. Nye has overlooked a significant development in the distribution of power in today's world. In many contexts, the distribution of *powers* matters more—has greater effect—than the exercise of smart power.

What should we call this kind of power? *Small power* is one possibility, but one that has a pejorative metaphorical thrust. *Prickly* might be a better metaphor. When certified experts exercise narrowly defined powers, with

---

[35] See, for example, Margaret A. Young, *Regime Interaction in International Law* (Cambridge: Cambridge University Press, 2012), and, for a critical assessment, Friedrich Kratochwil, *The Status of Law in World Society: Meditations on the Role and Rule of Law* (Cambridge: Cambridge University Press, 2014), chs 4, 6.

[36] See notably Andrew Abbott, *The System of Professions: An Essay on the Division of Expert Labor* (Chicago: University of Chicago Press, 1988).

[37] Onuf, *World of Our Making*, pp. 52–65; Onuf, *Making Sense, Making Worlds*, ch. 1.

localized effects ensuing, the result is just a pin prick. As these events accumulate, observers will look for proximate causes that they cannot see and might be tempted to call soft power. To do so is to hide a political judgement behind an appealing metaphor. Wherever we find power, there are politics. Who *does* get what, when, how?

PART II

Ethics: Doing What We Should

Without rules, there would be no society. Rules establishing what is valued in any given society, rules telling members of that society how they should generally conduct themselves to protect or advance values: these rules constitute a system of ethics for that society. We members of modern societies are disposed to call such rules *principles* in order to emphasize their significance, their margin-defining properties for society at large. We also tend to look askance at local rules at odds with ethical principles and condemn people who devise and follow such rules for their unprincipled conduct.

Chapter 5 got its start at a workshop, held at St Andrews in 2006, on rules in the use of force. The essay considers a hard case: the conduct of people who authorize and engage in torture. I suggest that even they are responsive to an elaborate set of rules: rules for selecting victims, rules for selecting torturers, rules on places for torture, rules on tools and techniques, rules on relations of victims and torturers, and rules on the presumptive value of torture in practice. While ethicists often treat any such rules as slippery slopes in the justification of torture, I further suggest that people are capable of drawing lines and imposing limits on their conduct and that this is central to the human disposition to make and use rules. There is, however, a noticeable tendency for what I call functional slippage in the institutionalized practice of torture. Such practices lose their observable structure as rules loosen and people rationalize their conduct in changing circumstances.

The next chapter also made its appearance in St Andrews, this time in 2008, at a conference on international political theory and for a plenary panel on Seyla Benhabib's work. In this essay, I show how this exceptionally influential political theorist could hope to derive universal principles of ethical conduct from a powerful critique of liberal modernity. I then suggest that Benhabib's struggle to save liberalism from itself falters because she fails to see that modernism in literature and the arts is an age-defining political project. Responding as it does to functional differentiation in modern society, rather than the rationalization of modern societies, modernist concerns subvert progressive liberal sentiments.

I launched Chapter 7 at a workshop, held in Brisbane in 2010, on hospitality as an expression of human sociality and perhaps a universal principle that could anchor a cosmopolitan ethics. The longest essay in this volume, it starts with Jacques Derrida's treatment of hospitality. Drawing from diverse literatures, I go on to argue that hospitality is indeed predicated on a human universal—the disposition to launch objects and observe the consequences of doing so. In every society this translates into giving things to others, but not always in expectation of receiving something of comparable value in return. I then argue that such gifts are status-markers; they mark off what I called 'social distance' (long before COVID-19) in every society. State leaders and diplomats in international society conspicuously engage in the asymmetric exchange of gifts as a measure of respect and deference.

I take the opportunity in Chapter 8 to sketch, initially for a lecture in Brasilia, four ethical systems of potential importance in our late modern world. Two of them lend themselves to universalizing claims. One of those, closely identified with Immanuel Kant, urges right conduct, and the other, identified with Jeremy Bentham, counsels good behaviour. Together they support liberal modernity and functional arrangements that I associate with modernity's modernist moment. In this essay, I give some attention to claims on behalf of a postmodern ethics before turning to virtue ethics—an ancient ethical tradition identified most of all with Aristotle but lately subject to much discussion. In other work I style this way of thinking positional ethics in order to emphasize virtues, once translated into duties, vary according to one's place in society.[1] Foreshadowed in Chapter 7, this stance distances itself from the universalizing claims of modern ethical systems.

At the centre of virtue ethics are the four cardinal virtues (wisdom or prudence, courage, justice, seemliness); centring them is Aristotle's concern for self-control. Every society depends on its members exercising self-control; raising children to control their conduct is crucial to societal survival. It is reductive to define self-control as calculative and unwarranted to claim that people in traditional societies lack patience.[2] Just for example, I am

---

[1] Nicholas Greenwood Onuf, *The Mightie Frame: Epochal Change and the Modern World* (New York: Oxford University Press, 2018), pp. 219–23.

[2] See Joseph Henrich, *The WEIRDest People in the World: How the West Became Psychologically Peculiar and Particularly Prosperous* (New York: Farrar, Straus and Giroux, 2020), pp. 38–41, 373–9, for an egregious example.

hard-pressed to imagine anyone more patient than Polynesian seafarers. Nor is it helpful to ignore self-indulgence as an unseemly feature of unseemly wealth in late modern capitalist societies. I have already suggested that virtuous conduct is relative to standing in society. When virtues become duties, the result is an ethical system better suited to the challenges that an overextended modernity faces in the decades ahead.

5

Rules for Torture? (2009)

Pandora's box

'Whatever one might have to say about torture, there appear to be moral reasons for not saying it'. This striking claim introduces Henry Shue's influential essay, first published in 1978, on 'Torture'. Just as bad press is better than no press at all, even to condemn torture is to draw attention to it, to dignify it, to imply that it falls within the bounds of moral discourse. This is, as Shue pointed out, a variation of the argument that one must never open Pandora's box of evil spirits. Nevertheless, 'Pandora's box is open'[1]—opened most conspicuously, and with unimpeachable moral authority, by Amnesty International with its *Report on Torture* (1975).

Here is Shue's unadorned summary of the report: 'scores of governments are now using some torture—including governments that are widely viewed as fairly civilized—and a number of governments are heavily dependent upon torture for their very survival'.[2] In the years since, many governments still use torture, which is to say, they deliberately inflict pain on individuals in their custody. Some governments have abandoned the practice, some did not survive, some have started the practice. That the government of the United States now engages in activities that seem like torture to many observers has attracted an enormous amount of attention. For the most part, observers condemn torture on moral and legal grounds. Governments rarely justify its practice or even admit to engaging in it, both because most government officials would prefer to avoid public condemnation and because international law, in the form of a widely ratified multilateral

---

[1]   Henry Shue, 'Torture', reprinted with elisions in Sanford Levinson, ed., *Torture: A Collection*, revised edn (Oxford: Oxford University Press, 2006), p. 47.

[2]   Ibid.

convention, requires that states treat torture as a criminal offence subject to extradition.[3]

In short, torture is an institutionalized practice in today's world. There are rules against torture, yet the practice continues, apparently unabated. It seems then that public discussion of torture is entirely warranted because the rules do not work and they should be made to work. Furthermore, most observers believe that discussion reinforces the widely shared conviction that torture joins slavery and genocide as the most egregious violations of human rights that we know. To suggest, however, that there are rules *for* torture—rules that people involved with torture make, follow, ignore and change—at least some observers might regard as morally dubious because it cloaks an unmitigated evil in the legitimating language of rules.

This objection is just the sort that Hannah Arendt provoked when she demystified the machinery of genocide.[4] Routine, normalized activities may not be morally defensible. Some legal rules may not be morally defensible; some rules may not be legal but are defensible; some rules are neither legal nor defensible. Whether rules are defensible depends on moral principles that are themselves contestable.[5] Whether any effort to identify rules for torture is defensible depends on the value one attaches to knowing why people engage in morally indefensible activities. Fine distinctions call for a dispassionate observer; feelings of horror and revulsion tend to obliterate such distinctions, and so does raising one's voice to condemn what one sees.

Many observers condemn torture because deliberately inflicting pain on someone else is reprehensible, and even more so when it is an officially authorized (if unacknowledged) practice that becomes institutionalized over time. Any such practice will be rule-informed; indeed processes of authorization and institutionalization describe the way rules are made available for social use. Yet few observers go on to ask what these rules are and what purpose they serve. In other words, they hesitate to ask why people

---

[3] United Nations, 'Convention against Torture and Other Cruel, Inhuman or Degrading Treatment or Punishment', 10 December 1984. The Convention entered into force on 26 June 1987 and has 142 parties [as of 16 December 2021, 173 parties], including the United States. According to Article 4(1), '[e]ach State Party shall ensure that all acts of torture are offences under its criminal law. The same shall apply to an attempt to commit torture and to an act by any person which constitutes complicity or participation in torture.' On extradition, see Articles 7–8. Also see Organization of American States, 'Inter-American Convention to Prevent and Punish Torture', 9 December 1985, for similar language. The Inter-American Convention entered into force on 28 February 1987; the United States is not a party.

[4] Hannah Arendt, *Eichmann in Jerusalem: A Report on the Banality of Evil* (New York: Viking Press, 1964).

[5] See further Anthony F. Lang, Jr, Nicholas Rengger, and William Walker, 'The role(s) of rules: Some conceptual clarifications', *International Relations* 20, 3 (2006), pp. 274–94.

are involved in the practice of torture, whether directly as torturers, indirectly as governmental officials, or obliquely as members of a society where torture is known to occur. More abstractly, they resist a functional analysis of torture as an institutionalized practice potentially implicating everyone.

As a result, much public discussion of torture as practised today is focused on torturers and their masters. And the individuals in this relatively small category seem to have the same obvious if morally fraught motive for engaging in torture: they want information that the subject of torture—hereinafter, victim—is unwilling to disclose. Most observers take this goal for granted. So do those few writers seeking to develop a moral defence of torture by imagining a situation in which torturing a mad bomber is the only way to prevent a major catastrophe. Nevertheless, history challenges the assumption that torture's purpose is to elicit information. Across epochs and cultures, people have been tortured most often to punish them for their misdeeds.

While so much discussion today focuses on interrogational torture, legal definitions of torture are not so limiting. Consider Article 1(1) of the United Nations' 1984 Convention against Torture:

> For the purposes of this Convention, the term 'torture' means any act by which severe pain or suffering, whether physical or mental, is intentionally inflicted on a person for such purposes as obtaining from him or a third person information or a confession, punishing him for an act he or a third person has committed or is suspected of having committed, or intimidating or coercing him or a third person, or for any reason based on discrimination of any kind, when such pain or suffering is inflicted by or at the instigation of or with the consent or acquiescence of a public official or other person acting in an official capacity.

Here we find three kinds of torture specified by reference to purpose: punishment, interrogation and intimidation. With punishment and interrogation, purpose and target coincide: the victim is the target. With intimidation, the purpose is to have an effect on other people, at least some of whom are meant to conclude that they are potential victims.

Article 2 of the 1985 Inter-American Convention to Prevent and Punish Torture also identifies these three same categories.

> For the purposes of this Convention, torture shall be understood to be any act intentionally performed whereby physical or mental pain or suffering is inflicted on a person for purposes of criminal investigation, as a means of intimidation, as personal punishment, as a preventive measure, as a penalty, or for any other purpose. Torture

shall also be understood to be the use of methods upon a person intended to obliterate the personality of the victim or to diminish his physical or mental capacities, even if they do not cause physical pain or mental anguish.

More vaguely, the United Nations' legal definition also refers to torture for the purpose of discrimination, and the Inter-American definition refers to methods that have the obliteration of personality as their purpose. In the former instance, discrimination may be less the purpose of torture than a basis for selecting victims. In the latter instance, the document does not make clear what purpose obliterating someone's personality might serve; an obliterated personality might be an incidental effect of torture undertaken for other purposes.

While these two treaties identify three distinct kinds of official torture, they leave open the possibility that other kinds of torture serve other purposes. Functional analysis generally starts with the observer stipulating a system of social relations for investigation, then asking what purposes, or functions, a particular practice might serve in that system, and only then looking for corroborating evidence. Everything hinges on the first of these operations. All systems are made up of functional parts forming a functioning whole, which is then a functional part of some larger whole. The more inclusively observers define the system, the more broadly they will look for evidence of functionally relevant practices. Looking broadly at the historical record, I see three additional kinds of torture.[6]

First are tests of faith. Inflicting pain to persuade victims to recant or disavow heretical beliefs, convert, or atone for their failings is not to be confused with coercive interrogation, even if both kinds of torture can result in a confession. In a test of faith, a confession is presumed to benefit the victim and, in an interrogation, the interrogator. Ordeals the outcome of which are believed to manifest a supernatural judgement may also count as torture of this kind.

---

[6] For broad surveys, see Henry C. Lea, *Superstition and Force: Essays on the Wager of Law—The Wager of Battle—The Ordeal—Torture*, 2nd edn (1870) (New York: Greenwood Press, 1968), pp. 323–459; George Ryley Scott, *The History of Torture throughout the Ages* (1939) (London: Kegan Paul, 2003); Malise Ruthven, *Torture: The Grand Conspiracy* (London: Weidenfeld & Nicolson, 1978); Edward Peters, *Torture*, expanded edn (Philadelphia: University of Pennsylvania Press, 1996). While Peters' book is the best of these surveys, it fails to consider non-Western practices; his annotated bibliography, pp. 188–210, is invaluable. Also see Ronald D. Crelinsten and Albert J. Jongman's extensive, well-organized bibliography in Ronald D. Crelinsten and Alex P. Schmid, eds, *The Politics of Pain: Torturers and Their Masters* (Boulder, CO: Westview Press, 1995), pp. 151–83.

Second are rites of membership, during which the infliction of pain can make the experience an indelible memory, bond victims with each other and their torturers, and even obliterate victims' personalities in the process of supplying them with new ones. Hazing is widely practised and officially condoned; sleep-deprived resident physicians in hospitals and doctoral students often complain, with some small justification, that they are being tortured. In the 17th century the Iroquois tortured prisoners, and then killed some but adopted others.[7] When the Greek junta institutionalized torture between 1967 and 1974, torture was an integral feature of the system for training torturers.[8] In both cases, those who survived the experience may well have experienced the so-called Stockholm effect, in which hostages end up identifying with their abductors.

Third is torture as public spectacle. While the ostensible purpose of torture in this instance may be punishment for the victim, it may also serve a larger purpose. Michel Foucault's unforgettable description of the torture in 1757 of a man who had attempted to kill Louis XV introduces a claim that 'the ceremonial of public punishment' reinforced the majesty of the crown and with it an extensive legal apparatus.[9] Foucault also suggested that modernity brought with it new penal practices. One may wonder, however, if graphic scenes of torture in movies and on television and the internet have not brought back torture as public spectacle.

The structure of torture

'The Structure of Torture': This the title Elaine Scarry gave to the first chapter of her extraordinary book, *The Body in Pain*. Scarry's book reminds us that the infliction of pain is the 'primary physical act' that makes torture what it is; this is its immediate, never-to-be-forgotten function. Her claim that torture also requires 'a primary verbal act, the interrogation', is plainly wrong. Scarry's summary characterization of the structure of torture does not require anyone, victim or torturer, to speak.

Torture is in its largest outlines the invariable and simultaneous occurrence of three phenomena which, if isolated into separate and

---

[7] Daniel K. Richter, *The Ordeal of the Longhouse: The Peoples of the Iroquois League in the Era of European Colonization* (Chapel Hill: University of North Carolina Press, 1992), pp. 33–36, 66–70.

[8] Mika Haritos-Fatouros, *The Psychological Origins of Institutionalized Torture* (London: Routledge, 2003), pp. 40–8.

[9] Michel Foucault, *Discipline and Punish: The Birth of the Prison*, trans. A. M. Sheridan Smith (New York: Vintage Books, 1979), p. 43. Also see Darius M. Rejali, *Modernity and Torture: Self, Society, and State in Modern Iran* (Boulder, CO: Westview Press, 1994), pp. 11–32.

sequential steps, would occur in the following order. First, pain is inflicted on a person in ever-intensified ways. Second, the pain, continually amplified within the person's body, is also amplified in the sense that it is objectified, made visible to those outside the person's body. Third, the objectified pain is denied as pain and read as power, a translation made possible by the obsessive mediation of agency.[10]

Adding a prior step (the victim must be detained) and a last step (torture ends with the victim's death or release) does not change the structure of torture or its function. The latter is *not* interrogation, which is an excuse or rationalization for the infliction of pain that happens to require speech; the asserted motive is a 'false motive'. Techniques for the conduct of torture produce pain as 'an actual physical fact'. This is what motivates their use and gives torture its actual function, a function unrelated to speech. The real motive for torture—especially for government officials who authorize torture—is to turn 'the objectified elements of pain into the insignia of power, ... into an emblem of the regime's strength'.[11]

In Scarry's conception, 'it is not the pain but the regime that is incontestably real'. As a 'display of the fiction of power', torture makes the regime or government real by unmaking the victim's world. Torture takes the actual infliction of pain as a series of events and gives them meaning as an ensemble of motivated activities; it 'endows agency with agency'. Agents know who they are, because they construe what they do and why they do it as a seamless whole, a reality featuring themselves as agents. The social construction of agency (as an objective condition) and the social construction of reality (as a subjective state) are indistinguishable as processes. Torture's ultimate function is the social construction of agency, and thus of agents' realities.[12]

For Scarry, torture is an 'ideal' illustration of how social construction works precisely because pain exposes the limits of language. By discriminating between ostensible, actual and real functions of torture, her structural characterization enabled her to order functions to suit her argument. Since structures are observers' constructs in the first instance, there is nothing wrong or peculiar in doing this. I see considerable value in Scarry's three-layered structure, all the more because it corrects my own tendency to privilege speech in processes in social construction. Yet any such characterization is

---

[10] Elaine Scarry, *The Body in Pain: The Making and Unmaking of the World* (New York: Oxford University Press, 1985), p. 28.

[11] Ibid., pp. 56, 58, 56.

[12] Ibid., pp. 56, 57, 58. Also see pp. 143–50, where the function of actualization ('material realization', p. 146) finds fuller expression.

arbitrary: it depends on the functions that an observer selects from the large number that any complex system is bound to reveal.

If, however, we ask what happens when agents act on observers' constructs (whether their own or others'), we shift attention from structure abstractly conceived to the institutions, or linked congeries of rules, that reflect agents' goals and guide their actions. Institutions express the 'reality' of diverse agents who have mixed motives that are often unclear even to themselves, who make their best guesses about other agents' motives and choices, who size up their circumstances continuously, who remember the past selectively and mimic it unreflectively, who find rules everywhere and follow them most of the time. In practice, ostensible, actual and real motives converge as publicly available reasons for agents to make the choices they do. Institutionalized patterns of practice present observers with a broadly discriminate set of functions that any 'structure of action' may be said to perform.[13] As practised in different societies, torture presents us with at least six distinctive institutional complexes performing identifiable functions for those societies.

People have motives; institutions perform functions. Much discussion of torture focuses on the people involved: victims and their rights; torturers, personality traits that motivate anti-social or even sadistic behaviour, and conceivably defensible reasons for such behaviour. After Arendt's controversial assessment of Adolf Eichmann's bureaucratic mentality and Stanley Milgram's notorious experiments on the common disposition to obey authority figures, some social psychologists have emphasized situational factors in making torturers what they are.[14] Anyone who is interested in social construction will also emphasize situational factors as the constituent features of the statuses, offices and roles that together confer agency on human beings. Yet an emphasis on situational factors, by itself, takes an institutional setting and its societal function as a given. If the institutionalized practice of torture has different functions in different societies, or even in the same society, then we need to identify, at least in a preliminary way, the properties of institutions that we would expect to find in functionally differentiated settings.

If, in other words, we think we know why torture is taking place (what function it performs in that society), we would want to know who is being tortured, where and how torture takes place, and who does it. Institutionalized torture requires victims, fixed sites, specialized tools and

---

[13] Ibid., p. 145.

[14] Arendt, *Eichmann in Jerusalem*; Stanley Milgram, *Obedience to Authority: An Experimental View* (New York: Harper & Row, 1974); Martha Huggins, Mika Haritos-Fatouros, and Philip Zimbardo, *Violence Workers: Police Torturers and Murderers Reconstruct Brazilian Atrocities* (Berkeley: University of California Press, 2002); Haritos-Fatouros, *The Psychological Origins of Institutionalized Torture*.

techniques, and dependable personnel. Moreover, we may be able to identify the actual rules specifying these features of the six functionally differentiated *kinds* of torture that I enumerated earlier. Some of these rules will tell agents how to conduct themselves—as victims, torturers, authorities.

Considered in functional-institutional terms, all such rules sort into the following *kinds*:

- rules for selecting victims and deciding when they need no longer to be tortured;
- rules for selecting torturers;
- rules on places for torture and public access to these places;
- rules on tools and techniques;
- rules on comportment.

This list is loosely constructed, as is my list of six kinds of torture (torture as punishment, for interrogation, as intimidation, as a test of faith, as a membership rite, as public spectacle). Other observers may construct different lists for different purposes. I claim only that the two lists broadly correspond in terms of ontological specificity and thus constitute a unified analytical domain. As such, it is suitably presented for analytical purposes as a matrix, with six rows (identifying kinds of torture) and five columns (identifying kinds of rules).

A six × five matrix yields 30 cells, each of which indicates what actual rules we should be looking for. Of course, we may not find rules belonging in every cell, either because we lack relevant evidence, or because the practice in question is not as fully institutionalized as we might have thought. If we find rules that do not fit in an appropriate cell, we have reason to re-evaluate our (always provisional) judgement about functions and their institutional correlates. With the matrix in hand, we could undertake a systematic study of torture as a functionally differentiated, institutionalized practice. Published interviews and trial transcripts would provide a good deal of reliable evidence. In effect, we are likely to find what we are looking for (and this is not a methodological problem because classification is not to be confused with theory testing). The extensive secondary literature would provide ample additional, more or less reliable evidence.

My intention here is to be suggestive, not systematic. Where direct evidence for the existence of rules is not readily available but the function of an institutionalized practice is discernible from the evidence we do have, we can make inferences and state plausible versions of these rules. For observers of preliterate societies, this is a standard ethnographic procedure. In this essay, I make functionally informed inferences, and I suggest a small number of plausible rules for torture. I corroborate some of them with evidence selectively drawn from the secondary literature.

I begin with torture as punishment. Rules for selecting victims will typically be formal and therefore relatively well known and unambiguous. If someone is known to have committed an offence for which the infliction of pain is the accepted form of punishment, then that person will be tortured. We might even say that some such people have selected themselves for torture by knowingly acting as they have. In many premodern societies, 'blood sanctions' are the standard mode of punishment, morally warranted as retribution or just deserts and publicly less burdensome than incarceration.[15] Rules typically call for sanctions corresponding in kind to the offence (an eye for an eye) and suggest that proportionality operates as a principle or meta-rule. Homicide demands capital punishment; regicide, treason, heresy and comparably heinous crimes may require punishment worse than death, or torture escalating to the point that execution will seem like an act of mercy.

Punishment takes place at fixed, often public sites dedicated to this purpose. By making other people less likely to commit offences punishable by torture, public awareness may be supposed to have a deterrent function—retribution and deterrence are complementary functional features of many institutions whose more general function is the maintenance of public order. Torturers and executioners will be trained and proficient in using standard tools and techniques; they uphold standards of conduct appropriate to their station and duties. Victims of high station are expected to conduct themselves with dignity; defiance may bring more pain. All such expectations reflect rules whose informality does nothing to vitiate their normative power.

When torture is undertaken to obtain information the victim is otherwise unwilling to give, torturers select victims whom they suspect have useful information about their intentions, acts they have already committed, or the intentions and acts of other people with whom they are associated. In medieval Western societies, inquisitorial torture rose in response to high standards of proof for criminal offences. In the absence of two eyewitnesses, a judicial official would authorize and supervise torture until the suspect confessed; typically the victim would have to repeat the confession afterwards to validate it as proof.[16] Interrogation accompanied by torture may take place in improvised facilities, for example on battlefields. Detention facilities reflect institutionalization, and even when these facilities are known to the public, torture itself is likely to be conducted in secret.

---

[15] John H. Langbein, *Torture and the Law of Proof: Europe and England in the Ancien Régime* (Chicago: University of Chicago Press, 1977), pp. 27–44. For a moral justification of retribution, and thus of torture, see Stephen Kershnar, *Desert, Retribution, and Torture* (Lanham: University Press of America, 2001).

[16] Langbein, *Torture and the Law of Proof*, pp. 45–60; Peters, *Torture*, pp. 40–73.

Widely considered a craft, effective interrogation requires training, while torture requires a different set of skills. Often periods of questioning and torture follow one after the other, in the process prompting the victim to identify with the interrogator (known to the public as 'good cop, bad cop' psychology). Perhaps the most important set of rules for torture to abet interrogation calls for the infliction of pain, as Scarry said, 'in ever-intensified ways' (quoted earlier). In Italy, for example, inquisitorial torture by means of the *strappado* (victims were suspended by a rope tied to their hands, which were tied behind their backs) proceeded in five grades. The anticipation of pain marked the first degree: victims were stripped and tied. The fifth degree maximized pain: weights were attached to suspended victims' feet. At some point, prisoners reached the limit of their ability to bear pain and confessed; at that point torture ceased.[17] We see here the operation of a meta-rule analogous to the requirement of proportionality. Torturers should inflict as much pain as is needed to elicit the desired information, but no more than is needed.

The *strappado* is one of innumerably many tools that torturers have devised in different times and places. Choice of tools seems to reflect persistent cultural differences, not to mention situational requirements. Where information is wanted quickly, torturers may begin by inflicting severe pain, but a quick confession may be less reliable than one obtained with patience and the progressive application of pain. Torturers may be trained to do their jobs with professional efficiency and detachment, but they may feign pleasure to diminish victims' sense of self-worth or will to resist, or indeed they may experience pleasure in inflicting pain on helpless victims. Knowing that torture is likely to be progressively more painful, victims must decide when to confess. A confession early in the process may not be credible, yet resistance devalues time-sensitive information and begs for an acceleration of the process. Where time is unlimited, the rules may call for sustained, less severe forms of torture. Extended, indefinite confinement itself can be effective as attenuated torture. As Scarry observed, walls become the torturer's 'weapon'.[18]

Walls have an ambiguous relation to torture when its purpose is intimidation. Here the actual victims of torture are not the real target. Instead torturers hope to intimidate victims' associates, people like the victims or the public at large. Governments are given to intimidation

---

[17] Ruthven, *Torture*, pp. 58–9. For a recent example (Greece, 1967–1974) involving three 'so-called "Plans," numbered according to severity', see Haritos-Fatouros, *The Psychological Origins of Institutionalized Torture*, pp. 57–8. 'These were applied progressively to a prisoner if he refused to confess.'

[18] Scarry, *The Body in Pain*, p. 45.

when they see treason everywhere: terror warrants terror in return; limits do not apply.[19] While interrogation generally calls for secrecy, finesse and some sense of proportionality, intimidation works even better when people have enough information about what is happening behind the walls to imagine what might be in store for themselves. Yet the unlimited brutality that intimidation encourages can have the effect of angering rather than intimidating the public.

Underlying torture as a test of faith is the conviction that the victim has failed to meet some absolute requirement, whether of belief or character, or to perform some absolutely necessary duty. Society does not and perhaps cannot impose such a requirement or duty. Instead it arises from what is taken to be a supernatural condition (or a natural condition with supernatural properties) that human beings have no choice but to submit to or help bring about. In this respect torture as a test of faith resembles the ordeal, or 'judgement of God', in which victims must meet a challenge, typically taking the form of torture by fire or water, that requires a supernatural intervention not to result in the infliction of horrendous pain.[20]

For tests of faith, there are no lesser offences, and proportionality is beside the point. The only remedy for heresy is confession, absolution and perhaps death. Torturers must be believers whose faith is beyond impugning; a priest (someone with privileged knowledge of the supernatural) is ideally suited to this awesome responsibility. Victims must have already exhibited signs of disbelief or flaws in character, which torture and confession will inevitably confirm. As with ordeals, tests of faith are often conducted publicly and the means by which pain is inflicted are likely to be ritually significant. Torturers must perform their tasks gravely. Victims cannot confess too readily or their sincerity will be doubted. Absolution or death cleanses the faithless and restores the world to its (super)natural order, even as the faithful must always watch for the next heresy.

While heresy presupposes membership in a community of faith, membership rites certify that new members have fully accepted the obligations of the community into which they are being accepted. Even if the members of the community do not insist on a supernatural warrant for their beliefs, rites of membership have the effect of setting members apart and reminding them of their obligations to each other. Torturers may include all members of the community, the occasion typically open to all members

---

[19] 'I recognize many excesses [meaning torture by security forces] because it was necessary to repress other excesses [by subversive forces]'. Wolfgang S. Heinz, 'The military, torture, and human rights: Experiences from Argentina, Brazil, Chile and Uruguay', in Crelinsten and Schmid, *The Politics of Pain*, p. 84, quoting a Chilean general.

[20] Here see Lea, *Superstition and Force*, pp. 201–321.

but closed to the outside world. Pain endorses the normative significance of the experience for torturers and recruits alike. Thus the torture must be substantial but not life-threatening or crippling, its form often decreed by ritual and tradition. Recruits should be subjected to torture in roughly equal amounts; those who cannot bear what others endure are castigated for their weakness and denied membership. Those who endure are bonded as a cohort and empowered by the promise of inflicting pain on the next cohort. Repeated at regular intervals, rites of membership attest to the community's continuous history and exclusive character.

Whenever torture is conducted in public, it may function as an incidental spectacle—as an entertainment or diversion for anyone who happens to be present. Sometimes torture is a blood sport, whether instigated by jaded emperors or schoolyard bullies for their own entertainment or institutionalized by an insecure government as a way of distracting a restless public. Such a government may count deterrence as an additional benefit. Victims are chosen not just for alleged offences such as treason or heresy, but also for personal qualities: they are said to be deviant or abnormal, seen to be defenceless or conversely, as with gladiators, seen to be able to defend themselves in entertaining ways. Victims may even be required to torture each other. Tools and techniques tend to maximize the visible marks of pain; stoning, crucifixion and exposure to wild animals are familiar choices. If torture is drawn out, it is only to heighten the audience's anticipation of a gruesome finale, making death itself anticlimactic. With agency reduced or eliminated, rules of comportment are minimal. All rules point to degradation and dehumanization as both the objective and the outcome of torture as public spectacle.

Slippery slopes, inverted worlds

Earlier I mentioned the mad bomber as an imagined situation in which torture might be morally warranted to obtain information. Anyone offering this example seems bound to offer an opinion on the problem of 'slippery slopes'. If torture is justified in this situation, is it justifiable in a slightly more ambiguous situation, and so on, until we end up believing that torture is routinely warranted?[21] Slippery slopes are everywhere—is detention for questioning the first step down (or up) a slope? Reversing the metaphor does not change the moral issue, even if it does imply that some slopes, such as the infliction of pain by degrees, are subject to rules and rational judgement.

---

[21] See Shue, 'Torture', pp. 56–9, and essays by Oren Gross, Alan Dershowitz and Elaine Scarry in the same volume.

If we look at the broad spectrum of functionally differentiated, institutionalized practices associated with torture, it is not so difficult to reconceptualize them as a long, continuous slope. Torturing the mad bomber is at the tip, even if there is no one actually up there. Next on the slope is detention for suspicious activity, by degrees vaguer and less substantiated. Then comes interrogation, in a general way inversely related to the grounds for detention: the vaguer the charges, the more coercive interrogation is needed to substantiate them. Interrogation gives way to intimidation, and intimidation gives way to the punishment of groups of people for the actual or imagined offences of a few of their members. Down the slope torture becomes more public by degrees. At the bottom, blood-soaked spectacles divert people more than deter them; degradation is complete.

I do not wish to suggest that people are incapable of drawing lines and imposing limits on slippery situations.[22] Indeed I believe this is at the very core of the human disposition to make and use rules. In effect, institutionalized practices terrace every slope that our senses and desires perch us on. Not every instance of interrogation descends into brutality, not every torturer becomes a sadist, not every government slips from coercive interrogation to intimidation, not every public emergency becomes a way of life. Nevertheless, there does seem to be a recurring and perhaps a general tendency for the institutionalized practice of torture to show signs of what we might call functional slippage.

We should recall that observers 'see' structures in social relations and 'find' functions that structures perform. This process goes both ways; neither structure nor function has to come first. The structures of torture that many observers have identified, typically relying on functional language, and the functions I have identified, relying as I have on the reports of many observers (and not just about the structures of torture), are *actual* only to the extent that people, here meaning agents, see them the same way and act on them consistently. When people act more or less consistently and see this happening (observers are agents when they act on what they see), rules emerge, and rules foster consistency in conduct.

Since people never see things exactly the same way, rarely act with complete consistency, and often disagree about the way they think things should be, functions are constantly subject to slippage. Institutionalized practices lose their observable structure. Rules seem to become looser, vaguer, more qualified and themselves inconsistent. Functional slippage

---

[22] See Michael Levin, 'Torture and other extreme measures taken for the general good: Further reflections on a philosophical problem', in Peter Suedfeld, ed., *Psychology and Torture* (New York: Hemisphere Publishing, 1990), pp. 89–92, for a similar argument about slippery slopes.

means mixed motives, changing circumstances and chronic disingenuousness. In societies where institutionalized practices and moral sensibilities seem most at odds, we should expect nothing else.

The long slope places several of the functions of torture in descending order—descending in moral terms. Torturing the mad bomber is most readily justified, torturing as public spectacle least justified. From this point of view, functional slippage is moral backsliding. If we have learned anything in the last century, it is that whatever we have built, morally speaking, we can destroy, and quickly: climbing up is harder than sliding down.

If torture is an 'inversion', as Scarry has claimed, an 'interruption and redirecting of a basic moral reflex', then that moral reflex would seem (at least to me) to be an acquired disposition, and not a natural one. People make their worlds by giving normative force to what they see and do and by generalizing normative content as moral meaning. Over the centuries we have come to see that 'intense pain ... destroys a person's self and world', and we have made our world morally meaningful, in part, by condemning the infliction of intense pain for most, but not all purposes—war remains the large and conspicuous exception. Torture we condemn because it destroys victims' worlds and, in the process, it threatens to destroy the world we have built together with so much effort and, yes, blood and pain.[23]

What we are disposed to call the modern world reflects an acute sense of, and commitment to, what we moderns think of as progress—material, social and moral progress as complementary features of a world unlike any other. The very possibility of torture inspires an almost panicky fear that such a world can be inverted, turned upside down. Functional slippage inspires an allied fear that we are reverting to an earlier world. Like other worlds, even those that we take to have been civilized, that world turned on different moral premises.

In the premodern world, human beings held different, reality-defining statuses, or stations, most of them from birth and for life. Stations institutionalized family position and relations among families in the first instance: bloodlines always mattered; purity was a regulative ideal. Every station had a fixed place, from high to low, in relation to every other. Honour attached to one's station; questions of honour formed a moral imperative pre-empting all other normative concerns. Dishonour was a fate worse than death or indeed any pain that one might suffer. Affronts to one's honour were to be avenged by inflicting pain, even at the cost of one's life; blood sanctions institutionalized blood-letting vengeance. Even

---

[23] Scarry, *The Body in Pain*, pp. 35–42, quoting p. 35; on war, see ch. 2. In short, 'torture uses, inverts, and destroys the trappings of civilization'. John T. Parry, 'Escalation and necessity: Defining torture at home and abroad', in Levinson, *Torture*, p. 153.

the slightest offence against the standing order affected one's standing and induced shame, which functioned as an all-purpose deterrent. Blood shed in sacrifice propitiated an awesome and demanding nature, fickle unseen spirits, a stern but sometimes forgiving God.

However stylized the description, this world was recognizably our own not so many centuries ago. Despite modernity's repudiation of its social and moral premises, despite our sense of moral progress, traces remain in quests for national glory and the carnage of war, images of the Crucifixion and the performance of the Eucharist. We see similar concerns in other great civilizations, and not just those that are gone. We see them in the tribes we take to be relics of humanity's earliest social arrangements, and in the gangs and clubs we take to be self-encapsulating reversions to an earlier way of life. In all such worlds, the infliction of pain serves functions that modernity has disavowed: punishment for offences of station, confirmation of the natural order of things through tests of faith, status assignments warranted through rites of passage and membership, a sense of power that comes from watching people lose not just their lives but, more importantly, their dignity.

The ritual infliction of pain is so entrenched in so many settings that it seems hardly appropriate to call this phenomenon an inversion. Perhaps the unprecedented normative requirements of the modern world should be considered an inversion (if we can free this term from its prejudicial connotations). We who believe ourselves to be modern also believe that blood rituals are normatively inadmissible because they violate intrinsic rights and serve no good (instrumentally useful) purpose. Yet the modern world experiences a surfeit of torture—far more torture than it 'needs', given the modest benefits of clandestine, sanitized torture as an adjunct to interrogation. The normative requirements of modernity notwithstanding, torture today tends to be public, even ceremonial. As such, it would seem to be functional (if we can free this term from its favourable connotations) for the public as a whole.

Rites of membership often require members to participate directly. Public punishment for grave offences and heresy has the effect of making many, if not most, members of society vicarious participants.[24] Even when torture as mass entertainment brings the crowd to a frenzy, the larger result is public passivity. While actual torture is condemned in the modern world, virtual torture is pervasive. Television, movies, video games, comic books and internet sites shower the public with images of deliberate violence and every

---

[24] See Rejali, *Torture and Modernity*, p. 12, for a graphic description of the fate of 30 Persian heretics in 1852. They were distributed to government ministers, nobles, military personnel, merchants, artisans, university students, servants and stable hands, tortured, marched in public and executed.

imaginable sort of human degradation. We are casual, sometimes involuntary participants in rituals of blood and violation.

At least in the United States, the onslaught of virtual torture has increased dramatically since 11 September 2001 and the war on terror.[25] Intimidation begets intimidation, humiliation calls for revenge, anxiety give rise to fantasies of domination. Nevertheless, the torture we see every day is rarely actual, Abu Ghraib notwithstanding. Instead it is sufficiently realistic (as we say) for us to suspend disbelief. We participate safely in a spectacle replete with familiar rules and return to a world where we smugly believe our moral reflexes are intact, even strengthened by the revulsion we felt.

For Scarry, the ultimate function of torture is to produce the illusion of power—the real powers of untrammelled agency. Yet virtual terror is a second-order illusion, as such attenuated by our conscious realization that what we see is, after all, only a series of manufactured images designed to play on our emotions. That we see so many images of the same sort makes us even more aware of their illusory character; a surfeit of images yields boredom, not power. Perhaps Scarry's argument is incomplete.

Scenes of torture, degradation and humiliation remind us of powers unseen, powers possessed by malevolent spirits and awesome monsters. For many people today, a supernatural world remains as real as it has been for most people in human history: a world of miracles and augurs, gods and heroes, angels and demons. Actual torture today—torture for interrogation and as intimidation—may indeed speak to our thirst for power, our need for the kind of agency that modernity denies us most of the time. Yet the virtual torture so pervasive today—torture as punishment, test of faith, membership rite or entertainment—fuses our attenuated actual power with the supernatural powers animating a world that modernity sought and failed to banish from popular consciousness.

---

[25] Between 1996 and 2001 in the United States, 102 'scenes of torture' aired on television during prime viewing hours, while 624 scenes aired between 2002 and 2005. Martin Miller, " '24" gets a lesson in torture from the experts', *Los Angeles Times* (13 February 2007), pp. E1, 14. Experts interviewed for the article advise producers to 'make scenes more realistic, not bloodier'.

6

The Ambiguous Modernism
of Seyla Benhabib (2009)

Seyla Benhabib has displayed a deeply normative concern for the origin, properties, condition and destiny of the modern world throughout her dazzling career. The great thinkers who figure so importantly in her work—from G. W. F. Hegel to the members of the Frankfurt School in *Critique, Norm, and Utopia* (1986), from Immanuel Kant to Hannah Arendt in *Another Cosmopolitanism* (2006)—drew her attention because their concerns collectively shaped the moral legacy of the Enlightenment. In the process their contributions to moral and political theory have illuminated and clarified her concern with the experience of modernity. Yet Benhabib's most direct consideration of modernity is to be discovered in the time between her early work reformulating Jürgen Habermas's effort to ground ethics in a theory of communicative action and her recent work on citizenship, multiculturalism, liberal democracy, cosmopolitan norms, and the future of the nation-state.

Two books from the 1990s capture this moment in Benhabib's career. One is her most frequently cited book, and her most forthright engagement with modernity as such: *Situating the Self: Gender, Community and Postmodernism in Contemporary Ethics* (1992). The other is one of her least cited books, a book dedicated to another thinker's puzzling engagement with modernity: *The Reluctant Modernism of Hannah Arendt* (1996). Together these books provide Benhabib with a platform for her multiple, tightly linked interests at the intersection of moral, political and international theory.

Whether this platform is adequate for the load it carries is a question I address here. Playing as I do on a book title, I hope to show that Benhabib's view of modernity is ambiguous. I believe that she has erected a position that shelters her from an ambivalence about modernity that many of us feel. I would further suggest her feelings may account for, but do not excuse, her lack of concern for 'the kind of ontological universe in which cosmopolitan norms can be said to exist'—the modern world as the only one of its kind—and undermine her efforts to show how cosmopolitan norms of justice 'shape, guide and constrain our political life'.[1] She is, of course, distressed by modernity's excesses and failings from a moral point of view, and behind them 'the metaphysical illusions of the Enlightenment', but she is convinced that modernity has within it the resources for its renovation.[2] The inconsistencies in her position run deeper than this sort of ambivalence, and reach back, through Habermas and Max Weber, to Kant.

I begin with a sketch of Benhabib's sense of what modernity is about. I turn then to what I think makes her position ambiguous. I conclude with a discussion of what I think is missing in her treatment of modernity. The gap I identify is strikingly pointed up when she uses the term *modernism* but does not talk about modernism at all.

I should emphasize that I do not address Benhabib's position on modernity with the philosophical rigour and subtlety it surely deserves. I offer an impressionistic account because I lack the philosophical training to produce anything better. Nor have I searched for assessments by scholars more competent to judge the philosophical issues than I am. Instead, I have asked myself why Benhabib's position on modernity seems to me, as a scholar in the field of International Relations, to be inadequate as *social theory*. I should also emphasize that my own views are very close to Benhabib's on many points, and I have come to recognize that what I find ambiguous in her standpoint is a source of ambivalence in myself. Indeed, if I had been astute enough to study her work when I first became interested in modernity, I would have understood much sooner and much better the challenge that the experience of modernity poses for social theory.[3]

Modernity

Benhabib adopts Weber's account 'of the emergence of modernity in the West as a process of "rationalization"' and "disenchantment"'.[4] Weber's account is so influential there would seem to be no other place to start. In the broadest possible terms, modernity took form in two phases, the first (disenchantment) culminating in the Enlightenment quest for universal

---

[1]   Seyla Benhabib, *Another Cosmopolitanism* (Oxford: Oxford University Press, 2006), p. 26.

[2]   Seyla Benhabib, *Situating the Self: Gender, Community and Postmodernism in Contemporary Ethics* (New York: Routledge, 1992), pp. 1–6, quoting p. 4.

[3]   And have benefitted in many other respects. For the record, I have cited Benhabib once before in my work, and once since. See *Making Sense, Making Worlds: Constructivism in Social Theory and International Relations* (Abingdon: Routledge, 2013), ch. 5; Chapter 7. That few of my colleagues in International Relations have done any better is a sad commentary on the barriers between fields of study.

[4]   Benhabib, *Situating the Self*, p. 68.

principles grounded in reason, and the second (rationalization) still transforming the world though the systematic use of instrumental reason. Yet Benhabib has another compelling reason for starting with Weber: this is also Habermas's point of departure in his characterization of 'reason and the rationalization of society'.[5] Given her view that Habermas initiated 'the broad philosophical shift from legislative to interactive reason', his brilliant reconstruction of Weber's account facilitates her own effort to complete this shift.[6]

On Habermas's account, the large question for Weber was whether the process of rationalization eventuating in Western modernity was an extraordinary development, to 'be relativized as a *special case* of cultural development', or merely an exemplary development, 'in which an essentially general phenomenon could appear for the first time'.[7] Acknowledging that Weber 'adopted a highly ambivalent position' on this large question, Habermas nevertheless concluded that 'a universalist position follows from Weber's conceptual approach'. Even if Weber had 'relativistic reservations', Habermas had none.[8] Nor does Benhabib.

Indeed, whether some values are defensibly universal or all values are relative to standpoint is, according to Benhabib, the question dividing postmodern and modern thinkers, including the many feminist thinkers who have come to 'feel ambivalent' about modernity's persistent metaphysical illusions. Benhabib does not share in this ambivalence. She believes instead that she has worked out a position 'that acknowledges the plurality of modes of being human, and differences among humans, without endorsing all pluralities and differences as morally and politically valid'.[9] She calls this position 'interactive universalism' and locates it 'within the hermeneutic horizon of modernity'.[10] Nevertheless, her interactive universalism might be seen as a clever patch job, one that suffices to hide her ambivalence from herself but not banish it from the minds of others such as myself.

To identify the constituents of Benhabib's position and to see if they can be assembled to do the work she asks of them, we need return to Habermas's universalist construction of Weber's position.

---

[5] Jürgen Habermas, *The Theory of Communicative Action*, 1, *Reason and the Rationalization of Society*, trans. Thomas McCarthy (Boston: Beacon Press, 1984).

[6] Benhabib, *Situating the Self*, p. 7 and see generally chs 1–2; Seyla Benhabib, *Critique, Norm, and Utopia: A Study of the Normative Foundations of Critical Theory* (New York: Columbia University Press, 1986), chs 7–8.

[7] Habermas, *Reason and the Rationalization of Society*, p. 179, emphasis in translation; also see Benhabib, *Situating the Self*, p. 69.

[8] Habermas, *Reason and the Rationalization of Society*, pp. 179, 180.

[9] Benhabib, *Situating the Self*, pp. 210, 153.

[10] Ibid., pp. 3, 6, 153, 164–5, 227–8.

The universalist position does not have to deny the pluralism and the incompatibility of historical versions of 'civilized humanity'; but it regards this multiplicity of forms of life as limited to *cultural contents*, and it asserts that every culture must share certain *formal properties* of the modern understanding of the world if it is at all to attain a certain degree of 'conscious awareness'.[11]

As modernity emerges, 'conscious awareness' reveals a 'formal stock of universal structures of consciousness expressed in the cultural value spheres that develop, according to their own logics, under the abstract standards of truth, normative rightness, and authenticity'. Just three in number, these universal structures or value spheres give form to 'scientific thought, posttraditional legal and moral representations, and autonomous art'. No doubt 'material values' and their 'historical configuration' are relative, but not 'those abstract ideas that are decisive for the inner logics of value spheres as such'—'ideas such as truth and success in the cognitive sphere of value; justice, normative rightness in general in the moral-practical sphere of value; beauty, authenticity, sincerity in the expressive sphere of value'.[12]

Weber recognized that value spheres appear to be 'irrational' in the sense that they may develop unevenly and in ways that bring abstract values into conflict.[13] In Habermas's opinion, this is an 'empirical question' and not the source of Weber's ambivalence. Instead, the source is Weber's failure to discriminate consistently between the differentiation of value spheres and the rationalization of worldviews, on the one hand, and the differentiation and rationalization of 'departments of life', on the other.[14] In addition to 'mystical contemplation', Weber specifically mentioned 'economic life, technique, scientific research, education, war, jurisprudence and administration' as departments of life. Any of them can appear to be irrational from the point of view of the other and all of them are capable of 'rationalizations of the most varied character'.[15] There is no limit to or logic in the proliferation of departments because it is a matter of a particular society's 'value contents', not an entailment of differentiated value spheres.[16]

As shall become clear, I have deep reservations about this highly formalized scheme that separates modernization (understood as differentiation and rationalization) into two substantially unrelated processes, one operating

---

[11] Habermas, *Reason and the Rationalization of Society*, p. 180, emphasis in translation.

[12] Ibid., pp. 180, 183.

[13] Ibid., p. 183, scare marks in translation.

[14] Ibid., pp. 183, 182.

[15] Ibid., p. 181, quoting Max Weber, *The Protestant Ethic and the Spirit of Capitalism*, trans. Talcott Parsons (New York: Scribner's, 1930), p. 26.

[16] Ibid., p. 184; recall 'cultural contents', quoted earlier.

at the level of strictly limited universal values and the other at the level of infinitely varied social practices and institutions. Habermas has no such qualms. His self-assurance seems to have reassured Benhabib, who expressly adopts the tripartite scheme of value differentiation in arguing that a communicative ethics, such as she endorses, cannot be 'morally neutral' but is nonetheless compatible with 'a framework of universal rights and justice'.[17] One way to substantiate my reservations about this scheme is to ask where it comes from.

On Habermas's account, Weber's three autonomous value spheres 'were gleaned inductively and treated in a descriptive matter'; they are 'the elements of culture that were, with the transition to modernity, differentiated out from the traditional residues of religious–metaphysical worldviews transmitted by the Greek and above all the Judeo-Christian traditions'. Yet Weber's discovery of three value spheres is not just a matter of reviewing the historical record. According to Habermas, 'it can only be understood against the background of the neo-Kantian philosophy of value, even though Weber himself made no attempt to order systematically and analyze from formal points of view' what he had gleaned from the record.[18] For my part, I cannot see the 'traditional residues' nearly as clearly as can I see early modern challenges to the single, teleologically unified value sphere that Scholastic thinkers had taken from Aristotle.

The strict separation of values from facts, including facts about values, initiated by David Hume and later made into a cardinal premise of positivist modernity offered one challenge to the unified value sphere handed down from Aristotle. The separation of emotion and reason offered a second challenge. As Albert Hirschman has suggested, the triumph of reason over emotion was inextricably related to the emergence of capitalism as a constellation of practices and institutions.[19] No less was the triumph of objectively corroborated facts over subjective beliefs inextricably related to the practice of justifying choices by reference to consequences and to the emergence of positive law and the apparatus of the state. The triumph of science and technology as first and final measure of modernity's success validated both challenges together, and the result has been a profusion of 'departments'—in universities, bureaucracies and productive activities, and in opportunities for artistic expression, self-actualization, social interaction and political participation. In short, I see the emergence of Weber's three value spheres not as intrinsic to the process of differentiation and rationalization,

---

[17] Benhabib, *Situating the Self*, pp. 41–6, quoting pp. 44, 46.

[18] Habermas, *Reason and the Rationalization of Society*, pp. 186, 165, 186 again.

[19] Albert O. Hirschman, *The Passions and the Interests: Political Arguments for Capitalism before Its Triumph* (Princeton: Princeton University Press, 1977).

forever after shaping the value contents of modern life, but as a canonical interpretation of the process at an early stage.

As Habermas intimated, it was Kant who made this interpretation possible and whose name accounts for its canonical status. Here we do not need a close examination of 'the neo-Kantian philosophy of value'. We need only recall the respective foci of Kant's three critiques: pure reason (the cognitive sphere), practical reason (the moral-practical sphere), and aesthetic judgement (the expressive sphere). At least to my knowledge, Kant never claimed that these three 'spheres' logically exhaust the materials calling for critical attention or that they form a unified system. Indeed, it seems to me that he approached them serially, moving from one critique to the next as he realized that the completion of each one left something else for his consideration. In this light, his late writings on a variety of topics suggest the possibility of additional critiques prompted by the rapidly shifting value contents of post-Enlightenment modernity.

Self and other

After Kant, the value contents of modernity expanded even more dramatically than they had during his lifetime. Benhabib fully appreciates the scale and importance of this development and is sensitive to its misinterpretation. Understood as 'the rise of the social', it distressed Arendt as the cause and consequence of the demise of the political. On Benhabib's interpretation, there are signs of an 'alternative genealogy of modernity' in Arendt's early work, one that acknowledges changing 'patterns of human interaction' and warrants calling Arendt a 'reluctant modernist' and not the 'nostalgic and antimodernist thinker' that most of us find in *The Human Condition* (1958).[20]

For Benhabib, Arendt's 'understanding of modernity and the place of politics under conditions of modernity' is unclear and quite possibly incoherent. It might be pointed out (as indeed Patrick Hayden has pointed out me) that we must go back to *The Origins of Totalitarianism* (1951) to appreciate fully the sources of Arendt's reluctance to embrace modernity. Insofar as imperialism, colonialism and racism gave modernity the boost needed for its spectacular rise, Arendt made a compelling case for her own reluctance. Yet the two books together make any effort to find in Arendt a clear 'understanding of modernity' all the more difficult. Limited to *The Human Condition*, however unfairly, Benhabib's 'rereading' is clear enough. '[M]odernity cannot simply be identified with the spread of commodity exchange relations and the growth of a capitalist economy; nor can modernity

---

[20] Sheila Benhabib, *The Reluctant Modernism of Hannah Arendt* (Thousand Oaks, CA: Sage, 1996), pp. 22–30, quoting pp. 22, 29, 28, 22.

be reduced to the spread of mass society alone. Modernity brings with it new forms of social interaction, patterns of association, habits, and mores.' These 'new forms' register 'transformations occurring in these spheres of modern societies'.[21] As used here, the term *sphere* obviously does not refer to Kantian value spheres. It does seem to refer to the explosion in the value contents of Western modernity and thus to the profusion of Weberian departments of life. Yet Benhabib does not actually say this in setting forth Arendt's understanding of modernity. Nor, as far as I can tell, does she elsewhere in her work.

Instead Benhabib elaborates the value contents of modernity insofar as they assist or inhibit the modern subject in the demanding task of situating herself in a rationalized world. This Benhabib does *not* do by situating the self in relation to the differentiation and proliferation of departments of life. Rather, she situates each self in relation to others—'concrete others'—who must situate their selves.[22] Even if the value contents of modernity are increasingly homogenized and commodified, they must differ in some degree for every one of us. Where there are concrete others, there are concrete differences. Where there are differences, there are grounds for anxiety, misunderstanding, disagreement, intolerance, hostility and selfishness, and there are opportunities to reduce anxiety, misunderstanding and so on. Human interaction transcends all spheres and departments.

By centring her position on the self and its relation to the value contents of modernity, and not on the social processes by which the value contents of modernity become rationalized and differentiated, Benhabib is well aware that she risks undermining a career-long effort to get 'beyond the philosophy of the subject'.[23] A general feature of modern Western philosophy, the preoccupation with the subject is especially marked in German philosophy from Kant and Hegel to the Frankfurt School and even Habermas, despite his shift to interactive reason. Introducing the self to the other, as G. H. Mead had, does not help (or at least help enough) because that other remains generalized. 'The standpoint of the generalized other requires us to view each and every individual as a rational being entitled to the same rights and duties we would want to ascribe to ourselves. In assuming the standpoint, we abstract from the individuality and concrete identity of the other.'[24]

Generalizing the other is a characteristic move in 'contemporary moral universalist moral psychology and moral theory'.[25] Such a move brings human

---

[21] Ibid., p. 29.
[22] See especially Benhabib, *Situating the Self*, ch. 5: 'The Generalized and the Concrete Other'.
[23] Benhabib, *Critique, Norm, and Utopia*, p. 343.
[24] Benhabib, *Situating the Self*, pp. 158–9.
[25] Ibid., p. 159; moral psychology here refers to Lawrence Kohlberg's work.

interaction into the moral-practical value sphere, where justice demands universally valid criteria for normative judgement.

> The standpoint of the concrete other, by contrast, requires us to view each and every rational being as an individual with a concrete history, identity and affective-emotional constitution. In assuming this standpoint, we abstract from what constitutes our commonality, and focus on individuality. We seek to comprehend the needs of the other, his or her motivations, what she searches for, and what s/he desires. Our relation to the other is governed by the norms of *equity* and *complementary reciprocity*: each is entitled to expect and assume from the other forms of behavior through which the other feels recognized and confirmed as a concrete, individual being with specific needs, talents and capacities.[26]

Beyond a general requirement to treat each other as human, no universal moral principle or procedure emerges from this description to guide our conduct. By equity, Benhabib must mean something more than an informal metric for evaluating the scope and content of legal rules in a liberal society. I suspect she has in mind a sense or feeling of fairness that people have about social relations in general, perhaps induced by their feelings (hurt, rage) when they think concrete others have treated them unfairly. What is not at all clear is how this sense of fairness plays out in a world where local standards operate within human communities and departments of life.

More specifically, it seems to me that status arrangements in many, perhaps most, communities sharply restrict the set of concrete others whose behaviour can trigger feelings of unfair treatment. Much the same can be said of reciprocity. In most communities, individuals can only reciprocate in kind if they are members of the same status set; *noblesse oblige* would lose all meaning and value if peasants could reciprocate. Furthermore, reciprocity would seem to invite mutual admiration (or vilification) at the potential expense of concrete others. Generalizing reciprocity is another name for generalizing the other; what complementarity can mean in this context I have no idea.

Even if 'ignoring the standpoint of the concrete other leads to epistemic incoherence in universalistic moral theories', affirming the standpoint of the other does not, *by itself*, assure the epistemic adequacy of that standpoint.[27] Adducing contextually relevant norms always finds a limit in contextual irrelevance. Moreover, identifying relevant norms shifts attention from the

---

[26] Ibid., emphasis in original.
[27] Quoting ibid., p. 161.

relations of selves to the departments of life. Effectively acknowledging as much, Benhabib returns to the universal standpoint with an 'enlarged mentality'—one that 'provides us with a procedure for judging the validity of our judgments'.[28]

What this return to the universal standpoint requires is clear enough, but what it gains for us is not. We should 'act in such a way as is consistent with respecting the dignity and worth of all individuals involved and a willingness to settle controversial matters through the open and unconstrained discussion of all'. Benhabib goes on to ask the very question I would ask: 'What does this mean concretely?' We cannot know, and not just because the procedure for judging judgements surely varies from department to department. 'Procedures do not dictate specific outcomes; they constrain the kinds of justification we can use for our actions, judgments and principles.'[29]

Universal rights and duties are necessarily specific in this sense. Especially in her recent work, Benhabib writes as if we already know the contents of these rights and duties. We know them to be universal. Recent developments confirm what we know: cosmopolitan norms of justice apply to 'individuals as moral and legal persons in a worldwide civil society'.[30]

I am not so sure. Faced with procedural indeterminacy, how can we be sure that we know that we have specified their contents conclusively? Why should we think these norms are anything more than the latest value contents of an ever more differentiated world? How do we even know that they are universal when we cannot be sure that the moral-practical value sphere, the sphere of 'justice' itself, is anything more than a particular social construction reflecting the value contents of an earlier time?

Modernism

Weber's account of modernity's development centres on our changing relation to the world or, more precisely, on our conscious awareness of our capacity to change the world, to rationalize its contents, by following the dictates of truth, right and beauty. There is, however, another way to identify what makes modernity distinctive, one that shifts emphasis from ontology to epistemology, from rationalization to representation. Postmodernists have developed this point of view with particular relish. In their view, the conceit that we can truly represent the contents of the world in our minds is at the heart of modernity's metaphysical illusions, practical follies and moral arrogance.

---

[28] Ibid., p. 186.
[29] Ibid., pp. 186–7.
[30] Benhabib, *Another Cosmopolitanism*, p. 16.

Benhabib takes this alternative view of modernity into account because it appeals to feminists who have come to believe that the philosophy of the subject can never be rid of its masculinist subjectivities. For convenience, she uses Jean-François Lyotard's familiar exposition, in which the contents of modernity are brought together in a 'grand narrative'.[31] Giving this grand narrative its coherence and direction is an 'episteme of representation', which Benhabib somewhat confusingly calls 'modernist', 'classical' and 'modern'.[32] Lyotard suggested that modernity produces 'functional knowledge'—knowledge that is 'an indispensable element in the functioning of society'—but also induces a turn to 'critical knowledge' that never goes far enough.[33] The emergence of 'two basic representational models for society', one functional, the other critical, reflects an inherent tension in the Enlightenment narrative; the rejection of the functional–critical binary marks the onset of the postmodern condition.[34] Against Lyotard, Benhabib aligns herself with critical thinking: the critique of the subject as spectator, of the world as an objective reality, of language as a reliable vehicle for representing the world.[35]

Benhabib writes as if the episteme of representation has indeed come to an end. A sustained, three-prong critique might seem to have pulled the rug out from under it. Yet the demise of the episteme has not rendered us incapable of telling better stories about our common condition, stories that salvage modernity's better tendencies. What then has critical thinking accomplished? Benhabib tells us it is 'the demise of rationalistic and transcendental philosophies from Descartes to Kant and Husserl'.[36] If critique has discredited the philosophy of the subject, then, following Lyotard, it must also have put itself out of business.

---

[31] Benhabib, *Situating the Self*, pp. 204, quoting Jean-François Lyotard, *The Postmodern Condition: A Report on Knowledge*, trans. Geoff Bennington and Brian Massumi (Minneapolis: University of Minnesota Press, 1984), p. xxiii, who also called it 'the Enlightenment narrative'.

[32] Ibid., pp. 204, 207 (modernist), 206–7 (classical), 207 (modern). As used here, the term *episteme* is Benhabib's, not Lyotard's. I suspect she took the term from Foucault, who identified a succession of epistemes—Renaissance, classical, modern—each giving modernity a new set of conditions for the possibility of knowledge. *Classical* would correspond to the time before Kant and to Weber's first phase in modernity's emergence, and *modern* to the time after Kant and Weber's second phase. Michel Foucault, *The Order of Things: An Archeology of the Human Sciences*, trans. A. M. Sheridan Smith (New York: Pantheon Books, 1971). In this scheme, Lyotard's grand narrative fits the modern episteme.

[33] Lyotard, *The Postmodern Condition*, p. 13; also see Benhabib, *Situating the Self*, pp. 204–5.

[34] Lyotard, *The Postmodern Condition*, pp. 11–14, quoting p. 11.

[35] Benhabib, *Situating the Self*, pp. 206–8.

[36] Ibid., p. 210.

If critique's success in its own terms makes critique superfluous, what should we do? Lyotard's answer is to abandon the functional–critical binary. The alternative is to view modernity as 'a functional whole'[37] without necessarily accepting his claim that the whole of modernity ended with the disintegration of its grand narrative. In my opinion, this is an alternative that Benhabib has slighted, perhaps because she has been so deeply immersed in the critique of the philosophy of the subject. I also suspect that she fails to see this alternative for what it is.

Consider Benhabib's marked tendency to use the terms *modern* and *modernist* interchangeably. Lyotard is a self-professed post*modernist* thinker, for whom the last chapter in the Enlightenment narrative is specifically *modernist*. By implication (an implication of little interest to Lyotard), the terms *classical* and *modern* describe earlier phases corresponding to Weberian phases in modernity's emergence. The demise of modernism spells the end of modernity as a functional whole—there is no next phase. As with many postmodernists, Lyotard took for granted that modernism has distinct properties dating from the late 19th century.

> The idea that society forms an organic whole, in the absence of which it ceases to be a society (and sociology ceases to have an object of study), dominated the minds of the founders of the French school. Added detail was supplied by functionalism; it took yet another turn in the 1950s with Parsons's conception of society as a self-regulating system.[38]

Benhabib might object that modernism refers to a movement in the arts—music, theatre, literature, poetry, painting, sculpture, architecture—in which representation turns in on itself to become its own and perhaps its only subject. As such, modernism would seem to have been a development of modernity within the expressive sphere of values, where the search for beauty and authenticity follows a logic of its own. During the 19th century, relentless rationalization in the cognitive sphere prompted an 'irrational' effort (see earlier) to save the expressive sphere from the mass production of cultural goods and correlative degradation of aesthetic standards. Indeed Benhabib has commented on this phenomenon.[39] Linking 'high modernism' in the arts to critical tendencies flourishing at the same time, she rather dramatically announced that Theodor Adorno and Max Horkheimer had 'a tortured vision of the project of the moderns', just as did Pablo Picasso,

---

[37] Lyotard, *The Postmodern Condition*, p. 11.
[38] Ibid.
[39] Seyla Benhabib, 'Critical theory and postmodernism: On the interplay of ethics, aesthetics, and utopia in critical theory', *Cardozo Law Review* 11, 5–6 (1989–1990), pp. 1435–49.

Max Beckmann, Paul Klee and Wassily Kandinsky.[40] I have no quarrel with this claim. I believe, however, that 'high modernism' is the tip of an iceberg.

Let me enlarge the modernist mentality. Beginning as early perhaps as the 1860s, and with increasing energy to the end of the inter-war period, the arts did indeed experience a revolution in the theory and practice of representation. Realism in the novel gave way to Virginia Woolf and then James Joyce, in painting to Paul Cézanne and then Marcel Duchamp. New modes of expression created opportunities and incentives to get inside the object at hand (including, of course, the objectified subject), to penetrate the hard surface of appearances, to find out how the object functions as a whole, to rearrange its parts and jolt the observer's senses, to open up the dynamics of differentiation and (dis)integration, growth and decay, to assign value to (devalue, revalue) what we never knew was there. To appropriate a slogan from modernist architecture, if form follows function, then the architect should turn things inside out; aesthetics is a matter of exposure.

In short, modernism is not just about representation. It is an injunction to represent function first (including the function of representation), just as Lyotard intimated. Among the 'founders of the French School' is the towering figure of Émile Durkheim, whom I would call the 'high modernist' of social theory. If Weber saw modernity as formalization (first phase) and rationalization (second phase), then Durkheim saw functional differentiation as the modernist third stage in modernity's trajectory. As in sociology, so in many other newly differentiated departments in modern life.

This is not the place to document the impact of modernism outside the arts.[41] It should suffice to say that modernism is a response to differentiation along functional lines, which is in turn a conspicuous feature of modernity's last century—whether interpreted as growth or decay. In my opinion, functional differentiation is the most conspicuous feature of modernity as it has globalized in recent decades. It is a less conspicuous feature of social theory, no doubt because the positivist, strictly modern preoccupation with things and their properties dominates the social sciences. It is substantially absent in critical thought, I suspect because critical thinkers confine modernism to the expressive sphere and because their preoccupation with

---

[40] Ibid., p. 1439.

[41] But see Roger Griffin, *Modernism and Fascism: The Sense of a Beginning under Mussolini and Hitler* (Basingstoke: Palgrave Macmillan, 2007) for an important study of fascism as 'political modernism'. Also consider Edward Said's brief but suggestive linking of imperialism and modernism: Edward Said, 'Notes on modernism' in *Culture and Imperialism* (New York: Alfred Knopf, 1993), pp. 186–90. To the extent that late 19th-century imperialism and 20th-century totalitarianism contributed to Arendt's understanding of modernity, she may indeed have been the reluctant *modernist* Benhabib had no reason to call her.

the subject blinds them to the ever more differentiated value contents of the world.[42]

Finally, functional differentiation is largely missing from Benhabib's work, and not just because she has immersed herself so deeply in critical thought. More and more, she has engaged liberalism in her project to rehabilitate modernity. As much as I appreciate her motives in doing so, I believe that she has not escaped the liberal tendency to underestimate the extent to which functions have fractionated and departments of life have proliferated in our late modern world. Affirming pluralism does not even begin to acknowledge what modernist modernity has wrought functionally and institutionally.

When Benhabib talks about global civil society, she makes the world a liberal place, surely flawed, but curiously empty.[43] A familiar meliorist project shows signs of replacing a flawed and ambiguous conception of modernity— an ambiguous conception, for all its flaws, reflecting the inescapable, multivalent complexity of modernity as we have come to experience it. It also suggests the danger of moral complacency. In these circumstances, for Benhabib to reaffirm at least some measure of ambivalence would be a welcome event.

---

[42] Habermas's work offers a large exception. While vol. 1 of *The Theory of Communicative Action* (1984) explicates the modern experience by reference to rationalization, vol. 2 (1987) turns to differentiation by engaging modernist sociology (even if the term *modernism* and its cognates have no place in his conceptual vocabulary). There he suggested

> that (1) we conceive of societies *simultaneously* as systems and lifeworlds. This concept proves itself in (2) a theory of social evolution that separates the rationalization of the lifeworld from the growing complexity of social systems so as to make the connection that Durkheim envisaged between forms of social integration and stages of system differentiation tangible, that is, susceptible to empirical analysis.

Jürgen Habermas, *The Theory of Communicative Action*, 2, *Lifeworld and System: A Critique of Functionalist Reason*, trans. Thomas McCarthy (Boston: Beacon Press, 1987), p. 118, emphasis in translation.

[43] For an alternative view, see Nicholas Onuf, 'Late modern civil society', in Randall D. Germain and Michael Kenny, eds, *The Idea of Global Civil Society: Politics and Ethics in a Globalizing Era* (London: Routledge, 2005), pp. 47–63.

7

Relative Strangers (2013)

The laws of hospitality

Hospitality is a fashionable topic in political and international thought. The most obvious reason for this development is the movement of people across national frontiers to escape persecution or privation in their own countries. The unplanned-for arrival of needy or enterprising strangers is hardly a new phenomenon. Nor is their disposition to make themselves at home. Yet in recent years immigration and its restriction have come to be seen as a social problem on a global scale—one that raises troubling questions about the duties we, as individuals or societies, have when faced with strangers.

Scholars have discovered that their predecessors have had little to say about the treatment of strangers. Thus they have seized on Immanuel Kant's brief and ambiguous remarks on 'universal hospitality' in *Perpetual Peace*.[1] This should be no surprise. With the recent resuscitation of liberalism in a cosmopolitan guise, Kantian ethics have been much in fashion and Kant and *Perpetual Peace* much discussed. Yet recent efforts to reach more deeply into early modern thought have, in my opinion, confirmed the paucity of relevant conceptual and ethical resources for help in thinking about hospitality in today's world of strictly bounded, presumptively sovereign nation-states.[2]

---

[1]   Immanuel Kant, 'Perpetual peace: A philosophical sketch', in Hans Reiss, ed., *Kant: Political Writings*, 2nd edn (Cambridge: Cambridge University Press, 1991), pp. 105–8; see Seyla Benhabib, *Another Cosmopolitanism* (Oxford: Oxford University Press, 2006), pp. 148–52, and Nicholas Greenwood Onuf, *Making Sense, Making Worlds: Constructivism in Social Theory and International Relations* (Abingdon: Routledge, 2013), pp. 150–3, for contrary interpretations.

[2]   Georg Cavallar, 'Vitoria, Grotius, Pufendorf, Wolff and Vattel: Accomplices of European colonialism and exploitation or true cosmopolitans?' *Journal of the History of International Law* 10, 2 (2008), pp. 181–209; Gideon Baker, *Politicizing Ethics in International Relations: Cosmopolitanism as Hospitality* (Abingdon: Routledge, 2011), ch. 3.

Among contemporary thinkers, Jacques Derrida is not just fashionable. His extensive work on hospitality is at the centre of the discussion of a cosmopolitan ethics not predicated on liberal premises. As Gideon Baker has remarked, Derrida's ethical stance is 'a significant departure from Kantian hospitality and from Kantian ethics generally'.[3] Derrida based his stance on a distinction that I believe most people would find entirely plausible. Hospitality is, or should be, utterly unconditional; it is to be extended to the stranger at the door, no questions asked. At the same time, hospitality is, in practice, always conditional; it is subject to rules in practice.

Derrida formulated this apparent contradiction in striking terms, with Kant very much on his mind.

> It is as though hospitality were the impossible: as though the law of hospitality defined this very impossibility, as if it were only possible to transgress it, as though *the* law of absolute, unconditional, hyperbolical hospitality, as though the categorical imperative of hospitality commanded that we transgress all the laws (in the plural) of hospitality, namely, the conditions, the norms, the rights and duties that are imposed on hosts and hostesses, on the men or women who give a welcome as well as the men or women who receive it. And vice versa, it is as though the laws (plural) of hospitality, in marking limits, powers, rights and duties, consisted in challenging *the* law of hospitality, the one that would command that the 'new arrival' be offered an unconditional welcome.[4]

Such is the 'double law of hospitality', which, for Derrida, 'defines the unstable site of strategy and decision'.[5] On Baker's interpretation of this summary claim (and following one of Derrida's most familiar themes), the double law presents the host with an undecidable choice that must nevertheless be decided. Every stranger's arrival is a singular event; 'there is always a decision to be made'. It follows from this line of reasoning that 'the ethics of hospitality must necessarily be particular to each case', and making a decision is a responsible act. 'Undecidability becomes a condition of ethical action rather than an obstacle to it.'[6]

While I am sceptical that deciding the undecidable constitutes a sufficient basis for an alternative to Kant's cosmopolitan ethics, my concern here is not

---

[3] Gideon Baker, 'The "double law" of hospitality: Rethinking cosmopolitan ethics in humanitarian intervention', *International Relations* 24, 1 (2010), pp. 87–103.

[4] Jacques Derrida, *Of Hospitality*, trans. Rachel Bowlby (Stanford: Stanford University Press, 2000), pp. 75, 77, emphases in original.

[5] Jacques Derrida, 'The principle of hospitality', *Parallax* 11, 1 (2005), pp. 6–9 (6).

[6] Baker, 'The "double law" of hospitality', p. 92.

the undecidable. Nor is it the decision, or even the moment of decision, when host and guest make themselves each other's hostage.[7] This is, I should point out, an extended moment, and one that shifts the ethical centre of gravity to the household (and by implication, the state), which 'shelters and duly domesticates the hostages within its walls'.[8] My concern instead is an ethics of 'straddling', as Derrida put it, 'the two regimes of hospitality'—an ethics 'depending on whether the living environment is governed by fixed principles of respect and donation, or by exchange, proportion, a norm, etc'.[9]

Regrettably, Derrida said little to clarify this remark. Whether it suffices for an alternative cosmopolitan ethics I will consider in the last section of this essay. In the next two sections, I will develop the implications of Derrida's suggestion that, by straddling the contradiction between absolute and conditional hospitality, two second-order regimes of hospitality present themselves, one based on respect and donation (the RD regime), and the other based on exchange and proportion (the EP regime). Even if we reject the term *proportion* as an indicative feature of the EP regime (not least because Aristotle used the term to suggest an unequal relation), the regime would seem nevertheless to depend on people owning what they have, on property (thus leaving the acronym EP intact). In any event, we should think of these regimes as ideal types. As the term *straddling* suggests, both regimes are likely to be in evidence, across social settings, in different proportions.

Kant, Derrida and just about everyone else who is writing about hospitality today take it to be a universal phenomenon, an entailment of human sociality in a world where people have separated themselves into households, bands and polities. Insofar as exchange is another consequence of human dispersion and social separation, it too will be construed as a universal phenomenon, but one to which hospitality is necessarily attached—by definition, strangers cannot deal with each other. In an age of discovery and commercial expansion, early modern writers held that nature itself demanded the right to visit and the duty to receive visitors; natural law made hospitality, like property, indispensable to exchange. Most contemporary observers take reciprocity to constitute an ethical principle undergirding any sort of exchange.

Insofar as reciprocity implies that parties to any transaction both give and take, as equals, for the purpose of that transaction, I accept its normative function in an EP regime. Yet I do not equate social relations with exchange

7 Jacques Derrida, *Adieu: To Emmanuel Levinas*, trans. Pascale-Anne Brault and Michael Nass (Stanford: Stanford University Press, 1999), pp. 55–7; Derrida, *Of Hospitality*, pp. 123, 125.

8 Onuf, *Making Sense, Making Worlds*, p. 155.

9 Derrida, *Of Hospitality*, p. 137.

and thus do not see any necessary symmetry between giving and giving back: I can give you some token of my esteem, or some trouble to be endured, or some piece of unsolicited advice, and take nothing from you in return. In such situations, I have no reason to think that you have conducted yourself inappropriately.

In an RD regime, gifts do not generally call for reciprocity—a 'countergift', to use Derrida's term. In a discussion of giving that parallels, not too surprisingly, his discussion of hospitality's paradoxical impossibility, Derrida held that giving back 'annuls' the gift. 'For there to be a gift, there must be no reciprocity, return, exchange, countergift or debt.' Nor must giving be a conscious act. '*At the limit, the gift as gift* ought *not to appear as gift: either to the donee or the donor.*'[10] Properly speaking, a gift taken exists only in the past tense: the act, the very moment, of giving annuls the gift. In this sense, the gift is unconditional in just the way that hospitality is.

Derrida made the case for unreciprocated giving, for 'the without-return of the gift', in a brilliant reading of Marcel Mauss's seminal monograph, *The Gift*. Because Mauss viewed ceremonial giving as a system of exchange, Derrida's concern was giving back, not unconditional giving. Gift and counter-gift compose a 'cycle of restitution', in which the rules specify conditions under which a gift is given in response to a gift taken. These rules constitute an EP regime in which, according to Derrida, the 'thing' given (which cannot be a gift) 'gives, demands, and takes time'.[11]

Derrida failed to consider giving in an RD regime, in which rules specify conditions under which a gift must *not* be reciprocated. If, for Derrida, the context is time—giving time/giving in time—and the consequence is deferral, then for my purposes, the context is space—giving things/fixing distance. Fixed distances form social space; 'social distance' seems natural to those who occupy the space thus formed and always has normative consequences.[12] In an RD regime, the foremost consequence is deference.

As with gifts, so with hospitality. An EP regime sets the conditions under which hospitality is to be reciprocated and a debt repaid. In an RD regime, hospitality does not require repayment. Instead, the regime's rules designate

---

[10] Jacques Derrida, *Given Time*, 1, *Counterfeit Money*, trans. Peggy Kamuf (Chicago: University of Chicago Press, 1992), quoting pp. 12–14, emphasis in translation.

[11] Ibid., pp. 48, 13, 41.

[12] Sociologists have measured what they call social distance for many decades, conventionally with a questionnaire that Emory Bogardus developed to ascertain how people in a stipulated group feel about other people in that group. While this instrument may tell us how social rank is perceived in a group, it relies on a subjective and affective conception of social distance that can tell us nothing about the way distance and rank are related *conceptually*—a primary concern of this essay. I am indebted to Elena Gadjanova for bringing the relevant sociological literature to my attention.

who is welcomed in the household under what conditions. In doing so, it establishes and maintains relative *distance* among households. In effect, the rules of conditional hospitality make people relative strangers in any given society. If, following convention, we take social *position* to be fixed by relative distance on a vertical axis, these same rules order societal statuses.

Foremost among the ceremonies and courtesies of hospitality among relative strangers is the gift or tribute, which signals where we stand, and not what we owe. According to Derrida, gifts result in deferral because they are, by nature, '*excessive in advance, a priori exaggerated*'.[13] I suggest that what might appear to be excessive for the purposes of reciprocity and parity in an EP regime (Derrida's frame of reference) would be entirely appropriate in an RD regime. In such a regime, gifts function as status-markers. A lavish gift generally signals high status for the donor; a lavish gift rejected suggests a status claim denied. When a gift is seen as unduly lavish but accepted anyway, the implied acknowledgement of the status claim embedded in the gift may be offset by the many other ways that regime participants can use the regime's rules to affect status assignments.

Evidently universal by virtue of sociality and separation, the RD regime would appear to consist of 'natural laws'—duties arising from a natural disposition common to humanity, but *not* by virtue of any necessary association with exchange. This is, I believe, the way that hospitality is understood in classical cosmopolitan thought, most clearly articulated by Cicero.[14] Because modern thought has had so little use for this conception of hospitality or its justification in natural law, I doubt that there is much to be gained by undertaking a conceptual history of the RD regime.[15] Instead I examine some small part of the recent literature in cognitive development. By doing so, I hope to show that our natural disposition is to see the world as composed of objects, many of which we possess only to alienate—to donate, to give to other people when we have no expectation of receiving anything back in turn or in kind.

This disposition is said to reveal itself in 'communal sharing'.[16] This we might call the CS regime, which is presumed to operate most conspicuously in small groups and difficult circumstances. It seems likely, however, that

---

[13] Ibid., p. 38, emphasis in translation.

[14] Cicero, *On Duties*, trans. Margaret Atkins (Cambridge: Cambridge University Press, 1991), pp. 22–3, 36–7, 87–9.

[15] But see Nicholas Greenwood Onuf, *The Republican Legacy in International Thought* (Cambridge: Cambridge University Press, 1998), pp. 47–57, and Nicholas Onuf and Peter Onuf, *Nations, Markets and War: Modern History and the American Civil War* (Charlottesville: University of Virginia Press, 2006), pp. 197–206, for relevant materials.

[16] Alan Page Fiske, *Structures of Social Life: The Four Elementary Forms of Human Relations* (New York: Free Press, 1991), pp. 13–14.

standing differences in how much group members can give will translate into differences in respect and thus contribute to social distance, in which case a CS regime will turn into, or persist as a recessive or episodic feature of, an RD regime. In any event, the natural disposition to give objects away does not determine the contents of the RD regime (or, for that matter, the CS regime). It does require us to live by *some* set of rules through which routine hospitality cements our social relations by making us relative strangers in known degrees.

The psychologists and cognitive scientists on whom I draw in the next section of the essay are notably indifferent to language as the medium through which rules are made and used. No doubt the reason for this is their common hostility to the assumption, at the heart of contemporary social theory, that cultures are infinitely variable and the mind is a blank slate.[17] In Kantian fashion, many of them assume (as I do) that we have only an indirect access to the world using evolution's gift of cognitive equipment. Even so, they ignore the social constitution of a common reality consisting of the individuated, imbricated realities of many brains working in tandem. Not only do they fail to see that the full range of 'natural' cognitive capacities in individual human beings work at cross purposes and demand coordination, they cannot see that the cognitive competence to orchestrate one's own mind does so for a multiplicity of minds, and that it can do so *only* because it is socially acquired, linguistically mediated and normatively realized.

I turn, therefore, to language in the next section to link the natural disposition to give things away to the rules of the RD regime. The gift's importance is never to be underestimated; it reveals itself as a grammatical construction. The dative case (from the Latin, *dare*, to give) tells us that in a well-formed sentence with a double object, the subject (which need only be human-like) refers to the one who acts (gives, throws), the direct object to whatever is acted on, and the indirect object to the object's recipient (which again need not actually be human). I use recent discussion of dative verbs to develop my thoughts on giving's importance for fixing the distance among relative strangers.

In the third section of the essay, I hold that international society consists of states-as-households and that the rules of the RD regime apply to heads of states and their duly appointed emissaries. I consider and reject James Der Derian's argument that diplomats mediate between estranged sovereigns.[18] I suggest instead that diplomats maintain the social distance

---

[17] See Stephen Pinker, *The Blank Slate: The Modern Denial of Human Nature* (New York: Penguin Books, 2002), for an extended, unremitting expression of this hostility.

[18] James Der Derian, *On Diplomacy: A Genealogy of Western Estrangement* (Oxford: Basil Blackwell, 1987).

among states-as-households. The many rituals and ceremonies that bring them together constitute their chief means for doing so. That outsiders consider these rituals arcane atavisms hardly troubles the people engaging in them in their everyday lives.

The fourth and concluding section of the essay returns to the ethics of hospitality, on which Derrida and other contemporary writers have fixed so much attention. Like honour, hospitality is a universal human concern manifest not in invariant principles but in codes of conduct, the contents of which vary from society to society but which no society can do without. These codes are the major constituents of what I call everyday ethics. Diplomacy is a demanding, sometimes nasty, even dirty world in which the self-esteem of its members is bound up in the requirements of deference and donation, honour and hospitality.

Objects in motion

Aristotle held that nature endows living things with the faculties necessary for them to fulfil their potential.[19] Animals have mental faculties, and, of course, a faculty for language distinguishes human beings from other living things. Aristotle's importance for medieval thought assured a continuing emphasis on mental faculties, which we also find even, or especially, in Kant but not thereafter, when cultural variability and positivist science dictated a modern preoccupation with the mind as a vessel to be filled. Only recently have scholars rediscovered mental faculties, renaming them 'domains of human cognition' or 'modular cognitive systems'.[20] There has since been raging discussion of domain specificity and modularity, much of it centred on daunting issues—how are domains bounded, how many modules does the mind possess?—that need not detain us.[21]

Noam Chomsky identified three domains: one specific to language, a second specific to physical objects, and a third specific to numbers. Music may constitute a fourth domain. Many scholars divide the second into three domains, each of which produces commonsense knowledge about physical objects: objects that only move when moved (folk physics), objects that

---

[19] Aristotle, *On the Soul*, in Jonathan Barnes, ed., *The Complete Works of Aristotle*, 1 (Princeton: Princeton University Press, 1984), pp. 641–92.

[20] Respectively: Noam Chomsky, *Rules and Representations* (New York: Columbia University Press, 1980), pp. 3–4; Jerry Fodor, *The Modularity of Mind: An Essay on Faculty Psychology* (Cambridge, MA: MIT Press, 1983), p. 2.

[21] See David Buller, *Adapting Minds: Evolutionary Psychology and the Persistent Quest for Human Nature* (Cambridge, MA: MIT Press, 2005) for a critical review.

move themselves (folk biology), and objects whose movements are goal-directed or intentional (folk psychology).[22] All three domains presuppose an ability to sort objects according to some discernible property (in speech, movement implies predication).

Insofar as classification is a core feature of folk biology, the latter might better be characterized as the domain where, after assigning properties to objects, we go on to classify them by reference to movement as a differentiating property, and then direct our attention to objects that seem to be able to move themselves (slowly, by growing, or more quickly, through locomotion). From an early age, children see—sense—what we adults take to be a world of objects. They see that like objects go together—put them together—in what we call categories. They see—single out—the relation between objects that we call *cause*. They are naturally disposed to perform these operations without any help from language, learning and culture.

In a much cited paper, Alan Leslie has suggested that children have a naïve theory of mechanical contact and the transmission of FORCE.[23] While using the term *theory* in this context is rather fanciful and the analogy between children's domain-specific knowledge and self-conscious theorizing is strained, its connotative sense more or less parallels *understanding* as that term and its cognates are used in ordinary language.[24] In other words, children seem to understand that inanimate objects can be made to move. 'From the point of view … of contact mechanical theory, launching is the simplest and most complete instance of the transmission of FORCE'; 'the two objects in launching are assigned different and imbalanced mechanical roles, one as pusher (transmitter of FORCE), the other as pushed (recipient of FORCE)'.[25] The act of launching is central to the large argument of this essay that we are naturally disposed to participate in an RD regime. I return

---

22 See, for example, David Premack and Ann Premack, *Original Intelligence: Unlocking the Mysteries of Who We Are* (New York: McGraw-Hill, 2003), pp. 2–37.

23 Alan M. Leslie, 'ToMM, ToBy, and agency: Core architecture and domain specificity', in Lawrence A. Hirschfeld and Susan A. Gelman, eds, *Mapping the Mind: Domain Specificity in Cognition and Culture* (Cambridge: Cambridge University Press, 1994), pp. 119–48. Leslie used the upper case to indicate a 'primitive notion' (p. 125).

24 Leslie is not alone in using the term *theory* for whatever children seem to know in a domain-specific way. See, for example, David Premack, 'The infant's theory of self-propelled objects', *Cognition* 36, 1 (1990), pp. 1–16; Alison Gopnik and Henry M. Wellman, 'The theory theory', in Hirschfeld and Gelman, *Mapping the Mind*, pp. 257–93; Paul L. Harris, 'Thinking by children and scientists: False analogies and neglected similarities', in ibid., pp. 294–315; Alison Gopnik and Andrew N. Meltzoff, *Words, Thought, and Theories* (Cambridge, MA: MIT Press, 1997).

25 Leslie, 'ToMM, ToBy, and agency', p. 133; see generally pp. 123–37.

to this act when I link the mechanics of launching—causing to go—and giving in performative speech.

Here is what we can say, more or less safely: before children are a year old, they begin to make associations. They realize that some objects are like other objects, and some are not. They sort objects by discernible properties, such as movement. They recognize that once objects are launched they tend to move continuously, smoothly in Euclidian space—in some direction that changes not at all or only gradually—until some other object stops or redirects it. They are intuitive taxonomists and naïve geometers, not Aristotelian teleologists or functional sociologists.

As mechanical theorists, infants may indeed understand that objects in motion bounce off each other, just as they understand that two solid objects cannot occupy the same space at the same time. They need not have any idea what interaction entails in the way of planning and strategic thinking, and I cannot imagine that they do. Infants have needs, but they have no goals except as imputed to them by observers. Launching an object is a mechanical event, for very young children a visually stimulating, perhaps an entertaining event subject to repetition. Giving some object away, giving it to someone else, giving it up: these are goal-directed activities that very young children cannot appreciate as such.

Only gradually do children come to realize that giving is a social and not just a mechanical event. As children construct themselves and others into self-possessed, wilful beings, they possess objects, including themselves, only in a weak sense. They participate in the RD regime unselfconsciously, if only to get along with other evidently wilful beings. Insofar as (dis)possession is a natural disposition, possession in the strong sense of ownership takes time and learning. So do autonomy, parity, reciprocity, exchange and fairness—all constitutive features of the EP regime.

If, indeed, very young children understand elementary mechanics, calling what they do understand goal-directed or intentional sows confusion. Furthermore, we as adults need to be clear about what we call *self*-propulsion to understand what infants actually do understand. Continuous (constant or gradually changing) motion by itself leaves the source of motion, its cause, unknowable. Starting is another matter, and so is stopping all of a sudden. For very young children, the compelling distinction is between launched and self-launching objects. We are hardwired to understand cause (in space and time) from a very early age—Kant got it right in his *Critique of Pure Reason*. Children soon realize that in a world of objects, there are two kinds of causes, external and internal. They cannot see which cause accounts for continuous motion until they fully understand goal-directedness.

It is wildly misleading to say, as Leslie did in an earlier paper, that 'infants possess a capacity for primary representation from the outset of development'—a capacity 'defined in terms of its direct semantic relation with the world'.[26] Even if we have a 'direct' relation to the world (say, through Kant's 'faculty of intuition'[27]), any 'semantic relation' is prima facie mediated by language. Representations are models, whether arrangements of objects or verbal constructions. They are built with or from representations, in an apparently infinite regress that can only end with the natural disposition to give names to what we think we see.[28]

At about the age that children begin to understand goal-directed beings and their interactions, they begin to develop their faculties for using words and numbers. In making models, in manipulating the world in their minds, they use imagination (to make associations), judgement (in dealing with rules) and reason (to reach beyond the limits of possible experience).[29] They master the relevant faculties with remarkable speed. That all these things happen at once can hardly be a coincidence.

Children begin to speak by repeating words that they hear in use. These words are typically nouns, the names for objects in their world. When they repeat verbs, they are making simple sentences to represent what is happening in their world of objects. In so doing they acquire beliefs, translate needs into desires, form goals and achieve them when others respond to their sentences. Verbs are key. 'A verb, then, is not just a word that refers to an action or state but the chassis of a sentence. It is a framework with receptacles for the other parts—the subject, the object, and various oblique objects and subordinate clauses—to be bolted onto.'[30]

Verbs come in different forms, which tell how to put sentence parts together. These coded instructions may well correspond to specific domains of human cognition, but they do vary from language to language, just as their interpretation varies from one speaker to another. Scholars typically estimate the reach of specific *verb constructions* (as linguists have traditionally called them—a revealing choice of terms) by offering examples and asking if they sound right to native speakers of the language. In what follows, I offer examples in English, which is my native language, judging what sounds right for myself. I assume my constructions will more or less correspond to the verb forms that native speakers of other languages are likely to put forward, because human beings tend to *represent* the world that we *see* pretty

---

[26] Alan M. Leslie, 'Pretense and representation: The origins of "Theory of mind"', *Psychological Review* 94, 4 (1987), p. 414.

[27] Immanuel Kant, *Critique of Pure Reason*, trans. Norman Kemp Smith (New York: St Martin's, 1965), p. 105.

[28] For an accessible overview, see Stephen Pinker, *The Stuff of Thought: Language as a Window into Human Nature* (New York: Viking, 2007), pp. 281–96.

[29] Kant, *Critique of Pure Reason*, pp. 141, 177.

[30] Pinker, *The Stuff of Thought*, p. 31. See generally pp. 25–87 for a fascinating disquisition on verbs and their analysis.

much the same way. At least this seems like a reasonable assumption for the world of objects in motion that very young children are naturally disposed to see—again, pretty much the same way.

Even the most elementary survey of verb constructions must take transitivity into account. In sentences with intransitive verbs, subjects are agents and the verb tells us that their acts are sufficient or complete as performed (thunder rumbled; doors open; wars start; I almost gave up). Recalling the child's world of objects, subjects are acting objects. Intransitive verbs have the effect of making motion into an object: an agent, which is an object positioned as the sentence's subject, launches a moving object. When verbs are transitive, subjects are agents performing acts, and having effects, on objects directly (lightning struck the embassy; the embassy guard opened the door), even at a distance (the ambassador saw the lightning; we gave thanks). Transitive constructions specify two objects, one represented as affecting the other.

As children, we are naturally disposed to see objects in motion, theorize cause and express what we see in sentences with transitive verbs. We are also disposed to locate moving objects in space and time (Ambassador, your husband called you), very often with help from additional instructions, variably coded as prepositions and adverbs (the foreign minister flew from Bangkok to Tokyo; call him back right away). Some transitive verbs have a subject and two objects, in which case we call them *dative* or *ditransitive*. They relate a subject as agent to an object (a noun in the accusative case) *and* that object to another object (a noun in the dative case). The causal effect is *indirect*, even when there is an observable connection (a moving object) between the source of motion and the object affected (the indirect object): the ambassador (object as subject) said (verb in dative construction) some harsh things (direct or first object) to the first secretary (indirect or second object).

At least in English, a few dative verbs can take two forms: the embassy guard threw the ball to the child; the guard threw her the ball (and, dropping the preposition *to*, it sounds perfectly natural to put the indirect object first). By contrast, it sounds wrong to say: the ambassador said me some harsh things; the guard opened the door to her. Using a direct object and a preposition or the double object interchangeably is a phenomenon that linguists call *alternation*. Malka Rappaport Hovav and Beth Levin classify alternating dative verbs as follows:

> *Verbs that inherently signify acts of giving*: give, hand, lend, loan, pass, rent, sell ...
> *Verbs of future having*: allocate, allow, bequeath, grant, offer, owe, promise ...
> *Verbs of communication*: tell, show, ask, teach, read, write, quote, cite ...

Verbs of sending: forward, mail, send, ship …

Verbs of instantaneous causation of ballistic motion: fling, flip, kick, lob, slap, shoot, throw, toss …

Verbs of causation of accompanied motion in a deictically specified direction: bring, take …

Verbs of instrument of communication: e-mail, fax, radio, wire, telegraph, telephone …[31]

Having given the dative case its name, *give* is the leading example of a dative verb. Among alternating dative verbs, *give* is the most common—according to one source, 53 per cent of the total in English usage—and the one that seems richest in metaphorical extension and social meaning.[32]

Alternation is a puzzle, a paradox, begging solution.[33] It is not to be found in languages, such as Russian, where word order is more flexible than it is in English.[34] How do we, as natural-born theorists and syntactically competent speakers, know which datives are alternating and, by implication, why they are and other dative verbs are not? In looking for an answer to these questions, linguists attach a great deal of importance to '*give* type verbs' causing possession and '*throw* type verbs' causing motion.[35] To throw (send, toss, bring, fax: all alternating verbs in the last four of Rappaport Hovav and Levin's categories) is to cause to go.

Classification implies an answer to my questions, a solution to the puzzle. As Stephen Pinker has put it, there is a shift in what the speaker thinks is happening to the objects of the world—'a conceptual gestalt shift between causing to go and causing to *have*'.[36] Here is his example: '*Give a muffin to a moose* means "cause a moose to go to a muffin," whereas *give a moose a muffin* means "cause a moose to have a muffin"'.[37] Pinker went on to observe that

this may seem to be hair-splitting, because causing-to-go usually results in causing-to-have. With a movable object, you have to cause it to go for that person to have it, and even immovable and intangible

---

[31] Malka Rappaport Hovav and Beth Levin, 'The English dative alternation: The case for verb sensitivity', *Journal of Linguistics* 44, 1 (2008), pp. 129–67 (134).

[32] Joan Bresnan and Tatiana Nikitina, 'The gradience of the dative alternation', in Linda Ann Uyechi and Lian-Hee Wee, eds, *Reality Exploration and Discovery: Pattern Interaction in Language and Life* (Stanford: CSLI Publications, 2010), p. 178.

[33] Pinker, *The Stuff of Thought*, pp. 58–60; Rappaport Hovav and Levin, 'The English dative alternation', pp. 129–33.

[34] Rappaport Hovav and Levin, 'The English dative alternation', p. 161.

[35] Ibid., p. 132.

[36] Pinker, *The Stuff of Thought*, p. 58, emphasis in original.

[37] Ibid., pp. 58–9, citation deleted.

possessions can be thought of as moving in a metaphorical sense. In this metaphor, possessions are things, owners are places, and giving is moving.[38]

Pinker then argued that inanimate objects cannot own things, and so we cannot say, for example, 'Annette sent the border a package' except by metaphorical extension.[39]

Even when we take metaphorical extension into account (personified governments maintain border facilities on behalf of the personified states to which these borders metaphorically belong), I think that there is something odd about these claims. When it comes to things—gifts in the usual sense of the term—we are naturally disposed to think we can choose to keep them as possessions, use them as we see fit, give them to someone else, or exchange them for other things of value to us. The ambassador gave her husband a hug; Annette sent the border station a package; the second secretary sold his replacement his car. And usually the alternate form sounds right (but not always: the ambassador gave a hug to her husband) because, as Pinker suggested, causing-to-go and causing-to-have are normally indistinguishable in effect (although giving a hug favours having over going). So far, so good.

Yet this is not all that happens. When subjects cause direct objects to go, they go somewhere and they have an effect *there*—on the indirect object. All three objects (subject, direct object, indirect object) *have* new properties. When we say *The president gave the ambassador a medal*, we mean to say: the president, who has medals to give out, gave one to the ambassador, so that the president now has one less medal (and one more medal-holder in his retinue), the medal has moved to a new location, and the ambassador has a 'new' medal. If we were to say instead *The president gave a medal to the ambassador*, we are shifting the weight of the sentence from the medal to the ambassador, on the view that we load what is most important in a sentence on its two ends.[40]

It would seem then that we use alternating dative verbs to indicate that the subject, direct object and indirect object have undergone a change in state. To *give* means to have the direct object in the subject's possession, to cause it to go, and to have an effect not just on the indirect object—the recipient—but also on the subject and the direct object, without implying that the indirect object, the recipient, owns or can alienate the direct object. Just as with inalienable possession in the genitive case (the ambassador's

---

[38] Ibid., p. 59.
[39] Ibid.; also see Rappaport Hovav and Levin, 'The English dative alternation', p. 138.
[40] Compare Rappaport Hovav and Levin, 'The English dative alternation', p. 156, on 'heaviness'.

right hand, motor reflexes, handshake), the indirect object, as recipient, may not own what it has been given (the ambassador's medal is not for the ambassador to give away). The indirect object *has* the properties (location and condition) that the subject gave it until some other subject *gives* it a new location and properties.

Alternating dative verbs always indicate changes in state, whatever the properties of the objects in question. Indirect objects of every kind, and not just inanimate objects, may be caused to change without being able to alienate whatever it is (direct object, gift) that caused them to change. As the object of giving, animate beings are not always free to alienate what they are given. Animals are obviously animate, but we are disposed to see them as owners only as metaphorical extensions of ourselves. We generally take our faculties to be inalienable gifts of nature; many of us hold certain rights to be inalienable.

The verb *give* identifies objects that, by having been caused to go (as mobile objects also known as gifts), *may* become possessions in the sense that liberal linguists seem to take for granted. Also, always and simultaneously, the verb *give* causes possession in the more fundamental sense of an object possessing new properties. As I have said, the subject as giver, the gift and the gift's recipient will have new properties, whether a change in location, condition or both. All gifts start off in the subjects' possession. Being alienable, they are caused to go and cause to have (despite what hair-splitting linguists say). Not all gifts cause to have in both senses of possession—once received, not all are alienable.

This distinction is *not* splitting hairs. For children theorists, objects have properties such as movement, agents cause objects to move, some moving objects have an effect on other objects, agents cause objects to have an effect on other objects: the verb *give* codes all of this information. As they learn to use their verbs, they learn that exchange is predicated on the alienation of mobile things, on giving things in order to get things. They participate as agents in the EP regime.

Yet this is not all that children learn. They also learn that many other kinds of social relations depend on the continuous supply of inalienable gifts. Gifts make us what we are through the effects that they have on us. In doing so, they constitute the RD regime and regulate our social relations by marking the differences among us and thus the distances between us, pair by pair, set by set.

When the president gives a medal to the ambassador, that act enhances (confirms, perhaps even diminishes) the president's esteemed position as someone who dispenses honours, the ambassador's esteem as honoured recipient, and the esteem in which all parties hold the medal as an honour and the occasion for its bestowal. Orientational metaphors reveal a natural disposition to position objects in space, at a distance from each other and the observer.[41] On a horizontal plane, social distance makes us all strangers to each other, but only relatively—we know where we stand. Rotate the axis, and we find our rank. Even as children we are naïve geometers who perform these operations effortlessly as we find our place in the RD regime.

On diplomacy

Not every instance of a gift given is equally important for the constitution and regulation of social distance. Giving the passing stranger a nod is less important than giving the ambassador a medal. Formal occasions for giving and acknowledging gifts—ceremonies, festivals, anniversaries, holidays—are especially important for social distancing, and they almost always involve hospitality under rule-specified conditions and the sharing of possessions—meals and memories, songs and stories, common concerns and good feelings. *Sharing* describes a situation in which the many give some of what is theirs to alienate, not to each other, but to the whole as a generalized indirect object. Egalitarian in its thrust, communal sharing may indeed be yet another natural disposition that human beings share, one that prompts the formation of a CS regime to mitigate social distance and vitiate any feelings of alienation that social distancing induces.

It is an ethnographic commonplace that humanity's evolutionary circumstances resulted in small bands of hunters and gatherers, some few of which have persisted to the present. As an ideal-typical social arrangement, such bands are said to share everything of value; whatever band members acquire they alienate immediately to the band as a whole.[42] Lacking alienable objects to separate them and to signify rank, band members have no need for the conditional hospitality and the rituals of giving and getting characteristic of an RD regime. Instead they form a rankless society—one that rewards or rankles no one in particular.

One need not accept the claim well known to evolutionary psychology that mating necessarily results in a 'dominance hierarchy' to be sceptical that living conditions were ever so simple: needs readily met, band size stable, strangers rarely encountered.[43] The natural, cultivable disposition to circulate esteemed objects, set conditions for hospitality, and calibrate social distance (in time by generations; in horizontal space by reference to kin, neighbours,

---

[41] The *locus classicus* on orientational metaphors is George Lakoff and Mark Johnson, *Metaphors We Live By* (Chicago: University of Chicago Press, 1980).

[42] See Jack Donnelly, 'The elements of the structures of international systems', *International Organization* 66, 4 (2012), pp. 609–43 (609–15), for an overview.

[43] On dominance hierarchy, see especially David M. Buss, *The Evolution of Desire: Strategies of Human Mating*, rev. edn (New York: Basic Books, 2003); and see Buller, *Adapting Minds*, pp. 201–345, for a critical assessment.

strangers; in vertical space by rank) will always find opportunities to assert itself. As a natural disposition, sharing is hardly likely to dominate social relations for long, even if we decide to cultivate it. Nor is communal sharing likely to disappear, even as we cultivate other natural dispositions making us relative strangers in rank-ordered sets.

How the rules of conditional hospitality and the circulation of esteemed objects instantiate social distance is, on examination, not altogether obvious. While my focus is on gifts as tokens of esteem and distancing mechanisms (and therefore the RD regime), most scholars focus on gift exchange as a (re)distributive mechanism, and not gifts as such. Focusing on the EP regime, they follow Mauss, who linked generosity and honour, most spectacularly in the potlatch.[44] Blessed with natural abundance and accumulating largess, the native tribes of the north-west coast of North America engaged in profligate hospitality, with families giving away their stores of goods in hopes of being seen as more generous and therefore worthier than their neighbours. The practice induced imitation, fostered reciprocity and resulted in a more egalitarian distribution of material goods through their destruction by consumption.

The rampant alienation of potlatch is not to be confused with communal sharing. The potlatch did nothing to reduce social distance beyond the ceremonial confines of seasonal hospitality. On the contrary, some families were always in a position to give more goods away, with greater honour their reward. We see this phenomenon repeatedly. Wealthy donors endow art museums and professorial chairs, always calibrating their generosity against the honour it accrues their names, the esteem it produces and the effect it has on their position in society. We also see its converse operating to the same effect. For hundreds of years, China's tributaries gave less tribute than the recipient could have extracted by other means, but the occasion for tribute conferred honour, connoted esteem and codified social distance.[45]

With Derrida, I see no reason to call this process *exchange*, as if it involved alienable possessions, or even *reciprocity*, as if some sort of parity is implied. Only when esteem is reified (as it often is: the ambassador's medal) and then commodified (as it is, much less often, in markets, such as for endowed professorial chairs) can there be exchange in the usual sense. Only when gifts are judged comparable in social value can there be reciprocity. Only then does the EP regime override or overlay the RD regime. Yet esteem,

---

44 Marcel Mauss, *The Gift: Forms and Functions of Exchange in Archaic Societies*, trans. Ian Cunnison (New York: Norton, 1967). On the potlatch, see pp. 31–7 and Derrida's *Given Time*, pp. 37–47, which reads Mauss against Mauss and his many followers.

45 David C. Kang, *East Asia before the West: Five Centuries of Trade and Tribute* (New York: Columbia University Press, 2010).

as a property, typically has different values for different people, depending on their relative positions in society. If the president gives the ambassador a medal, the effects on their esteem (self-esteem, esteem for each other, esteem in the eyes of others) will not be comparable. The RD regime prevails.

Unconditional hospitality is an unconditional gift. If there are rules of conditional hospitality, then there are rules on giving, taking, and giving back—as Mauss claimed, *separate* sets of rules telling people when and what kinds of gifts are obligatory, when and under what circumstances they are obliged to accept gifts, and whether accepting a gift creates an obligation to give a gift under what circumstances.[46] When a humble graduate student invites an exalted professor home for dinner, the professor is not obliged to invite the student to her home. Conversely, when an exalted professor invites a humble graduate student out for a beer, the student is not obliged to do the same or indeed to share the bill. Again, the RD regime prevails.

Few settings in the modern world make the rules of hospitality—the RD regime—clearer or more consequential than the relations between states manifest in the activities of chiefs of state, government ministers and other senior officers, and diplomats as standing guests in other states-as-households. When chiefs of states meet, the occasion is treated as festive day warranting extraordinary displays of hospitality and ritual exchanges—gifts, toasts, reassurances—affirming the formal parity of the states and their chiefs. The host initiates a carefully calibrated ritual of physical contact (by giving a hand, an embrace, a kiss). If two chiefs meet in neither one's country, they give and take back inalienable body parts in a single synchronized moment. Much the same holds for ministers and ambassadors on appropriately less elaborate scales. Expressions and tokens of mutual esteem foster solidarity and sharing within ranks, even as they confirm the distance between ranks.

While important rules make chiefs, ministers and ambassadors formally equal at each rank, there are additional rules, many of them informal, acknowledging them to possess or assigning them different attributes, all of which have the effect of differentiating them within ranks. When the ambassador of a large country in a major capital hosts a grand reception and invites many dignitaries, the ambassador of a smaller country is not obliged to host an equally grand reception. Indeed, it would be presumptuous for the ambassador of the smaller country to do so. Finally, there are all sorts of informal rules for social relations across formal ranks. When the president gives the ambassador a medal, the ambassador should give her thanks to the president (confirming her esteem for him) and her thanks to her staff (raising its members' esteem for her). That there are so many rules, that so many of them are informal, suggests that mastering the code of hospitality

---

[46]   Mauss, *The Gift*, pp. 37–41.

in the relations of states takes time and skill—protocol matters because social distance is a large concern in those relations.

The general features of the RD regime in the relations of states go back to the 15th century. At that time, sovereigns were steadily tightening their control over lesser lords, with a proportionate increase in the former's majesty— the property of inspiring awe.[47] This process also saw the transformation of the sovereign's lords from warriors to courtiers,[48] and the institution of permanent embassies.[49] Before the last of these developments, occasional visitors representing sovereigns and their interests were of two sorts: those with symbolic duties such as delivering a message or gracing a ceremony, and those with powers to negotiate. Permanent embassies effectively ended a distinction already tenuous in practice, and resident ambassadors assumed a variety of duties taking them to their hosts' courts.[50] Together, resident ambassadors constituted the diplomatic corps, defined as such by set rules for the corps' members—rules for presenting credentials, rules assuring respect for each other, rules for dealing with notables and officials of every rank, rules granting ambassadors local privileges and immunities.

The large effect of these closely related developments was to order social distance within the proto-states of Europe on the same vertical axis and to routinize the ongoing conduct of relations among them. Over time, the shift from state sovereigns to sovereign states has done little to change the RD regime or working relations among states' agents within and across ranks. Judging from Garrett Mattingly's account, the first book on diplomatic practice (Bernard du Rosier's *Ambaxiator breviologus*, 1436) failed to discriminate in any systematic way between what diplomats are, as honoured members of a ranked society subject to an elaborate code of hospitality, and what they do, as agents engaged in relations on behalf of sovereigns.[51] Indicatively, the two most important manuals on diplomatic practice to appear before the last century—Abraham de Wicquefort's *L'ambassadeur et ses fonctions* (1680) and François de Callières's *De la manière de négocier avec les souverains* (1716)—refer to the diplomat as 'an honorable spy'.[52] Both consider rank and conduct to be inseparable features of the 'art' of diplomacy.

---

[47] Onuf, *The Republican Legacy in International Thought*, pp. 113–38.

[48] Norbert Elias, *Power and Civility: The Civilizing Process*, 2, trans. Edmund Jephcott (New York: Pantheon, 1982), pp. 258–70.

[49] Garrett Mattingly, *Renaissance Diplomacy* (Baltimore: Penguin, 1964), pp. 55–70, 87–93.

[50] Ibid., pp. 25–7, 94–102.

[51] Ibid., pp. 30–8.

[52] H. M. A. Keens-Soper and Karl W. Schweizer, eds, *The Art of Diplomacy: François de Callières* (New York: Holmes & Meier, 1983), p. 80, citing Wicquefort's book and quoting Callières's.

Only gradually did later commentators develop the distinction between ceremony and the conduct of relations—communicating wishes, negotiating differences—and view the latter as the diplomat's primary function. Harold Nicolson, as the 20th century's most influential diplomatic participant-observer, could emphasize negotiation as the diplomat's primary function, at least in theory, all the while concerning himself with the personal qualities of an ideal diplomat, just as his predecessors had.[53] Indeed he also wrote a book on good behaviour and civility.[54] The prevailing sentiment today is that diplomats are, and have always been, communicators and negotiators first and foremost, their practical responsibilities warranting their privileges and immunities.[55] Their ceremonial duties come a distant second, their high standing suiting them to the social whirl of frivolous activities.

Diplomatic privileges and immunities are long settled in international law. The manual on diplomatic practice now most widely in use, *Satow's Guide to Diplomatic Practice*, devotes only a few pages to the diplomatic corps.[56] In contrast, we find hundreds of pages devoted to international law and institutions, as if these rules are the only ones that diplomats really need to know. The contemporary literature on diplomacy is, for the most part, a pastiche of diplomatic history, personal anecdotes and half-hearted efforts to situate diplomatic practice in the larger context of foreign policy making and international theory.[57]

A recent exception to this general tendency is Christer Jönnson and Martin Hall's *Essence of Diplomacy*, which systematically considers diplomacy from an institutionally oriented theoretical perspective. Influencing this book is an earlier, conspicuous exception: James Der Derian's masterpiece, *On Diplomacy*.[58] Its subtitle, *A Genealogy of Western Estrangement*, announces a debt to Michel Foucault. The book is not at all a conventional history of diplomacy, much less a manual for diplomats on the rules of the RD regime.

---

[53] Harold Nicolson, *Diplomacy* (New York: Harcourt Brace, 1939); and Harold Nicolson, *The Evolution of the Diplomatic Method* (London: Cassell, 1954); also see Derek Drinkwater, *Sir Harold Nicolson and International Relations: The Practitioner as Theorist* (Oxford: Oxford University Press, 2005), pp. 94–102.

[54] Harold Nicolson, *Good Behaviour: Being a Study of Certain Types of Civility* (London: Constable, 1955).

[55] Christer Jönnson and Martin Hall, *Essence of Diplomacy* (Basingstoke: Palgrave Macmillan, 2005), pp. 67–97.

[56] Paul Henry Gore-Booth, ed., *Satow's Guide to Diplomatic Practice*, 5th edn (London: Longman, 1979), pp. 161–73. I have yet to inspect Ivor Roberts' 6th edition (Oxford: Oxford University Press, 2009), which is too recent for wide use [when I wrote this essay a decade ago].

[57] See Paul Sharp and Geoffrey Wiseman, eds, *The Diplomatic Corps as an Institution in International Society* (New York: Palgrave Macmillan, 2007), for one of the better examples.

[58] As Jönnson and Hall acknowledged, *Essence of Diplomacy*, p. 18.

It is, however, an inspired, altogether original treatment of the conditions and consequences of social distance in international relations.

Der Derian's general point is close to the one I have put forward here: 'it is as much the "petty" rituals and ceremonies of power as it is the "great" events of power politics or the famous developments of international law which define diplomacy'.[59] Der Derian's point of departure is the unfolding of a 'diplomatic culture' incipient in the Western world from its earliest moments. That culture acquired the rituals and ceremonies so evident even today when states emerged together but separately in the 15th and 16th centuries.

> Like the bridges of medieval cities, the diplomatic culture begins as a neutral link between alien quarters, but with the disintegration and diffusion of a common Latin power, it becomes ... a discursive space where representatives of sovereign states can avoid the national tolls of the embryonic international society while attempting to mediate its systemic alienation.[60]

Der Derian's explication of this development hinges on concepts—*alienation* and *mediation*—conspicuously deployed in this passage.[61]

Der Derian's extended treatment of alienation reminds us that the Latin infinitive *alienare* means 'to make something another's'.[62] This is, of course, entirely consistent with the way I have been using the term *alienate* and makes it generally synonymous with *give*, to which I have already given so much attention. Der Derian focused his attention on economic and juridical senses of the term established in Roman and early modern practice (in effect, elements of the EP regime), and on the use of the term in Christian theology, before turning to G. W. F. Hegel as the master theorist of alienation understood in the contemporary (modern and postmodern) sense of separation. To simplify Der Derian's subtle discussion, Hegel construed alienation as intrapersonal estrangement brought on by consciousness and interpersonal estrangement brought on by history. In a parallel dialectic to reunify mind and history, mediation is the middle term, the mode of synthesis. Estrangement, with its feelings of indifference or hostility, brings not just recognition but mediation—metaphorical movement across the space that separates us all.

---

[59] Der Derian, *On Diplomacy*, p. 114.

[60] Ibid., pp. 42–3.

[61] Ibid., pp. 13–26; James Der Derian, 'Mediating estrangement: A theory for diplomacy', *Review of International Studies* 13, 2 (1987), pp. 91–110.

[62] Der Derian, *On Diplomacy*, p. 13; 'Mediating estrangement', pp. 96–7.

For Der Derian, diplomacy is mediation between estranged peoples.[63] In the diplomatic culture that emerged half a millennium ago, mediation is not just metaphorical movement; diplomats as mediators come and go, with an elaborate code of hospitality to regulate their movements and mark the places where mediation takes place. In Der Derian's words, 'ceremony and the ritual for receiving and dispatching ambassadors ... sanctioned the *movement across political boundaries*'.[64] As metaphorical movement, mediation depends on giving and taking, in the first instance discursively and thus metaphorically, but with the potential or consequence of moving valued objects.

Der Derian emphasized gift exchange in the deep origins of the diplomatic culture.[65] As a medium for establishing parity between mediating parties, and eventually an acknowledgement of the sovereign equality of states, gift exchange has always had a powerful ritual significance. This is the case whenever parity within a rank or social stratum needs to be confirmed—as it must to anchor the EP regime. Yet it hardly exhausts the circumstances in which gifts (objects caused to go) are taken (have an effect on the recipient) so as to constitute and regulate social distance between ranks.

Diplomatic culture is rife with gift-giving that has these effects, notwithstanding the formal parity of states. No one expects parity in giving or gifts as objects. Der Derian's emphasis on mediation puts reciprocity first and not the 'one-sided nature of the power relation'.[66] By contrast, I hold that ranking is the most important business to be transacted by diplomatic mediators. As I have endeavoured to show, gifts broadly understood are a primary medium for calibrating and codifying ranks and thus a central feature of the RD regime.

All gifts are valued, some negatively. Some gifts are hostile by design (Trojan horses), some are rejected. By extension, promises are deferred gifts; threats are gifts withheld or gifts not wanted. This is the stuff of diplomacy, all of it affecting social distance, only some of it constituting exchange in the usual sense of the term.

Der Derian's misplaced emphasis on mediation as reciprocity, parity and exchange betrays an undisclosed assumption that liberal modernity (the EP regime broadly construed) has generally displaced an old RD regime of aristocratic practices. The insular world of diplomacy is an exception, lagging behind large changes in the structure of international society. 'The most obvious example of diplomatic cultural lag is the formation and retention

---

[63] Der Derian, *On Diplomacy*, pp. 34, 110.
[64] Ibid., p. 34, emphasis in original.
[65] Ibid., pp. 67, 72. Also see Jönnson and Hall, *Essence of Diplomacy*, pp. 45–8.
[66] Der Derian, *On Diplomacy*, p. 72. So does Jönnson and Hall's emphasis on communication in *Essence of Diplomacy*.

of aristocratic manners and norms in diplomacy in a period when merchant capitalism and bourgeois nationalism were taking off.'[67] For Der Derian, the time needed to internalize structurally induced changes accounts for the lag. Yet the persistence of the RD regime to this very day suggests something more than a lag in learning.

Even more, the persistence of diplomacy's old ways suggests that Der Derian has gratuitously separated diplomacy (as process) and international relations (as structure) merely by introducing the notion of lag. As I have said several times now, the rituals of diplomacy constitute and regulate the social distance among states. For observers (diplomats, scholars, people in general), the patterns that these distances exhibit *are* the structure of international relations.[68] In good measure, this structure remains as stable as it has seemed over the centuries because diplomats at every rank constantly manage the distances among states that they are charged with representing.

Codes of conduct

Throughout this essay, I have referred to the RD, EP and CS regimes in the singular. Sometimes I have done so to indicate that they are ideal types, sometimes to identify a specific regime exhibiting properties of one or another ideal type. I do not wish to suggest that there is only one such regime of each type, reflecting specific natural human dispositions or faculties and operating universally with some accommodation to local conditions. By definition, a regime is a set of rules more or less durably linked to each other by derivation or specification from more general rules or principles. However general, these rules are *social*; as such their reach is limited to a finite set of social relations—societies are regimes in the first instance.[69] To revert to Derrida's language, regimes are always conditional. Thus we can identify any number of regimes, each one mixing a host of rules that we might identify, one by one, with RD, EP and CS regimes. Each hybrid regime is unique; each overlaps and interacts with other regimes in specific social settings.

That human beings come equipped with natural dispositions that manifest themselves very early in our lives might suggest—has suggested to many observers for a very long time—the existence of unconditional duties or universal natural laws. Such natural (and not just social) principles are said to dictate the content of the many regimes constituting and regulating social

---

[67] Der Derian, *On Diplomacy*, pp. 31–3, quoting p. 33.

[68] On this conception of structure, see Onuf, *Making Sense, Making Worlds*, ch. 6.

[69] Nicholas Onuf, *International Legal Theory: Essays and Engagements, 1966–2006* (Abingdon: Routledge-Cavendish, 2008), pp. 302–4.

reality. Just perhaps, hospitality is a natural disposition and unconditional hospitality is a general good and universal duty. Very young children distinguish faces and imitate facial expressions. According to Alison Gopnik, these faculties develop into a capacity for empathy.[70] From natural empathy to unconditional hospitality is a short step. Even if this turns out to be the case, I do not believe we can infer the specific contents of regimes from such principled formulations. Thus the duty of unconditional hospitality can tell us nothing about the specifics of conditional hospitality, the contents of any given RD regime—this is exactly the thrust of Derrida's double law of hospitality.

In my opinion, recent efforts to jump from Kant (as if he had unambiguously formulated a universal duty of unconditional hospitality) to the contents of an immigration regime are simply fatuous for this very reason. Moreover, natural dispositions often pull in different directions. If empathy is a natural disposition, so is Hobbesian fear as an evolved, entirely reasonable response to danger. Unconditional hospitality requires an open door; fear commends a closed door. In other words, the links between natural dispositions and particular rules are far too tenuous to call any such rules natural or necessary. 'Natural reason' notwithstanding, general principles, which are so often at odds with each other, are the weak link in these chains of association and derivation. How can conflicting general principles be universal in scope and equally compelling normatively?

The quest for universal principles and binding inferences is the programmatic core of modern ethics. Given the importance of liberalism for modernity, it can be no surprise that this quest centres on the general principles of the EP regime as an ideal type—as I said earlier, autonomy, parity, reciprocity, exchange and fairness. At least in recent times, relative indifference to the RD regime as an ideal type has pretty much spared it from efforts to generalize such virtues as fortitude and magnanimity, which have always been calibrated by status: higher standing and greater virtue should go hand in hand. Nor do we find any sustained interest in deriving binding content for particular RD regimes from such principles.

While the recent revival of virtue ethics suits the RD regime by emphasizing personal traits, I have something more in mind. After all, unconditional hospitality is arguably a universal duty. The demands of respect and honour may also have the same unconditional properties and result in Derrida's double law, since every society has at least one RD regime—a code of honour *and* of hospitality, however different in reach, content and effect. I have elsewhere argued that honour is a constituent feature of what

---

[70] Alison Gopnik, *The Philosophical Baby: What Children's Minds Tell Us about Truth, Love, and the Meaning of Life* (New York: Farrar, Strauss and Giroux, 2009), pp. 202–5.

I called everyday ethics.[71] Here I maintain that we should extend everyday ethics to include the requirements of conditional hospitality and the many rituals of giving that make us relative strangers in known degrees.

The ethical status of the RD regime as an ideal-type can only be realized in specific RD regimes. All such regimes function as normatively weighty codes of conduct. In practice, I should point out, the same holds for the EP regime. Whatever we might say about universal principles, specific codes of conduct, often formalized as law, significantly shape our immediate ethical situations.

Codes of honour and hospitality constitute an everyday ethics for people in every society and every walk of life because people know what rules are—what they are for, why they are to be followed, when they can be broken, how they relate to each other. On the evidence, Gopnik has concluded that very young children, as born imitators, understand what rules are about, implicitly before they are two years old and explicitly by the time they are three.[72] Such claims recapitulate Hans Kelsen's *grundnorm* as a human universal: we ought to behave as we customarily have behaved.[73] Whether we have a natural disposition to understand normativity, becoming linguistically competent provides the necessary equipment.

Any speaker who knows how to modify verbs with such auxiliaries as *can, may, would* and *should* (or their equivalents) knows that she is imagining (un)desirable states of affairs. Normativity is latent in this sort of competence.[74] A more explicit awareness of obligation may have to be learned in different ways in diverse social settings. The rules of any specific RD regime *give* children the practice with rules that they need to get along in their worlds. More than this, I suspect, the rules about gifts that are such central features of every RD regime teach children and remind adults that normative force is relative, whatever modern ethicists say.[75]

As we have seen, not every gift compels reciprocity. Every gift given or received tells us who (we should think) we are, what we (should) value, where we (can) stand, and does so with fine discrimination. If relative normativity makes us relative strangers, it gives us the relative comfort of being strangers

---

[71] Nicholas Onuf, 'Everyday ethics in international relations', *Millennium: Journal of International Studies* 27, 3 (1998), pp. 669–93.

[72] Gopnik, *The Philosophical Baby*, pp. 222–5.

[73] Hans Kelsen, *General Theory of Law and State*, trans. Anders Wedberg (New York: Russell & Russell, 1961), pp. 110–1, 120.

[74] Note that my claim here is more cautious than John R. Searle's claim to the effect that speech acts have 'deontic powers' and normative effects by their nature. *Making the Social World: The Structure of Human Civilization* (Oxford: Oxford University Press, 2010), pp. 80–6.

[75] Also see Onuf, *International Legal Theory*, pp. 464–6.

in familiar ways. The RD regime so conspicuous, so important, in diplomatic culture and international relations—two aspects of the same world—works this way in order for diplomats to be able to mediate the relations of states. Other RD regimes conspicuously constitute and regulate social reality in non-modern worlds (excepting perhaps hunting and gathering bands). RD regimes are pervasive; we find them even where EP regimes seem to dominate. Rearing children readies them for a world of objects where location—position, social distance—always matters.

8

Ethical Systems (2016)

Many worlds, four worlds

There are many worlds. Continually experiencing a 'world inside my head', I charitably concede that there is another, somewhat different world in your head and, by extension, everyone else's. If we abandon this subjective sense of many worlds, and the strict philosophical idealism that this way of thinking implies, there are still many worlds.

Seen from the inside, worlds have horizons. Visualized from the outside, worlds are wholes composed of many parts, including people who see the world (the world in their heads) more or less the same way. Society becomes the background condition for all the things or objects that members of society talk about. Broadly speaking, this is a phenomenological conception of world as worlds, and one that I subscribe to myself.

There is, of course, a contrary claim, to the effect that there is only one world—the real world consisting of all things. Most of us are philosophical realists, for whom this claim seems indisputably right. In such a world, no society (with the possible exception of some hunter-gatherer societies) is ever wholly self-contained; all things in the world are caught up in a web of (causal, functional, constitutive) relations. This is an Aristotelian formula—every whole is a part of some larger whole. We who live in what we call, somewhat paradoxically, the modern or Western world depart from this formula when we insist that the world we live in is the only world there is—the sum of all things.

Indeed, we have it both ways. There is *our* objectively discernible, subjectively valorized modern world. There is another objectively discernible world of many worlds, or, as we are inclined to say, the rest of the world. Taken together, these two worlds—the modern world and the rest of the world—constitute an ostensible objective reality (ostensibly objective, ostensibly real) we also call the earth, planet or globe.

Here I am concerned with the three worlds that members of the modern world think they see: our world, the rest of the world, and the world as the largest possible whole. I am also concerned with the possibility of a fourth world. This is *not* the world so many of us see at hand—one in which, thanks to globalization, all has become modern, or indeed, postmodern. I rather doubt that tendencies already manifest in the modern world will result in any such outcome.

Instead, I foresee a fourth world—a straitened world—coming about when global capitalism collapses in the next few decades, infrastructure undergoes irreversible deterioration, and immiseration engulfs what we moderns call the middle class. I expect these developments to precipitate large-scale civil violence and perhaps major wars, all of which will help to accelerate the coming of the next world, a postmodern world that will in some respects resemble the world that came before. Some readers will find these claims shocking; others will notice that they have a Marxist provenience. All of you will recognize them to be a matter of conjecture; evidentiary support for them will be highly controversial.

Many theories, four theoretical frameworks

I take a theory to be an ensemble of related, abstractly stated propositions about *some* world. Taken together, these propositions purport to tell us about how that world works. Again I am using functional language that owes a great deal to Aristotle. There are other, more familiar ways of talking about theory, generally involving 'cause' as a mechanical metaphor rather than 'function' and 'constitution' as organic metaphors.[1]

If we assume that the workings of any society are hugely complex, as I do, then we are likely to formulate many theories that are, at best, only obscurely related to each other (whether causally, functionally or constitutively). In the circumstance, we are forced to rely on a small number of competing theoretical frameworks by which to arrange our theories (or merely theoretical hunches). We judge these frameworks by their apparent relevance, coherence and plausibility.

When we look at the modern world and ask how it works, four theoretical frameworks immediately present themselves. One grants priority to the system of nation-states. We students of International Relations usually call this framework realism. A second framework is liberalism (or, in International Relations, liberal institutionalism); it emphasizes a system of values centred on individual autonomy, equality and freedom of choice. While realism sees sovereign states engaged in perpetually hostile relations,

---

[1] I should have gone on to say: *function* and *constitution* predicate overlapping kinds of causal complexity—one presupposes cause directed to some end or goal, the other identifies causal loops establishing or reinforcing some condition that may be the goal.

liberal institutionalism confers on states the values that liberalism ascribes to human individuals in their social relations.

The third framework we in International Relations have tended to minimize, except when we talk, rather confusedly, about governmentality—too often, with a confused Michel Foucault as a source of inspiration.[2] It directs attention to the rational organization of daily life. The last framework is one I have already invoked. Its large concern is the way social functions are defined and divided as modern life has become ever more complex.

For many social theorists the organizational framework is indicatively *modern*. David Mitrany's work aside, scholars in International Relations have largely ignored the functional framework, which I take to be distinctively *modernist* ('form follows function').[3] If the proximate source of the organizational framework is Max Weber, the proximate source of the functional framework, which gave rise to structural-functionalism in anthropology, sociology and comparative politics, is Émile Durkheim. What we in International Relations call constructivism is a framework that draws selectively on all four frameworks, but mostly to qualify and contain the first framework by emphasizing the constitutive features of all social relations.

Now, it should be clear that moderns view modernity as a world apart. By convention, all those societies *not* modern are *traditional*. Some traditional societies may be highly bureaucratized (thereby exhibiting a degree of organizational and functional development only recently achieved by modern societies). They may sustain relations with neighbours that resemble 'the state of war' among modern nation-states, though generally with less evident institutionalization. (Imperial relations with neighbours are far more likely to be institutionalized.)

Most importantly, no traditional society seems to have developed the theory and practice of liberalism. I think this claim is substantially correct. It is the other side of the coin that bears inspection. Are modern societies liberal? Obviously not all, as the recent experience of several Asian societies makes utterly clear. Latin America is an ambiguous case because there has been long exposure to liberal values and a robust sense of individualism. The larger question is this: Did liberalism prevail even in those few societies said to exemplify the triumph of the principle that all human beings are free and equal by nature?

---

[2] Michel Foucault, *Security, Territory, Population: Lectures at the Collège de France, 1977–1978*, trans. Graham Burchill (Basingstoke: Palgrave Macmillan, 1978).

[3] See especially David Mitrany, *A Working Peace System* (Chicago: Quadrangle Books, 1966). Also see Chapters 6 and 11 on modernist modernity.

I have commented on this 'revolution' elsewhere.[4] Here I want to emphasize an often unstated implication of the claim that modern liberalism emerged from the momentous events of the late 18th century. Modern liberalism displaced and defeated the old regime of status-ordering; social standing ceased to determine the distribution of opportunities and rewards available to members of society. As an alternative formulation, appearances, always associated with rank, no longer mattered in the way that tradition says they must.

The point is important, so let me repeat myself. In principle, status no longer matters in the modern world. Individuals have been rendered equal in their social relations; organizations are free to serve 'rational' ends. In practice, actual modern societies work best when they suppress status and its corrupting effects. By contrast, traditional societies are *always* status-ordered.

I am sceptical that modern practices ever fully dispatched status as an ordering principle.[5] I am convinced that the last three decades have seen a resurgence of status concerns among the members of modern societies, that these concerns have significantly affected the way modern societies actually work, and that the large cause of this tendency has been the downward trajectory of global capitalism in producing material welfare—a tendency most obvious in the United States. I should also point out, as some realists have recognized, that the system of relations among states preceded modernity and has always exhibited a traditional preoccupation with status.

One conspicuous feature of the decline of global capitalism as a slow-motion crisis is the widening gap between the rich and the poor in modern societies. This sorry state of affairs is a harbinger of the next world—the straitened world to come. Local conditions may mask this development, but only in the short run. Long-term decline of global markets will adversely affect productive activity and distributive mechanisms in every corner of the globe. Insofar as capitalism is global in reach, there is no escaping the demise of liberal modernity.

Many rules, four ethical systems

Every society is saturated in rules. Many of those rules (I would call them instruction-rules) tell people how to conduct themselves.[6] Often these rules are tacit, typically they are specific to that society, even if similar rules are

---

[4] Nicholas Onuf, 'Recognition and the constitution of epochal change', *International Relations* 27, 2 (2013), pp. 121–40.

[5] Nicholas Onuf, 'Late modern civil society', in Randall D. Germain and Michael Kenny, eds, *The Idea of Global Civil Society: Politics and Ethics in a Globalizing Era* (London: Routledge, 2005), pp. 47–63.

[6] See Chapter 3 for a brief discussion.

found in other societies. In so-called traditional societies, these rules tend to be specific in another sense: they apply specifically and differentially to people whom the rules have already differentiated by rank, status, standing or social position (I use these words more or less interchangeably). In effect, each rule specifies a duty *and* a duty-holder at one and the same time.

Thus traditional societies are said to value honour and hospitality, which means that they have well-developed codes specifying honourable and hospitable conduct by reference to social position. While I have argued that such codes constitute an everyday ethics to be found in *every* society,[7] they would not seem to constitute an ethical system in *any* society, chiefly because ethical systems are generally said to make universal claims about acceptable or appropriate human conduct. By this criterion, the Ten Commandments constitute a stern code of conduct specific to God's chosen people (or, more specifically, to men as heads of households—or so I interpret the last two Commandments). That this code now applies to a huge community of believers does not make its contents universal; no logic or method by which to universalize these or any other rules is implied.

Much the same can be said of Confucian ethics. Many commentators suggest that *ren* or benevolence is roughly equivalent to virtue (excellence—see later). Associated with *ren* are more specific virtues, such as sincerity, loyalty and piety. In my view the resemblance is as misleading as it is intriguing. Fei Xiaotong has argued that ancient Chinese society never produced 'an all-encompassing ethical concept'; *ren* is simply 'a compilation of all the ethical qualities of private personal relationships'. These relationships are familial in the first instance, and family relations are inalterably asymmetric or status-ordered. According to Fei, their 'most important feature is certainly *ke ji fu li* (subdue the self and follow the rites)'.[8] Where there are rites, there are rules—exquisitely detailed rules from which no deviation is tolerated.

One of the innovations of the modern world is precisely the idea that ethical conduct need not depend on an internalized set of rules. Instead ethical conduct depends on a general, rationally mandated procedure for discovering a few universal rules—rules applicable to humanity as a whole, rules that any reasonable person can satisfactorily apply to any possible situation. Two such ethical systems dominate modern thought. One is attributable to Immanuel Kant, the other to Jeremy Bentham.

The first, deontological ethics, grants autonomy to each of us—freedom to legislate for ourselves—and demands that we treat others as ends and

---

[7] Nicholas Onuf, 'Everyday ethics in international relations', *Millennium: Journal of International Studies* 27, 3 (1998), pp. 669–93.

[8] Fei Xiaotong, *From the Soil: The Foundations of Chinese Society*, trans. Gary Hamilton and Wang Zheng (Berkeley: University of California Press, 1992), pp. 75–6, 74.

not means to an end. The second, consequentialist ethics, grants us equal value as human beings and demands we act so as to achieve the greatest good for the greatest number of us. Liberals prefer the Kantian system and see it manifest in the promulgation of human rights. People working in organizational contexts prefer some version of Bentham's system and see it realized in the quest for efficiency and proportionality. In principle, the two systems are radically incompatible; in practice, most moderns are adept at switching from one to the other as circumstances require.

Neither of the two modern ethical system seems to fit modernist conditions, in which functional differentiation produces ever more specialized spheres of skilled activities. Functional compartments cut across modern organizational arrangements even as functionally skilled personnel appropriate those arrangements for internal use. Lacking an ethical system that suits a functionally fragmented world, we see an emphasis on professionalization. As we all know from personal experience, professionalization is effectuated through detailed codes of conduct highly reminiscent of traditional codes, which candidate-professionals internalize in the course of intensive training.

Focused on aesthetic matters, the postmodernist movement has generally ignored the social side of modernism and its ethical implications. As postmodernism provoked a more general critique of modernity and a concern with what comes after modernity's demise, postmodern scholars have articulated a third ethical system without being clear as to the continued relevance of modern ethical systems. Its general subject is otherness. In this context, they have seized on one feature of the modern world—displacement from one's homeland—as demanding a universally warranted response and finding that response in the traditional value of hospitality.[9] In my view, postmodern resistance to universal claims, combined, oddly enough, with reliance on Kant's brief remarks on hospitality as a universal duty, undercut any sense that postmodern ethics function systematically, either as an alternative to modern ethics or as traditional codes of conduct.

There is, however, a candidate for a fourth ethical system. It goes back to Plato and Aristotle, and yet it has been subject to a significant revival in recent decades. Called virtue ethics, it is routinely juxtaposed to modern ethical systems because it locates the normative thrust of conduct in character and education, and not in rules, whether universal or local. Arguably it is an alternative to any kind of ethics. If instead we think that internalizing examples of, and exhortations about, desirable character traits is no different from internalizing rules, then any list of virtues constitutes a highly coded code of conduct. I am inclined towards the latter view myself.

---

[9] Also see Chapter 7.

Virtue ethics has a long association with republicanism as a political theory episodically institutionalized in practice. Like virtue ethics, republican theory goes back to Plato and Aristotle—notwithstanding their many differences. Republicanism found its golden age in Rome, experienced a major revival in the Renaissance and Enlightenment, set the stage for liberalism, and was then eclipsed by modern developments. Along with virtue ethics, republicanism has enjoyed a recent revival, if only in theory.[10]

Virtue ethics has much to offer today's world of functional differentiation and even more as this world gives way to the next world of straitened circumstances. To see how this is so, I need to show how virtue ethics can be considered an ethical system, and not just a list of desirable character traits. Such a system is by no means evident in classical Greek texts. Cicero took us in the right direction, and Adam Smith pretty much got us there. Cicero and Smith were both republican thinkers with strong Stoic sympathies. By implication, republicanism may also find a place in a straitened world.[11]

Virtue ethics, four cardinal virtues

Virtues are many. Yet four have assumed a canonical status. They are the cardinal virtues: wisdom and/or prudence, courage or bravery, justice, and temperance or moderation. Convention holds them to derive from Plato, who linked virtue to what translators anachronistically call 'class' (*Republic*, 427e, 435b). Rulers should be wise, warriors courageous, workers temperate (thus reflecting the rational, spirited and appetitive parts of the soul); together they constitute a just society. Thus it would seem that the virtues can only be unified in or by an ideal society—one that is perfectly just.

The *Republic* offers a social theory that is conspicuously status-ordered. While Plato had much to say about wisdom, he gave relatively little attention to virtue as such. Aristotle's social theory is less conspicuously (or perhaps more complexly) status-ordered than Plato's, and his treatment of virtue is far more extensive. For Aristotle, virtue (excellence, *aretē*) is simultaneously a disposition to seek excellence (faculty, capacity, potentiality, *dunamis*), an activity (*energeia*) or way of being excellent, and

---

[10] Nicholas Greenwood Onuf, *The Republican Legacy in International Thought* (Cambridge: Cambridge University Press, 1998), ch. 2; and Nicholas Onuf, 'Organizing for good: Republican theory in a changing world', *The Global Community: Yearbook of International Law and Jurisprudence 2013*, pp. 507–33. Note that I do not limit republicanism to the currently fashionable 'neo-Roman' version associated with Philip Pettit, *Republicanism: A Theory of Freedom and Government* (Oxford: Oxford University Press, 1997), and Quentin Skinner, *Liberty before Liberalism* (Cambridge: Cambridge University Press, 1998).

[11] I do not pursue this possibility here, but see Onuf, 'Organizing for good'.

even the state (*hexis*) of excellence achieved and thus worthy of praise (*Nicomachean Ethics* 1109b30-1)—all fitting together in his teleological worldview. Virtue relies on deliberation and choice. There is, however, no direct sense of necessity or obligation attaching to virtue in any of these senses. Insofar as ethical conduct depends on rules, virtue ethics is not up to the job—unless knowing what is excellent implicitly depends on rules for evaluating conduct.

For Aristotle, virtue is a whole with many parts, or readily distinguishable virtues. In the *Nicomachean Ethics*, Books III–VI, he offered a laundry list of virtues. If the cardinal virtues have a 'unity' (as is often claimed), then they are, for Aristotle, unified only in the trivial sense that their presence in varying degrees, along with many other virtues, describes any individual human being's character. The cardinal virtues are not unified in such a way as to constitute a principle or generalizable standard of worth. Much less are they ordered as a set of principles such as is implied by the modern idea of an ethical system.

In Aristotle's laundry list of virtues, courage comes first, then temperance (*sōphrosunē*). Discussion of generosity, magnificence and magnanimity follows. Only then does he turn to justice. Generosity, magnificence and magnanimity apply disproportionately to high-status individuals. Aristotle had much less to say about the 'homely' virtues associated with people of lesser status (starting with women), such as fidelity, humility, modesty and thrift. Breaking with the logic of the four-virtue scheme, he treated 'virtues of character' and 'virtues of thought' separately. The latter include prudence and wisdom.

In Greek thought, natural goodness or well-being (*eudaimonia*) might serve as a high principle, but it is hard to formulate as such (rather than as a tendency or disposition) and little help in choosing a course of action when specific virtues from Aristotle's list point in different directions. In practice, choice would seem to be substantially situational or contingent. This sort of ethics has no compelling answer to the charge of relativism. By contrast, modern ethical systems insist that some few rules should be framed abstractly enough to be credibly universal, that is, applicable to humanity as a whole, thereby sidestepping the issue of depending on local, contingent rules. Hence the appeal of Kant's categorical, but strictly procedural, imperative (act as if the maxim of your action were universal/a law of nature) or Bentham's utilitarian calculus (act so as to maximize the greatest good for the greatest number).

In Hellenistic Stoicism, discussion of ethics settled on the cardinal virtues and the claim that each virtue depends on the other three to be existentially and normatively complete. They constitute the ideal life lived according to nature. In this way of thinking, the cardinal virtues are analogous to the cardinal directions (north, east, south, west). North (wisdom) points to reason (*logos*), east (courage) to passion (*pathos*), south (justice) to lawful nature (*phusis*), and west (temperance) to the constraining features of society (*nomos*). Thus the wisdom–justice axis and the courage–temperance axis are intersecting binaries; at the point of intersection are human beings (*anthrōpoi*), in full possession of their faculties and pulled in all four directions at once. One must balance these tendencies, as circumstances require, to live well.

Implied is self-control (*kratein*) at the centre of a ring of cardinal virtues. Aristotle had made the lack of self-control (typically translated 'incontinence') a central theme in his ethics (*Nicomachean Ethics*, Book VII), and this emphasis seems entirely consistent with our contemporary understanding of Stoicism. (I should register here my misgivings in using the term *self* so anachronistically.) It does not, however, unify the virtues and constitute virtue ethics as universalizable ethical system, unless we believe that self-control is all that matters—as an end in itself that trumps all other ends.

Much influenced by Hellenistic Stoicism, Roman thinkers adopted the four-virtue scheme. Cicero's treatment in *On Duties* is exemplary. In this text, written as advice to his son, the virtues become duties (*officia*) together constituting honourable conduct. The correspondence between virtue and duty is not characteristic of classical Greek thought. Nor is duty's relation to rules specifying duties. The closest Greek equivalent to duty would seem to be *kathekon*, which the Stoics understood to mean 'appropriate action'.[12] Given Cicero's belief in natural law, it follows that a status-order mandated by nature would assign normative weight to the virtues associated with rank or position in that status-order.

For Cicero, the cardinal duties are *sapientia*, not to be confused with *prudentia* (or 'knowledge of things that one should pursue and avoid'), *magnitudo animi* (or greatness of spirit), *iustitia* and *decorum*. While the cardinal virtues are 'bound together and interwoven', they have no unity in themselves. Instead it is 'the power of reason' that 'unites one man to another'.[13] Thus the fourth virtue is better translated as seemliness than as decorum.[14] As a virtue, *decorum* or seemliness is appropriate conduct in a given social arrangement, or being true to one's position or status in society. Notice the shift from temperance as a disposition offsetting passion to seemliness as a social concern. In Cicero's scheme, all four duties apply to all human beings but relatively; duty is the aggregate of duties; position correlates with the burden of duty.

---

[12] Cicero, *On Duties*, trans. Margaret Atkins (Cambridge: Cambridge University Press, 1991), Notes on Translation, p. xlv.

[13] Ibid., pp. 59, 7, 6.

[14] Ibid., Notes on Translation, p. xlvi.

While St Thomas Aquinas made the cardinal virtues (*virtutes cardinals*)—*prudentia, fortitudo, iustitia, temperantia*—basic to Scholastic ethics (*Summa theologica*, I-II, Q. 61), he seems to have denied the normative thrust that Cicero gave them. Much influenced by Aristotle, St Thomas appealed instead to our capacity for reason. Notwithstanding his attempt to show how the four cardinal virtues are related in and through good conduct, they remain discrete. Joining them are the so-called 'theological virtues' of faith, hope and charity, which are gifts of God's grace.[15]

If Christianity speaks to and for the oppressed, then faith, hope and charity might be construed as low-status counterparts to magnanimity, magnificence and generosity. In practice, the cardinal virtues apply chiefly to men and the theological virtues to women. The many virtues are not unified because God (or God's love or God's will) is already the source and meaning of unity. Thus the virtues join God's commands in guiding Christian conduct, but they do not in themselves constitute an ethical system of universal principles.

Ethics as virtuous conduct is a major concern in humanist/Renaissance discourse. Niccolò Machiavelli is only the most famous writer of that time to consider virtuous conduct—famous, of course, for disowning the Scholastic point of view. As a republican thinker, Machiavelli directed attention to *virtú* as '*grandezza dello anima*'.[16] More specifically, to avoid the contempt of his subjects, the prince 'should contrive [*ingegnarsi*, do one's best] that greatness, spiritness, gravity and strength [*grandezza, animosità, gravità, fortezza*] are recognized in his actions'.[17] Here, it seems, virtue is an ordered composite of the several virtues. Machiavelli's emphasis on spirit and spiritedness suggests a link to self-control, magnanimity and a sense of proportion, but not moderation.

Protestantism emphatically shifted emphasis from virtue to duty. Self-control conceptualized as conscience comes to the fore. John Milton, a republican Calvinist, here assuming the voice of God, offers a powerful example in *Paradise Lost* (1667), Book III, lines 191–7:

> To prayer, repentance, and obedience due,
> Though but endevord with sincere intent,
> Mine eare shall not be slow, mine eye not shut.
> And I will place within them [human beings] as a guide

---

15 *Catechism of the Catholic Church* (New York: Doubleday, 2003), pp. 495–502; *catechism* and *kathekon* have the same Greek root.

16 Niccolò Machiavelli, *Il Principe* (Turin: Einaudi, 1961), p. 30.

17 Ibid., p. 67; Niccolò Machiavelli, *The Prince*, trans. Harvey C. Mansfield, 2nd edn (Chicago: University of Chicago Press, 1998), p. 72.

My Umpire CONSCIENCE, whom if they will hear, Light after
light well us'd they shall attain,
And to the end persisting, safe arrive.

What Weber called 'the Protestant ethic' resonates with a Stoic sense of
duty—the virtues as duties, unified as one's vocation or calling: 'The only
way of living acceptably to God was not to surpass worldly morality in
monastic asceticism, but solely through the fulfilment of the obligations
imposed upon the individual by his position in the world [*Lebensstellung*].
That was his calling.'[18] Let me emphasize: '… obligations imposed upon the
individual by his *position* [*Stellung*] in the world'.

In early modern thought, Smith articulated a distinctive ethical system in
The Theory of Moral Sentiments (1759). Given Smith's reputation as father of
liberalism, I should emphasize that he was indeed a republican thinker and
no advocate of the principle of natural equality. In his view, social inequalities
are given by nature:

The objects with which men in the different professions and states of
life are conversant, being very different, and habituating them to very
different passions, naturally form in them very different characters
and manners. We expect in each rank and profession, a degree of
those manners, which, experience has taught us, belong to it. But as
in each species of things, we are particularly pleased with the middle
conformation, which, in every part and feature, agrees most exactly
with the general standard which nature seems to have established for
things of that kind; so in each rank, or, if I may say so, in each species
of men, we are particularly pleased, if they have neither too much, nor
too little of the character which usually accompanies their particular
condition and situation.[19]

The Aristotelian emphasis on continence or self-control reveals itself in the
Stoic counsel of equanimity. For Smith 'self-command' is central to ethical
conduct, not to mention 'self-approbation'.

The man of real constancy and firmness, the wise and just man who
has been thoroughly bred in the great school of self-command, in the
bustle and business of the world, exposed, perhaps, to the violence and
injustice of faction, and to the hardships and hazards of war, maintains

---

[18] Max Weber, *The Protestant Ethic and the Spirit of Capitalism*, trans. Talcott Parsons
(New York: Scribner's, 1930), p. 80.
[19] Adam Smith, *The Theory of Moral Sentiments* (Indianapolis: Liberty Fund, 1984), p. 202.

this control of his passive feelings upon all occasions; and whether in solitude or in society, wears nearly the same countenance, and is affected very nearly in the same manner.

The degree of the self-approbation with which every man, upon such occasions, surveys his own conduct, is higher or lower, exactly in proportion to the degree of self-command which is necessary in order to obtain that self-approbation.[20]

For Smith and other early modern republicans, self-control is listening to one's conscience (the internalized, impartial observer). This is a stern demand but does not give the virtues any unity, or order one's duties, so as to guide conduct in every situation.

Instead we are guided by the admiration with which others respond to our conduct. If we are vicious (as Aristotle insisted, every virtue has a contrary vice), then it is the contempt and indignation of others that guides us. Admiration, contempt and indignation are the social mechanisms for operationalizing Smith's ethical theory. Their force stems from our need to be praised.

> The jurisdiction of the man within, is founded altogether in the desire of praise-worthiness, and in the aversion to blame-worthiness; in the desire of possessing those qualities, and performing those actions, which we love and admire in other people; and in the dread of possessing those qualities, and performing those actions, which we hate and despise in other people.[21]

I suggest that Smith accomplished something that none of his predecessors could in their quest to unify the cardinal virtues. By making self-control a human universal explained by our common need for praise and hinting at the normative consequences of praise and blame, he transformed virtue ethics into an ethical system. This system produces rules, which Cicero simply stipulated, but it does so in a way that we now attribute to customary practices. These rules may well instruct us individually to conduct ourselves as if individuality were a property of the collectivity and not ourselves. If we all respond to praise and blame more or less the same way, this pattern of responses duly acquires normative weight. Indeed it becomes a source of law—arguably its primary source.[22]

---

[20] Ibid., pp. 146, 147.
[21] Ibid., p. 131.
[22] Hans Kelsen, *General Theory of Law and State*, trans. Anders Wedberg (New York: Russell & Russell, 1961), pp. 110–15.

Virtue ethics today, four pathologies

As an ethical system, virtue ethics does not imply a unity of virtues even in the weak sense of a given set of virtues ordered by importance. Priority is relative not only to position in any society, discernible as such, but also to the conditions in which that society is obliged to operate. It is the one ethical system that takes every society to be status-ordered. Every status-order places everyone to whom it applies in a fixed position in relation to everyone else.

We visualize that order vertically, as an ascending (or descending) set of steps. For this arrangement we typically use the term *rank*. We also use this term for the typical arrangement of offices in an organization; office often entails a corresponding social position (see later). Every one of us has a position in one or another status rank, of which we are then a member, on equal terms with everyone else holding that same rank. We know or find our position—our place, rank, standing or station in society—by reference to the titles, honours, privileges, liberties and immunities that 'society' has assigned to us. They may be ours by circumstance over which we have no control or we may be said to have earned them. They may or may not be revocable or indeed alienable. Exercising them may or may not degrade or enhance them.

The content of one's duties corresponds to social or worldly position. We can identify our duties first by constructing a checklist of virtues (starting with the four cardinal virtues), and then by asking how those virtues, framed by reference to one's position and conditioned by circumstances, translate into duties. For convenience, those duties may be codified. Presumably any reasonable person can do this (as indicated by the first of the cardinal virtues); everyone is doing it all the time. Self-control is taken for granted. Fulfilling our duties is virtuous, expected by all (that is, people in all positions) and backed by the positive sanction of admiration or negative sanction of disapproval experienced as shame.

As a general matter, those who have the least standing in any society have the fewest or least demanding duties. Everyone holds those in the highest positions to the highest standards, and we all know that this expectation is warranted. Those who have the highest positions in society have the most privilege as well as the greatest burden of duty. Privilege permits or creates opportunities for bad, vicious or corrupt behaviour arising from lack of self-control. Some versions of republican theory takes corruption to be the great danger in the organization of politics, a danger liberals are disposed to overlook and powerless to combat.

Recall that virtue ethics, as an ethical system, does not order the virtues by normative weight. Yet it is possible to formulate some limited generalizations about the way particular societies rank the cardinal virtues (as against Plato's status-order for an ideally just society). Members of traditional societies will generally give priority to seemliness or propriety and to courage. In modern societies, wisdom (rationality) and justice are favoured; courage and seemliness are seen as faintly irrational or atavistic. When societies are stable, justice and seemliness prevail (even when seemliness is not recognized for what it is); when times are turbulent, prudence and courage are valued more.

As the world as a whole slides into grinding poverty, massive inequity and chronic violence, deontological and consequentialist ethics will lose their appeal. Indeed, their natural constituencies will disappear. Functional compartmentalization will capture organizations, and loosely federal arrangements such as favoured in republican theory may prevail in the best of circumstances. The nation may endure as an emotional anchor for depleted populations.

If any ethical system speaks to such a future, it can only be virtue ethics. Offering, as it does, different combinations of virtues for different situations, virtue ethics offers something in every situation short of complete social collapse. In some conspicuous situations, Machiavelli's greatness of spirit will trump the other virtues. In troubled times, prudence (and the perseverance it implies) will, in my opinion, win out more often than not. If status-orders stabilize locally, then the traditional preference for seemliness and courage may well prevail.

There are, however, four pathologies that I see already, and too often, in our allegedly modern yet status-ordered world. Decline is likely to aggravate them, in the process discrediting virtue ethics. Let me comment briefly on each. These pathologies are not peculiar to individuals. Corporate entities (nations, professions, functional organizations, cyber-communities, villages and so on) are readily afflicted.

Stasis. Modern thought holds that traditional societies are static—they resist change (and note the classical Greek sense of stasis as strife-ridden). In the first instance, status-orders are fixed in and by dense webs of rules; and one individual's social position is determined at birth; one's actions (for example, heroism) and events (for example, war) only exceptionally alter this social reality. I should point out that republican theorists from Aristotle to Machiavelli to the US founding fathers grappled with the issue of stasis by virtue of ascription. They argued that those who rule should be those whom nature has given the talents or capacities to rule: an aristocracy of merit.[23]

Modern thinkers have always been sceptical that this republican solution to the problem of stasis actually ever works for long. Only if societies accept

---

[23] See, for example, Thomas Jefferson's letter to John Adams, 28 October 1813, in Lester J. Cappon, ed., *The Adams-Jefferson Letters* (Chapel Hill: University of North Carolina Press, 1959), pp. 387–92.

the principle of natural equality will merit find its reward and societies be ruled by those whom others take to have a talent for rule. Needless to say, modern liberals hold this principle dear. So do most moderns adept at life in a world of organizations, at least to the extent that they see merit rewarded in organizational settings.

Contrary to modern hopes, status-ordering may be less visible in modern circumstances, but it has never gone away. Successful organizations give rise to correlative status-orders. They tend to reward merit with higher status in the organization. Status based on achievement and duly rewarded is sticky the way status always is, gradually taking on the properties of ascription. Individuals with high status use that status to reward those to whom they ascribe various attractive, promising or useful traits rather than their achievements.

The same dynamic operates in the professions, in which status-ordering has always dominated. Even as the professions have organized around meritorious performance, they have reinforced the static properties of an ascriptive status-order. The world of scholarship is a telling example. In my view, there is no solution to this pathology, which can only worsen as this world transitions to the next world.

To put the point in the broadest possible terms: virtue is its own reward. This is what my Yankee relatives used to say (evidently quoting the Roman poet Claudius Claudianus). Better to say: self-control actualized as virtuous conduct and the praise that such conduct brings are reward enough. But are they? As an ethical system, virtue ethics is flawed to the extent that this not the case for most people most of the time.

Machismo. Modern thought holds that traditional societies give undue emphasis to honour or respect. Their members respond to insults and even more subtle signs of disrespect with a fury out of proportion to the 'slight' (as this very metaphor suggests). Insofar as respect attaches to one's social position, and social position determines one's identity, we might say that proportionality takes on different proportions. Acting in the name of honour is virtuous—appearances matter—but only if self-control is maintained and that society's honour code is followed. As at least some of us moderns concede, such conduct is *not* pathological.

I have already suggested that a sense of proportion (or balance: think Aristotle) figures differently in virtue ethics. The cardinal virtues must be in held in balance, and this requires the ongoing, ever recalibrated exercise of self-control. Out-of-proportion/out-of-control prudence turns into procrastination and indecision, decorum into empty, resource-depleting ritual, justice into self-righteousness and vigilantism, courage into machismo. For every virtue a vice. I emphasize machismo, or courage where none is called for, because it is simply the most obvious of this family of failings.

Latin cultures bear witness to the excesses and attendant social costs of machismo.[24] They are hardly the only societies where it is to be found. Just for example, the fad for extreme sports and stunts now besetting the modern world illustrates machismo run riot. National leaders are especially prone to this pathology. We should not be surprised. What we in International Relations call 'international society' arose before the modern world fully emerged and continues to bear many of the features of a traditional society.[25]

Paternalism. Progressive modern thinkers have long coupled paternalism and authoritarianism, for example, in leadership styles. More generally assumed is the analogy between the household and society: in traditional societies, father figures rule unchallenged. We might construe the republican preference for rule by those best suited to rule as an antidote to traditional authoritarianism, but, for most liberals, hardly an adequate one. Lately, however, paternalism has earned some respectability in liberal circles as a response to modern excesses.[26]

In the contemporary international society, paternalism is a chronic, systemic condition, but rarely discussed as such. Drawing on a substantial literature in applied ethics, Michael Barnett has recently directed attention to 'international paternalism'.[27] He is hardly alone; the concern with paternalism suffuses postcolonial studies, and it extends to the feminist critique of patriarchy. It is also increasingly a theme among scholars investigating the ethics of international development.[28] While Barnett, just for example, lamented liberal 'neglect of the underlying social relations that generate the positions of superiority and inferiority and a sense of *noblesse oblige*',[29] he had nothing to say about virtue ethics or republican theory and its affirmative sense of what *noblesse oblige* involves as an ethical matter.

It would seem that paternalism is generally a pejorative term for an integral feature of virtue ethics, which is, after all, predicated on societal status-ordering. As such, it offends liberal sensibilities. Nevertheless, recent concern for responsibility in the relations of states suggests an awareness that circumstances warrant some measure of paternalism. Principle 7 of

---

[24] See Matthew C. Gutmann, *The Meanings of Macho: Being a Man in Mexico City* (Berkeley: University of California Press, 1996) for an important discussion.

[25] Also see Chapter 7.

[26] Cass R. Sunstein, *Why Nudge? The Politics of Libertarian Paternalism* (New Haven: Yale University Press, 2014), offer a prominent example.

[27] Michael Barnett, 'International paternalism and humanitarian governance', *Global Constitutionalism* 1, 3 (2012), pp. 485–521.

[28] Here David Kennedy's *The Dark Side of Virtue* (Princeton: Princeton University Press, 2005) is a landmark.

[29] Barnett, 'International paternalism and humanitarian governance', p. 49.

the Rio Declaration on Environment and Development (2002) offers a conspicuous example.[30]

> States shall cooperate in a spirit of global partnership to conserve, protect and restore the health and integrity of the Earth's ecosystem. In view of the different contributions to global environmental degradation, States have common but differentiated responsibilities. The developed countries acknowledge the responsibility that they bear in the international pursuit to sustainable development in view of the pressures their societies place on the global environment and of the technologies and financial resources they command.

Much discussed, the principle of common but differentiated responsibilities is nonetheless overshadowed by the United Nations initiative and alleged new norm called 'responsibility to protect' (R2P). States are said to have primary responsibility, notably through the Security Council, but 'the international community' acting through global civil society 'should, as appropriate, encourage or assist states to exercise this responsibility'.[31] More plausibly, R2P is a continuing manifestation of the republican idea of guardian or trustee, an office linked to status. The guardian is a stand-in father, manifest in an executive organ acting on behalf of 'the international community' as a status-order.

On the evidence of a recent book titled *Special Responsibilities*, some scholars in International Relations have started to evaluate hegemony of the United States as a matter of 'special responsibilities', that is, responsibilities that are differentiated by reference to an asymmetric distribution of power.[32] Needless to say, this is a familiar concern: the great powers have always been said to have great responsibilities, and the post-Vienna Concert system merely formalized the status-order warranting this state of affairs.

We might conclude, then, that paternalism is perhaps a pathology from a liberal point of view, but that the appropriate exercise of responsibility is not. The term *appropriate* indicates the continuing relevance of virtue ethics. As we slip into the next world, we may expect an increase in need and calls for help. Whether this will eventuate in an increased sense of responsibility

---

[30] Issued by the United Nations Conference on Environment and Development, 3–14 June 1992, A/CONF.151/26, 1, Annex 1.

[31] United Nations, '2005 World Summit Outcome', General Assembly Resolution 60/1, 16 September 2005, § 138.

[32] Mlada Bukovansky, Ian Clark, Robyn Eckersley, Richard Price, Christian Reus-Smit, and Nicholas J. Wheeler, *Special Responsibilities: Global Problems and American Power* (Cambridge: Cambridge University Press, 2012), pp. 6–7.

among those corporate entities (states, social movements) in a position to help will surely depend on how fast things go bad.

Infantilization. One might think that infantilization results from out-of-proportion paternalism. I identify it as a pathology in its own right both because of what I take to be its importance in the ostensibly liberal modern world and because it is so little noticed. The important exception to this generalization is recognition of infantilization as an effective technique for colonial administration: treat natives as children and they will act like children, unable to care for their basic needs and properly dependent on their colonial masters.[33] The contemporary practice of treating African states as 'quasi-sovereign' tells us that infantilization persists in postcolonial settings.[34]

More germane perhaps is infantilization in 'advanced industrial societies'. This condition and its pathological effects are notably evident in Japan. There the cult of the 'cute' (*kawaii*) and the pervasiveness of an imbecilic youth culture in an ageing society constantly assaults the visitor's sensibilities. Why don't those kids just grow up?

The obvious if incomplete answer is that infantilization serves an important social function. In Japan, infantilization may function to cordon off a country still deeply traditional in many respects from the many perils of modernity in its organizational mode. While Japan may be a special case, infantilization is easy enough to identify in other modern, and ostensibly liberal, societies (where Japanese youth culture is widely emulated). Privileged members of a liberal society given to excesses of various kinds are increasingly committed to protecting their children from a world that is growing harsher by the year. And not just children. Arguably the events of 11 September 2001 infantilized everyone in the United States. As a character in a Thomas Pynchon novel says: 'Can't you feel it, how everybody's regressing? 11 September infantilized this country. It had a chance to grow up, instead it chose to default back to childhood.'[35]

Good conduct takes hard work; no ethical system can make it easy. Children can only learn how to exercise self-control and balance the cardinal virtues by being exposed to the world, however harsh it has become. Indeed they risk never learning, thereby becoming dependent on others for the rest of their lives. To exempt people (groups, states) from assuming a position in any society's status-order can only be construed as irresponsible. As this world slips into the next, no good can come from such a practice.

---

[33] See Uday S. Mehta, 'Liberal strategies of exclusion', *Politics & Society* 18, 4 (1990), pp. 427–54, on the liberal rationale for this technique.

[34] Robert H. Jackson, *Quasi-States: Sovereignty, International Relations and the Third World* (Cambridge: Cambridge University Press, 1990).

[35] Thomas Pynchon, *Bleeding Edge* (New York: Penguin, 2013), p. 336.

PART III

Semantics: Saying What We See

Chapter 9 is a tribute to James Rosenau. I presented it on a panel honouring Rosenau at a conference in San Francisco in 1996, which I had helped to organize and which eventuated in a richly deserved *Festschrift*. In this essay, I review what Rosenau had to say about theorizing and report on the echoes of David Hume's sceptical voice in Rosenau's defence of Enlightenment values and commitment to the methods of modern science. I turn then to an influential book he wrote in the wake of dramatic changes in the political arrangements of the modern world. Called *Turbulence in World Politics* (1990), this book documents a significant shift in Rosenau's theoretical concerns.

Turbulence defeats easy claims about causation and undercuts generalization. The cumulative impact of turbulence is transformative—an epochal change in the contours of modernity. 'Writ large', an aggregate of small, local changes indicates a global contest between mindless habit and adaptive behaviour—one that would likely displace the modern world's political arrangements. This is a striking and potentially illuminating claim. There are, however, two problems with the way Rosenau developed it.

In pursuit of science, Rosenau consistently underrated the normative sphere in social life. As a result, he underestimated the durability of the modern system of states—the mighty frame, as I have called it elsewhere. Second, Rosenau mistook the surge in some people's analytic skills as a novel development. Instead, it is an integral feature of the modernist epoch, gaining momentum for a century and fully implicated in late modernity's functional arrangements supporting the system of states. In the end, Rosenau could not see what lies beyond politics at different scales because he failed to free himself from the habitual language of Enlightened politics—a universalizing language inadequate to the contest between never-squelched tradition and overweening modernity. In that contest, incivility, calumny and wilful ignorance have since become the norm, violence valorized, and the centre's absence conclusively demonstrated.

In 2009, the editors of a modest Danish journal (no longer published) asked me to write a brief essay for a project imaginatively called 'The Nines'. They had noticed that major statements of international theory appeared in the ninth year of most decades in the last century. My year was 1989, in which had appeared the first major effort to stake out the premises and possibilities of poststructuralism in the field of International Relations—a symposium volume titled *International/Intertextual Relations*. Something of a fellow traveller myself, I gave it a sympathetic if critical reading. For poststructuralists, the world is a text subject to as many readings as there are readers. In my view, every text is embedded in a story; modernity is a grand narrative. Poststructuralists may be able to resist grand narratives, but I cannot. And so I say in Chapter 10.

I drafted Chapter 11 for a small conference on state-building in 2011. The conference took place in Belgrade, which is, of course, centred in a part of the world where state-building was, and remains, an urgent concern. At that time, I had reworked the periodization of modernity informing Michel Foucault's archaeology of knowledge and identified six epochs in the unfolding of the modern world: the Renaissance (c. 1500–1650), followed by the classical (c. 1650–1800), modern (c. 1800–1900), modernist (c. 1900–1970) and late modern (c. 1970–) epochs. At the same time, I had come to think that concepts are always metaphorical in source and use. The occasion afforded me a chance to combine these two concerns. We moderns use metaphors deriving from our bodily experience in the world to describe our political arrangements; in the Introduction to this volume, I use the terms *friction* and *resistance* as metaphors for this phenomenon. Each of six epochs has favoured its own metaphorical complex, which successively have supported the modern state in a world of states.

In 2015, my plenary address at a conference in Taormina, Sicily, set out my views on what we do as scholars. On the way to becoming Chapter 12, these views were much influenced by my collaboration with two wide-ranging, dedicated and accomplished scholars in editing the *SAGE Handbook of the History, Philosophy and Sociology of International Relations*. As I tack from the field's brief history to large philosophical concerns, and from there to its sociological features, and then make the same circuit a second time, it becomes all too clear that what we do most of the time is talk. We talk (and read, and write) about our models, values and skills—as I do in this volume.

The story of Chapter 13 is simple enough. I prepared some remarks on my career as a constructivist for a workshop, held in Los Angeles in 2015, sizing up a quarter-century of constructivism in the field of International Relations. I used the opportunity to insist that the 'question of foundations' is never off limits; that we humans are cognitively equipped to fill the world with 'moderate-sized dry goods' gives constructivism a distinctive flavour. Suitably revised, these remarks ended up as the Foreword to an excellent symposium volume called *Constructivism Reconsidered*.

9

Writing Large (2000)

[M]ost students in the international field have not treated their
subject as local politics writ large.

James Rosenau[1]

Students in the international field see *Turbulence in World Politics* as a dramatic
shift in James Rosenau's thinking about world politics, brought on by
dramatic changes in the world of politics.[2] Rosenau thinks about politics
in dramatic terms.[3] He has even written a publicly performed play. Despite
decades of work in which he has developed and tested his ideas in the manner
of normal science, Rosenau has proven himself better attuned to the dramas
of the last few years than any other major figure in the field.

It does not do, however, to conclude that Rosenau has abandoned a
magnificent body of work, or repudiated its conceptual underpinnings, in
favour of a new 'turbulence paradigm'. Even if Rosenau speaks in terms that
suggest such a paradigm shift, we ought not to be fooled by his dramatic
inclinations.[4] Just before *Turbulence in World Politics* appeared, Rosenau

---

[1] James N. Rosenau, *The Scientific Study of Foreign Policy*, rev. edn (London: Frances Pinter,
1980), pp. 243–4.

[2] James N. Rosenau, *Turbulence in World Politics: A Theory of Change and Continuity*
(Princeton: Princeton University Press, 1990). After this essay was completed, Rosenau
published *Along the Domestic-Foreign Frontier: Exploring Governance in a Turbulent World*
(Cambridge: Cambridge University Press, 1997). Even if I had seen this large, rich book
beforehand, I believe that I would still have written the essay much as it now appears.

[3] James N. Rosenau, *The Dramas of Political Systems: An Introduction to the Problems of
Governance* (North Scituate, MA: Duxbury Press, 1972); James N. Rosenau, ed., *Global
Voices: Dialogues in International Relations* (Boulder, CO: Westview Press, 1993).

[4] James N. Rosenau and Mary Durfee, *Thinking Theory Thoroughly: Coherent Approaches to
an Incoherent World* (Boulder, CO: Westview Press, 1995), pp. 31–5.

claimed to be an unrepentant behaviouralist.[5] So he remains [and did so until his death in 2011].

What then in Rosenau's thinking has changed so dramatically? I suggest that changes in the world forced him to formulate, for the first time systematically, the behavioural theory underlying all of his work. How can someone who counts thinking theoretically among his 'longstanding habits' *not* have done so long ago?[6] After all, Rosenau's early study of 'calculated control' presents a tightly organized conceptual framework, elements of which occupy an important position in *Turbulence in World Politics*. Yet by Rosenau's own reckoning, this piece presents no theory: 'it does not explain why international affairs unfold as they do'.[7] Even with respect to foreign policy, Rosenau claimed to offer nothing more than a 'pre-theory'.[8] His modesty stems from the conventional positivist assumption that normal science conducted within the terms of an increasingly refined conceptual framework would eventuate in a general theory whose propositions had already passed the test of scientific scrutiny. When the world began to change far more dramatically than existing frameworks seemed to be able to account for, Rosenau was jarred from his theoretical slumber.

Rosenau declared his new stance on theory in a long, highly visible review essay, which he published several years before *Turbulence in World Politics* appeared. 'The need for theorizing—good and bad—is especially acute in world politics today. Change is so pervasive in both the internal and external lives of communities and nation-states that old formulations no longer feel comfortable.'[9] Under review was 'the best of "bad theory"'. Rosenau called for a better alternative—'grandiose theory'—meeting grandiose requirements.[10]

The term 'grandiose' is itself rather grandiose. 'Grand' might have been a better choice, both for the ambition 'to roam across theoretical vistas' and for the demands placed on those daring to do so. Four of the criteria for good grandiose theory 'come straight from the philosophy of science'.

[5]   James N. Rosenau, 'The scholar as an adaptive system', in Joseph Kruzel and James N. Rosenau, eds, *Journeys through World Politics: Autobiographical Reflections of Thirty-four Academic Travelers* (Lexington, MA: Lexington Books, 1989), p. 64.

[6]   Ibid., p. 59. Also see James N. Rosenau, 'Thinking theory thoroughly', in Rosenau, *The Scientific Study of Foreign Policy*, pp. 19–31.

[7]   James N. Rosenau, 'Calculated control as a unifying concept in the study of international politics and foreign policy' in Rosenau, *The Scientific Study of Foreign Policy*, pp. 242–82.

[8]   James N. Rosenau, 'Pre-theories and theories of foreign policy', in Rosenau, *The Scientific Study of Foreign Policy*, pp. 115–69.

[9]   James N. Rosenau, 'Before cooperation: Hegemons, regimes, and habit-driven actors in world politics', *International Organization* 40, 4 (1986), pp. 849–94 (849–50).

[10] Ibid., p. 851. Cf. Quentin Skinner, ed., *The Return of Grand Theory in the Social Sciences* (Cambridge: Cambridge University Press, 1985).

Nevertheless, they do not require 'operationalized hypotheses or systematic data', at least initially.[11] Such a requirement would effectively prevent theorizing on an appropriately grand scale.

Another three criteria constitute 'the substantive core' of Rosenau's 'theoretical predispositions'. Rosenau's substantive criteria ensure that a properly grandiose theory reaches across 'macro and micro levels of aggregation'.[12] While these criteria would seem to favour neither level over the other, the complexity of micro–macro interaction forces the grandiose theorist to start somewhere. Ever the behaviouralist, Rosenau's clear preference is the micro level.

Habit

Constituting the micro level are 'habit-driven actors'—'both officials and citizens who strive for goals and respond to challenges in habitual ways'. Habits differ, as do their 'bases', but everyone has a 'habit function'. So-called rational actors are 'habituated' to making self-consciously rational choices. Indeed, no actor can be dismissed as a mindless victim of habit. According to Rosenau, *the readiness to learn is part of an actor's habit pool*.[13]

Rosenau makes habit an abiding feature of human behaviour. Perhaps not consciously, he follows an august predecessor in doing so: David Hume, whose analysis of causality helped awaken Immanuel Kant from his self-described dogmatic slumber. Hume argued that we experience the 'constant conjunction' of objects, events, or properties in nature, leading us to infer a 'necessary connexion', or causal relation, between them. Yet we can never demonstrate that such conjunctions are necessary because we have no way of knowing if they will continue to take place in the future. Only by experiencing them can we know for sure, and this is so no matter how often we have experienced them in the past. In Hume's words, 'there can be no *demonstrative* arguments to prove, *that those instances, of which we have had no experience, resemble those, of which we have had experience*'.[14]

Lacking arguments, why are we so confident that constant conjunctions will continue as they have? Hume's answer is *habit* (a term he used interchangeably with custom). 'All inferences from experience ... are effects of custom, not of reasoning'.[15] We come to expect what we are accustomed

---

[11] Rosenau, 'Before cooperation', pp. 853–5.

[12] Ibid., pp. 855, 861.

[13] Ibid., pp. 861–2, 864, emphasis in original.

[14] David Hume, *A Treatise of Human Nature* (1739–1740), 2nd edn rev. P. H. Nidditch (Oxford: Clarendon Press, 1978), pp. 87, 89, emphasis in original.

[15] David Hume, *An Enquiry concerning Human Understanding* (1748), ed. Peter Millican (Oxford: Oxford University Press, 1900), p. 32.

to experiencing. Indeed the principle *'that like objects, plac'd in like circumstances, will always produce like effects'* is a product of experience. Having 'establish'd itself by a sufficient custom, it bestows an evidence and firmness on any opinion, to which it can be apply'd'.[16]

Hume's inference that habit causes us to infer causal relations from the evidence of constant conjunctions is, by his own account, unproven and unprovable. Nevertheless, Hume bestowed considerable firmness on his opinion by calling habit a 'principle'—one that 'determines' our causal conclusions.[17] Even more striking is Hume's claim that 'habit is nothing but one of the principles of nature, and derives all its force from that origin'. This principle seems no more justified than the principle that nature is uniform, which Hume had dispatched as an argument for causality.[18] Yet Hume seems to have believed that nature is uniform. Our ability to recognize and act on this condition sets us apart from animals. Like us, they are guided by the habit of drawing inferences from experience, as well as by instinct. Unlike us, they do not make arguments about the state of nature, or about anything else.[19]

The principle that nature is uniform is not just an argument, but an article of faith for positivist science. It encourages us to formulate scientific laws or, in Hume's terms, 'general rules', and theories, or arguments, purporting to explain the existence and operation of these general rules.[20] Science depends on generalization. More precisely, science makes the process of generalization a collective undertaking guided by general rules.

Hume thought that generalizing from our experiences is the first and foremost of our habitual activities. The difficulty comes when we seek to generalize in the face of ambiguous or contradictory evidence. As Hume noted, 'when any cause fails of producing its usual effect, philosophers [clearly including himself] ascribe not this to any irregularity in nature; but suppose, that some secret causes, in the particular structure of parts, have prevented the operation'.[21] In such instances, we ought to assign probabilities not to nature, but to our assessment of its causal relations.[22]

In generalizing, we are prone to mistakes. Following 'certain and infallible rules', scientists make fewer mistakes than the rest of us perhaps, but they do make them because of their 'uncertain and fallible faculties'. Haste causes mistakes, as does narrow-mindedness. A particular failing that the rules of

---

[16] Hume, *A Treatise of Human Nature*, p. 105, emphasis in original.
[17] Hume, *An Enquiry concerning Human Understanding*, p. 32.
[18] Hume, *A Treatise of Human Nature*, pp. 179, 89.
[19] Ibid., pp. 176–79; Hume, *An Enquiry concerning Human Understanding*, pp. 76–8.
[20] Hume, *A Treatise of Human Nature*, p. 141.
[21] Hume, *An Enquiry concerning Human Understanding*, p. 42.
[22] Hume, *A Treatise of Human Nature*, pp. 130–72; Hume, *An Enquiry concerning Human Understanding*, pp. 41–3.

good science seek to prevent is the formulation of a general rule before the evidence warrants. Hume's term for a rashly formulated general rule is prejudice.[23]

To generalize with Hume: everyone generalizes all of the time. It is a universal habit, but not one that is uniformly practised. We can learn to generalize better by being self-conscious about the process, by learning from our mistakes, and by formulating rules in aid of generalization. Rosenau's position is identical.

Consider four of Rosenau's nine rules for 'creative theorizing' about 'international phenomena'.[24]

- To think theoretically one must be able to assume that human affairs are founded on an underlying order.
- To think theoretically one must be predisposed to ask about every event, every situation, or every observed phenomenon, 'Of what is it an instance?'
- To think theoretically one must be tolerant of ambiguity, concerned about probabilities, and distrustful of absolutes.
- To think theoretically one must be consistently ready to be proven wrong.[25]

The first rule simply and unequivocally reaffirms the principle of the uniformity of nature in the most inclusive sense. The second rule makes generalization a maximally self-conscious activity. As any of Rosenau's students will attest, he attaches great importance to the question, Of what is this object, event, property or relation an instance? 'Of all the habits that one must develop to think theoretically, perhaps none is central than the inclination to ask this question at every opportunity.'[26] The third rule seeks to combat prejudice and its concomitants. The last rule reaffirms Hume's claim that we can never prove anything anyway.

Implicit in the Hume-Rosenau position on habit as a human universal that can be cultivated to good effect is the division of humanity into two groups. There are those who generalize rashly, without sufficient attention to evidence. There are those who generalize circumspectly but effectively in solving nature's 'secrets' or 'puzzles'.[27] Just this division made Hume an emblematic figure in the Enlightenment of the 18th century.

---

[23] Hume, *A Treatise of Human Nature*, pp. 181, 142, 146.
[24] Rosenau, 'Thinking theory thoroughly', pp. 20–31. They are reproduced in Rosenau and Durfee, *Thinking Theory Thoroughly*, pp. 178–90.
[25] Ibid., pp. 23, 25, 27, 30. On Rosenau's list these are rules 3, 4, 6 and 9.
[26] Ibid., p. 25.
[27] 'Secrets' is Hume's term: 'nature has kept us at a great distance from all her secrets'. Hume, *An Enquiry concerning Human Understanding*, p. 24. 'Puzzles' is Rosenau's. Another rule

Philosophers and other enlightened individuals of the time saw selves free from the thrall of tradition—of superstitious beliefs, mindless habit and blinding prejudice. Superstition wilfully misreads nature, mindless habit refuses change for the better, prejudice resists correction. Worst of all from Hume's point of view is the widespread belief in miracles. By definition, a 'miracle is a violation of the laws of nature'.[28] Believing an event to be a miracle denies the possibility of a natural explanation for the event. Miracles appeal to the gullible masses, who 'receive greedily, without examination, whatever soothes superstition and promotes wonder'.[29]

As far as I know, Rosenau has never attacked traditional, popular beliefs the way Hume did. Nevertheless, the behavioural theory that he systematically formulated in *Turbulence in World Politics* exhibits a strongly Humean tendency to differentiate between an enlightened few with exemplary habits, and the mass of ordinary people who are unable to rise above their bad habits. Even if habit is the source of all learning and progress, habits that drag humanity down constitute the great problem to be vanquished, the puzzle to be solved, at every level of human aggregation.

Habdaption

In *Turbulence in World Politics*, Rosenau reaffirmed the importance of habit in understanding human behaviour. There is, however, a subtle change in the way he formulated this proposition. All people are simultaneously rational about some situations of choice and habit-driven about other situations. When rational, they learn from experience and adapt to changing circumstances; when habit-driven, they respond to situations unreflectively and repeat the same patterns of behaviour even when circumstances have changed.

> Empirically, in short, the vast preponderance of officials and citizens are both rational and habitual, both intellectual and emotional, and our understanding of turbulence in world politics is thus more likely to be advanced if we employ a perspective that posits individuals as falling between two ideal types. What is needed is a model organized around a central premise in which the form and direction of micro action is conceived to spring from a combination of habits that perpetuate continuity and orientations that allow for thoughtful estimates and

---

for thinking theoretically requires that we be 'genuinely puzzled'. Rosenau, 'Thinking theory thoroughly', p. 29.

[28] Hume, *An Enquiry concerning Human Understanding*, p. 83.

[29] Ibid., p. 91.

are open to change. It is the shifting balance between rote behavior and adaptive learning that forms the conditions of postinternational politics. To reflect this model, it seems worthwhile to coin a new term that expresses the synthesis of habitual and adaptive responses. Hence forth, where appropriate, we shall refer to individuals as *habdaptive* actors and to their location on the continuum between rote behavior and adaptive learning as their *habdaptive* function.[30]

Rosenau seems to have revised his earlier view that people, as creatures of habit, are habitual learners. In this new formulation, some people are adaptive learners, while others learn habits and then stop learning. The former have 'developed analytic skills', 'complex cognitive maps', 'active and refined cathectic capacities', 'questioning compliance orientations' and 'performance criteria' for their 'legitimacy sentiments'. Conversely, the latter have 'rudimentary analytical skills', 'simplistic cognitive maps', 'dormant and crude cathectic capacities', 'unthinking compliance orientations' and 'traditional criteria' for their 'legitimacy sentiments'.[31]

Rosenau's Enlightenment opposition of tradition and enlightenment is analytically rudimentary, crudely cathectic (indeed, highly prejudiced in its cathectic thrust), and, two and a half centuries after Hume, thoroughly traditional. Nevertheless, its utility for Rosenau is undeniable. The simple proposition that everyone is habit-driven is no foundation for theory. Taken together, the propositions that everyone combines habitual and adaptive behaviour but in different proportions, and that these proportions can shift individually and in aggregate, constitute a model. With this model in place, Rosenau had positioned himself to formulate a theory of behaviour applied to the circumstances of world politics.

As stated in *Turbulence in World Politics*, the theory itself has a simple grandeur.

[T]he possibility of change on the part of the habdaptive actor … underlies a prime argument of this book: that turbulence has engulfed world politics partly, even largely, because citizens and officials have moved away from the habit end of the learning continuum and toward the adaptive end. The movement may be no more than minimal—on the order of one JND [just noticeable difference]—for any individual, but the aggregative consequences of the movement are not minimal at all. On the contrary, the breakdown of habits is a major reason for the transformation of the state-centric system.[32]

---

[30] Rosenau, *Turbulence*, p. 228, emphasis in original; two footnotes deleted.
[31] Ibid., Table 9.1, p. 211.
[32] Ibid., p. 228.

Rosenau's habitual reluctance to declare himself theoretically is still in evidence—why not call this 'prime argument' the 'grandiose theory' that it is? On the other hand, Rosenau's habitual preference for probabilistic formulation is to be commended. The introduction of 'just noticeable difference' (JND) as a 'measurement unit' is regrettable, and not just because it is methodologically misleading.[33] Claiming that the aggregate effects of just noticeable changes 'are not minimal at all' is unwarranted. Why cannot the many individual changes in habdaptive actors offset each other, with the result of little or no noticeable change at the level of the aggregate?

Turning first to the methodological difficulties with JND as a measurement unit, we might ask, just noticeable to whom? When differences are just noticeable to observers (this was clearly Rosenau's frame of reference when he introduced the concept of JND early in the book), different observers may not agree on what they have observed, errors in observation are most likely, and changes in observers' instrumental capacities can dramatically change the field of noticeable differences. Furthermore, the fact that some observer just notices a change in an individual's behaviour has no demonstrable relation to the degree of individual change needed for Rosenau's theory to work. Individual changes that are too subtle or minute for any observer to notice may nevertheless aggregate to major change. Conversely, the observer may notice all sorts of changes in all degrees and not know which ones are responsible for the aggregate pattern of change.

If individuals whose behaviour has changed are the ones who do the noticing, then Rosenau's theory has acquired a significant additional term. Reference to JND is not just a methodological aside that interrupts the statement of the theory. Instead it is an important if cryptically formulated proposition linking individual changes to aggregate change. When individuals begin to notice changes in themselves, then these changes (the changes noticed and the additional change represented by the act of noticing) add up to major change. In order to maintain the theory's simple grandeur, we should construe an additional term as a necessary one: major movement depends on people's noticing that they—themselves and all those whom they can observe closely—have begun to change.

I am not at all sure that Rosenau intended to make self-awareness an integral feature of his theory, even if his conception of rational, adaptive behaviour includes just this property. From a positivist point of view, measuring self-awareness is highly problematic, and offering JND as a measurement unit is not even close to a solution. More to the point, making individual self-awareness a necessary condition for major change would not seem to comport with Rosenau's theoretical disposition to emphasize

---

[33] See ibid., pp. 32–3, for JND as a measurement unit.

the unintended consequences of small changes. If people begin to notice changes in their behaviour and act on what they have noticed, then these second-order changes are hardly unintended, whether and to what degree, from any observer's point of view, they are noticeable.

Change

Rosenau set his theory up as an alternative to the standard liberal theory of unintended consequences, which of course is Adam Smith's invisible hand and the entire edifice of modern microeconomics.[34] This theory asserts that small, noticeable changes in behaviour yield aggregate conditions that have the effect of encouraging small change by others in a compensatory direction. If many individuals begin to demand more of some good, other individuals produce more of this good until supply and demand have returned to balance. Major movement is dampened, precisely because everyone notices small differences and responds accordingly.

Rosenau would likely say (indeed, may have said somewhere) that the liberal theory of unintended consequences is a good theory. He would also say that it is unduly grandiose. It fails to account for a major class of unintended consequences—those that have amplifying rather than dampening effects. By implication, the standard liberal theory makes habit its centrepiece. People have learned the habit of calculating marginal utilities, and that is all they ever need to do.

Rosenau's habdaptive actors engage in other kinds of behaviour less calculating, but far more likely to produce macro-level change. To make space for a theory that features an elastic habdaptive function, Rosenau needed to explain why any rational person would abandon habits when they are so obviously useful. Change itself—'changing circumstances'—is the key. There are two sorts of changes in circumstances that prompt a change in an actor's habdaptive function: '(1) when external stimuli are persistently and startlingly new; (2) when new skills and orientations develop within the actor'. External stimuli that are likely to prompt a significant, readily noticed shift towards learning include war, revolution or a rapid change in the material conditions affecting daily life. 'Internally induced habit change is illustrated by effects of the microelectronic revolution on people's analytic capabilities'.[35] Both sorts of change are much in evidence in today's world.

The kind of behaviour that changing circumstances prompt people to learn differs from the habit-driven behaviour that markets rely on and economists concern themselves with. Implicitly Rosenau has reaffirmed the

---

[34] Cf. ibid., p. 51.
[35] Ibid., pp. 233–5.

liberal division of political and economic domains. For Rosenau, 'politics is conceived of as activities in which one actor … seeks to modify or preserve the behavior patterns of functionally distant others'.[36] This is what Rosenau has always called 'calculated control'. Not just calculated, but self-consciously oriented to the achievement of specific consequences, control thus conceived would seem to be the antithesis of habit-driven behaviour yielding an orderly set of unintended consequences.

Yet even here habit enters the picture. Enduring relations of control are authoritative, authority being 'that set of premises and habits on which macro leaders are entitled to rely to obtain automatic compliance from their followers'. After reviewing the reasons that 'people accord legitimacy to acts of authorities', Rosenau concluded that compliance is mostly 'a matter of habit; repeated instances of compliance become deeply ingrained'.[37] Hume held the same view: 'men, once accustomed to obedience, never think of departing from that path, in which they and their ancestors have constantly trod, and to which they are confined by so many urgent and visible motives'.[38]

According to Rosenau, a shift along the continuum from habit to adaptive learning undermines authority. 'It is in the deterioration of habit that authority crises originate: the more the membership moves away from automatic acceptance and toward outright rejection, the more is an authority relationship subjected to strain'.[39] When challenged, authority is far more likely to be dislocated than destroyed. When compliance orientations shift from unthinking to questioning, the 'locus of control' tends to shorten.[40] In particular, states become '[m]ore decentralized, less coherent and effective'; their '[a]uthority more diffuse, hierarchy weakened'; and their '[c]itizens more defiant, loyalties more tenuous'. In a compensating movement, subgroups become '[m]ore numerous, centralized, coherent, and effective'; their '[a]uthority more concentrated, hierarchy strengthened'; their '[m]embers more compliant, committed, and loyal'.[41]

In our time, states are losing ground to subgroups, many (but not all) of which are 'located within states and at least technically subject to their authority'.[42] Size matters. States reap economies of scale due to their large size but depend on the uniform habits of a passive citizenry to be able to operate

---

[36] Ibid., p. 184.

[37] Ibid., pp. 186–7.

[38] David Hume, 'Of the origin of government', in *Essays: Moral, Political, Literary* (1741–2), p. 38; also see Hume, *Treatise*, p. 566.

[39] Rosenau, *Turbulence*, p. 190.

[40] Ibid., Table 9.1, p. 211.

[41] Ibid., Table 6.1, p. 119.

[42] Ibid., p. 133.

on the scale they do. Active learners find small groups and organizations more responsive to their concerns. For them, local politics pay off, with at least some chance of achieving intended consequences at the local level.

Republican theory has always concerned itself with the size problem in politics. Hume thought the best solution was a pyramid of representative bodies—a solution James Madison seconded in *Federalist* No. 10, as did Rosenau in *Turbulence in World Politics*, if only in passing.[43] Yet contemporary republicans doubt that voting for representatives sufficiently activates habit-dominated citizens or satisfies active, adaptive citizens with consequences worthy of their intentions. Having studied the problem of mobilizing citizens between elections, Rosenau would seem to have had the same misgivings.[44]

Contemporary republicans have turned their attention to social movements that challenge as well as mediate the state's authority. So has Rosenau. As *Turbulence in World Politics* makes clear, Rosenau is a republican thinker who has come to believe that local politics writ large can only go so far in saving the state from the perils of scale. Now more than ever local politics have global consequences.

The largest such consequence is, for most citizens, hardly intended, indeed hard to imagine. The world itself is bifurcating. A 'multicentric world' of 'sovereignty-free actors' has begun to take its place alongside the 'state-centric world' with which we have long been familiar. Whether one world will prevail over the other, bifurcation continue, or a cyclical pattern set in is a matter of speculation.[45] The theory predicts a range of outcomes depending on the extent to which citizens experience a change in their habdaptive functions.

Rosenau observed that one's preferences are likely to affect one's assessment of the possibilities. His preference is bifurcation.

> It has the potential for a creative reconciliation of all the great antitheses of politics—the conflicts between order and freedom, between the will of majorities and the autonomy of minorities, between individual needs and collective welfare, between technological innovation and cultural integrity, between growth and stability, and between change and continuity.[46]

---

[43] David Hume, 'Idea of a perfect commonwealth', in *Essays*, p. 516; Douglass Adair, '"That politics may be reduced to a science": David Hume, James Madison, and the Tenth *Federalist*', *Huntington Library Quarterly* 20, 4 (1957), pp. 343–60; Rosenau, *Turbulence*, p. 241.

[44] James N. Rosenau, *Citizenship between Elections: An Inquiry into the Mobilizable American* (New York: Free Press, 1974).

[45] Rosenau, *Turbulence*, pp. 249–53, 445.

[46] Ibid., p. 461.

Thus concludes *Turbulence in World Politics*, its theory offered not just to explain turbulence in today's world, but to reassure us, and perhaps even bring bifurcation to fruition as an intended consequence of one scholar's adaptive learning.

Skill

Rosenau's behavioural theory of politics explains stable, predictable relations of authority by reference to mindless habit. It explains our own era of turbulence by reference to a general change from habit-driven behaviour at the micro level to adaptive behaviour. Great change at the micro level is, as far as Rosenau is concerned, a recent phenomenon that is easy enough to substantiate. Not only is turbulence a conspicuous feature of our times but, thanks to television, the evidence is constantly before our eyes, stimulating us to think politically as never before. Far more important is the spectacular increase in analytic skills engendered by the microelectronic revolution. This is, indeed, a 'skill revolution'.[47]

Rosenau's behavioural theory starts with change in actors' habdaptive functions and ends with a bifurcating world. One might object that he significantly weakened his theory, or at least the claim that it stands grandly on its own terms, by finding the cause of behavioural change in worldwide changes in material conditions. Presumably these changes are the result of (somebody's) adaptive learning at an earlier interval. Thus stated, the theory suffers from infinite regress, and the charge that its point of departure—recent behavioural change—is glaringly arbitrary.

Rosenau's implicit answer to this charge is that the skill revolution is just that—a revolution that has no precedent As a step-level shift towards adaptive learning for a very large number of people, its consequences are world shaking. Rosenau has considered the obvious criticism that the effects of the skill revolution are anything but equal. Some people have privileged access to the means for improving their analytic skills, others have much less access. The point, however, is aggregate change. As Rosenau and Mary Durfee put it, 'the gap between the two ends of the skill continuum may be no narrower than in the past'. Nevertheless, 'the advancement in the competencies of those at every point on the continuum is sufficient to contribute to a major transformation in the conduct of world affairs'.[48]

At first glance, this claim is empirical and, as such, contestable. Indeed, the gap between the two ends of the skill continuum may be wider now

---

[47] Rosenau and Durfee, *Thinking Theory Thoroughly*, pp. 35–7. Rosenau seems not to have used this phrase in *Turbulence*.

[48] Ibid., pp. 36–7. Also see Rosenau, *Turbulence*, pp. 364–7.

than in the recent past. Possibly the gap is growing so dramatically that the world's bifurcation is an unintended consequence, not the sort of bifurcation that Rosenau has had in mind. After bifurcation, one world would consist of materially privileged, analytically skilful people. The other is a nether world, made up of all those have been left behind analytically and materially, despised or pitied for their bad habits and retrograde attitudes by those who have abandoned them.[49]

The issue is not simply empirical. Implicitly, Rosenau's theory makes habit the rule and adaptive learning an exception. Habit reigns because we are all good at repetitive behaviour, which is, often enough, socially efficient. Adaptive learning is exceptional because it is hard work for individuals and costly to society. Rosenau seems to believe that the material changes underlying the skill revolution somehow annul time-tested propositions that are embedded in the structure of his theory. Without offering a compelling amendment to the theory— a set of propositions to the effect that microelectronics has altered our capacity to learn and rid us of the tendency to revert to habit—Rosenau's empirical claims fail to convince for theoretical reasons. If he is right, then his theory cannot be very good.

Normativity

Rosenau's behavioural theory of politics is undeniably grandiose. I believe, however, that something is missing—something Hume might have supplied—that would make it a better theory without undue cost to its simple grandeur. Adding self-consciousness is neither warranted on Humean grounds (although there may be Kantian grounds for doing so) nor, as I observed earlier, is it methodologically tractable for anyone with positivist commitments. Instead, Rosenau's theory would benefit from the addition of a normative element. I am not suggesting that Rosenau make his theory any more normative than he already has (that is, make it 'value theory'; *Turbulence in World Politics* is 'value-explicit').[50] An early proponent of the distinction between facts and values, Hume nevertheless made a great deal of the fact that values systematically affect human conduct.[51]

---

[49] See Robert B. Reich, *The Work of Nations: Preparing Ourselves for 21st Century Capitalism* (New York: Alfred Knopf, 1991), for a popular assessment along these lines.

[50] Rosenau, 'Thinking theory thoroughly', p. 22; Rosenau, *Turbulence in World Politics*, p. 33. Rosenau finally turned to normative matters in *Along the Domestic-International Frontier*, pp. 174–88, but even there has not made them integral to his grandiose theory.

[51] According to Hume, 'morality consists not in any relations, that are the object of science; but if examin'd, will prove with equal certainty, that it consists not in any *matter of fact*'. *A Treatise of Human Nature*, p. 468, emphasis in original. See, however, Arnold Brecht's sceptical assessment of Hume's contribution to the fact-value distinction: *Political*

Rosenau did include 'normative prescriptions' in a laundry list of factors contributing to every actor's habit pool.[52] He also speculated that turbulence fostered the emergence of new 'global norms'.[53] To illustrate this trend, he offered an especially Humean instance—increasingly actors at every level insist on scientific criteria in evaluating truth claims. Nevertheless, Rosenau failed to consider where norms come from, and why they might matter more (given their origin) than other factors making up anybody's habit pool. Instead, norms belong to a residual category of macro phenomena—call it culture—that somehow bears on every actor's habdaptive function.

Hume, by contrast, used the proposition that people are creatures of habit to explain both how norms happen to be everywhere and, if only by implication, why norms matter when people have habits to guide them. Armed with a Humean understanding of normativity, we can then rewrite the terms of Rosenau's habdaptive function to avoid the gratuitous, though Humean, opposition between the benighted beholders of tradition and the enlightened seekers of truth. The key to this move is recognition that behaviour is always, necessarily social. Individuals have habits but share customs. The latter are habits writ large.

To acquire a habit, people must engage in repetitive behaviour. If two people simultaneously engage in behaviour that is mutually beneficial, or one imitates another, and they and others repeat the behaviour in question to further benefit, all begin to generalize from the experience and then to count on its repetition—by everyone, for everyone's benefit. In Hume's compelling analysis, the process of generalizing from observed regularities of conduct (a process exactly analogous to that of inferring cause from regularities in nature) assures us that 'the sense of interest has become common to all our fellows, and gives us a confidence of the future regularity of their conduct'.[54]

The product of our collective generalizing is a rule or convention 'which arises gradually, and acquires force by a slow progression, and by our repeated experience of the inconveniences of transgressing it'.[55] According to Hume, conventions account for language, property and everything else that makes society possible. Even '*natural*' justice is '*invented*': 'it derives its origins from human conventions'. The 'force' that conventions acquire is normative; expectation gives rise to obligation. 'They are contriv'd to remedy like

---

Theory: The Foundations of Twentieth-Century Political Thought, Princeton: Princeton University Press, 1959), pp. 539–41.

[52] Rosenau, *Turbulence in World Politics*, p. 229. The 1986 version of this list referred to 'cultural norms'. Rosenau, 'Before cooperation', p. 861.

[53] Rosenau, *Turbulence in World Politics*, p. 425.

[54] Hume, *A Treatise of Human Nature*, p. 490.

[55] Ibid.

inconveniences, and acquire their moral sanction in the same manner, from remedying those inconveniences.'[56]

Normativity seems natural because we—people in general—think that we should behave as we customarily have behaved. We habitually come to this generalization from the particulars of our daily lives, and not from the requirements of any particular moral system.[57] People slip from fact to value, and back again, with amazing facility and splendid insouciance. We do so, in my opinion, because we know how to use language to have people (ourselves included) act as we think they should. Hume's brilliant analysis of promising as a performative use of language suggests instead that the relevant cognitive skills precede language and its invented rules, even if our linguistic abilities strengthen those skills.[58]

For Rosenau's purposes, it does not matter why people are so adept at traversing the fact–value divide—why we are so quick to draw normative conclusions from observed regularities and so sure of ourselves when we do so. He need only accept that, as social beings, we make rules just as readily as we form habits. Furthermore, we make rules on the expectation that we, and others, will follow them. Ruled as we are by habit and instinct, we are even more ruled by our rules.

Following rules is, often enough, a matter of habit. It works well for us. We also know when it works better for us to disregard a rule. Or to evade a rule. Or to claim that it is not a rule or at least not applicable to us. Or to change a rule or claim that others' evasions or endeavours have already changed it. Or to follow the rule to the letter but not in spirit, or follow it in spirit but not to the letter. Pierre Bourdieu has called this ensemble of activities '*habitus*'—'the durably installed generative principle of regulated improvisations'.[59] Bourdieu claimed it a mistake to speak of rules—'a euphemized form of legalism'—where *habitus* is in evidence. Bourdieu was mistaken—misled, actually, by a too formal conception of rule as 'an institutionalized call to order' that people are bound to follow.[60] People deal with rules all the time. However formal these rules are and whatever the institutional support for them, we do so with consummate skill and a high degree of self-awareness. We are quite aware, for example, that disregarding

---

[56] Ibid., p. 543, emphasis in original.
[57] Cf. Hans Kelsen's 'basic norm'. *Principles of International Law*, 2d edn, rev. Robert W. Tucker (New York: Holt, Rinehart and Winston, 1967), pp. 556–65.
[58] Hume, *A Treatise of Human Nature*, pp. 516–25.
[59] Pierre Bourdieu, *Outline of a Theory of Practice*, trans. Richard Price (Cambridge: Cambridge University Press, 1977), p. 78. Bourdieu chose the term *habitus* 'to set aside the common conception of habit as a mechanical assembly or preformed programme, as Hegel does when in the *Phenomenology of Mind*, he speaks of "habit as dexterity"'. Ibid., p. 218, n. 47.
[60] Ibid., p. 17.

an informal, local, and provisional rule is likely to weaken the rule, or that making a rule more formal and general will contribute to the likelihood of its being followed. Intending such consequences is an integral feature of our collective normative competence.

No doubt people vary in their normative skills. Nevertheless, all of us who are able to get along as social beings possess this skill abundantly. To paraphrase Rosenau and Durfee, the gap between two ends of the normative skill continuum is far narrower than it is for the continuum of analytic skills. Nor would it matter if the gap in normative skills changes, for it is unlikely to change enough to have any revolutionary consequences.

It does matter who has the institutional position to make rules formal and their violation costly, just as it matters what the people in this position want for themselves and others. It matters that particular sets of rules are difficult to learn and costly to teach. For example, rules for obtaining and using analytic skills, like the rules of science, are notoriously demanding, even if some of these rules are needlessly arcane, practically irrelevant or routinely disregarded by those who know them. It matters that informal rules colonize formally ruled environments, making it doubly difficult for outsiders to know how to conduct themselves.

These are political matters, all of them affecting whether and to what degree the rules accompanying the microelectronic revolution are likely to narrow the gap in analytic skills around the world or, as an unintended consequence, to exacerbate it. I doubt that the gap will narrow because the normative competence that we all possess so abundantly seems, perversely enough, to foster asymmetrical distributions of privilege and control. That we are all so good with rules means that some people always rule over others. This is less a complication for Rosenau's theory than a setback for his normative preferences. In practical terms, it suggests that, with modest alteration, his theory can help to account for turbulence wherever it occurs *and* the way people respond to it, not just individually, but socially.

10

Intertextual Relations (2009)

For reasons that need no explaining, 1989 is surely the most memorable of the last 50 years of international relations. 1989 was also a signal year for International Relations as a field of study, thanks to three books expressly written to challenge the way scholars think about their subject. Two of these books—Friedrich Kratochwil's *Rules, Norms, and Decisions* and my own *World of Our Making*—are now reckoned as founding texts for the contructivist movement in International Relations, along with two papers of Alexander Wendt's.[1] The third book is *International/Intertextual Relations*, which James Der Derian and Michael Shapiro edited, and to which they and a dozen other scholars contributed.[2]

While all three books reflect philosophical and theoretical developments that had originated in Europe and already unsettled disciplines from literature to sociology, *International/Intertextual Relations* is the most open in its challenge to prevailing ways in International Relations. Its authors drew on a pantheon of variously provocative French thinkers—Roland Barthes, Jean Baudrillard, Jacques Derrida, Michel Foucault, Julia Kristeva, Jacques Lacan, Jean-François Lyotard—with extraordinary fluency and not just a little flamboyance. Although Nietzsche looms in the background, the conspicuous absence of such fashionable figures as C. S. Peirce, Ludwig Wittgenstein and Thomas Kuhn, not to mention a long century of post-Kantian philosophy,

---

[1]   Friedrich V. Kratochwil, *Rules, Norms, and Decisions: On the Conditions of Practical and Legal Reasoning in International Relations and Domestic Affairs* (Cambridge: Cambridge University Press, 1989); Nicholas Greenwood Onuf, *World of Our Making: Rules and Rule in Social Theory and International Relations* (Columbia: University of South Carolina Press, 1989); Alexander E. Wendt, 'The agent-structure problem in international relations theory', *International Organization* 41, 3 (1987), pp. 335–70, and 'Anarchy is what states make of it: The social construction of power politics', *International Organization* 46, 2 (1992), pp. 391–425.

[2]   James Der Derian and Michael J. Shapiro, eds, *International/Intertextual Relations: Postmodern Readings of World Politics* (Lexington, MA: Lexington Books, 1989).

suggests an unusually tight focus for an edited volume, though hardly a uniform one. While the constructivist texts from 1989 ranged more widely, none of these three books give an adequate sense of the impact of feminist scholarship at the time. Had Cynthia Enloe's *Bananas, Beaches and Bases* appeared a year [or even a few weeks] earlier, it would have contributed even more to the sense that 1989 was a banner year for the field.[3] I should also note that 1989 is the year Francis Fukuyama published 'The end of history?'[4]—a piece undoubtedly read by more students of international relations than any book published that year.

Of the contributors to *International/Intertextual Relations*, nearly half are political theorists (William Connolly, Jean Elshtain, Timothy Luke, Diane Rubenstein, Michael Shapiro, R. B. J. Walker), no doubt reflecting one source of contagion in the hermetic community of scholars identifying with International Relations as a field. Alfred Fortin seems to have studied with Shapiro but took his doctoral degree in health politics. The others trained in the field, for the most part as political scientists (Hayward Alker, Richard Ashley, Thomas Biersteker, James Der Derian, Roger Hurwitz, Takashi Inoguchi, Bradley Klein). That all but two contributors were trained in the United States (Der Derian in Britain, and Walker in Canada) and only two were located elsewhere in 1989 (Inoguchi and Walker) will seem odd if not inconceivable today. All but Fortin and Klein remain active as scholars, as did Alker until his sudden death in 2008.

The book had its beginning in a number of panels, including one Ashley organized with David Sylvan, at an International Studies Association convention, 'fittingly' held across the street from Disneyland in 1986.[5] Participants attending each other's panels unexpectedly discovered common interests. (And, on an unrelated panel at the same conference, Wendt presented his 'Agent-Structure' paper and I what was to become a chapter in my 1989 book.) The year 1986 also saw the publication of *Neorealism and Its Critics*, with Robert Keohane as editor and Ashley a contributor.[6] Ashley's paper, 'The Poverty of Neorealism', had already occasioned a good deal of rancorous discussion when it appeared in 1984 and prompted Robert Gilpin, in defending realism, to call Ashley a 'Kafkaesque prosecutor'.[7] In 1987–8, Ashley continued to publish prolifically and, with

3   Cynthia Enloe, *Bananas, Beaches and Bases: Making Feminist Sense of International Politics* (Berkeley: University of California Press, 1990).
4   Francis Fukuyama, 'The end of history', *The National Interest*, 16 (1989), pp. 3–18.
5   Der Derian and Shapiro, *International/Intertextual Relations*, p. x.
6   Robert O. Keohane, ed., *Neorealism and Its Critics* (New York: Columbia University Press, 1986).
7   Robert G. Gilpin, 'The richness of the tradition of political realism', in Keohane, *Neorealism and its Critics*, p. 302.

Walker, edited a special issue of the *International Studies Quarterly* called 'Speaking the Language of Exile: Dissident Thought in International Studies' (1990). Der Derian, Klein and Shapiro contributed papers, and Ashley's concluding paper with Walker was his last substantial contribution to what Yosef Lapid had already stylized 'The Third Debate' in 1989.[8] As if there were nothing left to debate, the 'dissidents' got comfortable with 'exile' and the field moved on; Walker's *Inside/Outside* (1993) marked the passing of a remarkable moment of challenge, controversy and containment in the field.[9]

Postmodern/poststructural

The subtitle of *International/Intertextual Relations* is *Postmodern Readings of World Politics*. In the editors' Preface and Acknowledgments, the very first sentence refers to 'continental philosophical and intellectual practices that have been loosely construed as postmodern and poststructural'. Merely modern scholars in International Relations (and other fields) are understandably given to using the terms *postmodern* and *poststructural* loosely to indicate what they are pretty sure they are not. Yet Der Derian and Shapiro used these terms interchangeably and inclusively to challenge the philosophical and intellectual practices constituting 'the Enlightenment foundation of international relations'. Notwithstanding their claim that 'poststructuralism' had undertaken 'a rigorous analysis of the language and methods of international relations', *these* poststructuralists made a point of using key terms rather loosely to 'resist identity-mongering'. In other words, the 'prefixal "post"' is all that matters.[10]

Most scholars in the social sciences have come to acknowledge that every term has many meanings, that meanings are never fixed, and perhaps even that meaning is ultimately subjective. No doubt scholars will always use language loosely—broadly, suggestively and often metaphorically—to give themselves latitude in framing their inquiries and marking their stances. Yet indiscriminate use of the terms *postmodern* and *poststructural*, not to mention *postpositivist* (which Lapid seems to have introduced to the field in 1989) and *postmodernist* tells me that the situation has worsened over two decades and warrants a modest attempt at clarification. Polysemous language and intersubjective barriers to effective communication are

---

[8] Yosef Lapid, 'The third debate: On the prospects of international theory in a post-positivist era', *International Studies Quarterly* 33, 3 (1989), pp. 235–54.

[9] R. B. J. Walker, *Inside/Outside: International Relations as Political Theory* (Cambridge: Cambridge University Press, 1993).

[10] Der Derian and Shapiro, *International/Intertextual Relations*, p. ix.

integral features of the human condition. Nevertheless, we, as scholars, should actively resist the careless and uninformed use of language among ourselves.

Applied to scholars generally, and not just in International Relations, *postmodern* is the most inclusive of these terms in common use. It connotes a repudiation of, resistance to, or, at minimum, severe reservations about modernity's Enlightenment foundations—conceptions of self, knowledge and reality. Most of the contributions to *International/Intertextual Relations* are clearly postmodern. Whether this term applies to scholars who are ambivalent about the Enlightenment's legacy, critical of modernity's various features, or persuaded that modernity, as an existential condition, is undergoing a transformation qualitatively unlike anything in its history is less clear. Quite a few scholars of this ilk prefer the term *late modern* for the world (as did Connolly[11]) and for themselves.

All too often we find the term *postmodernist* where *postmodern* is appropriate, at least in the social sciences. In *International/Intertextual Relations*, both Der Derian and Connolly made this mistake in their chapters. The mistake is understandable, given that *modernism,* named as a literary movement dating roughly between 1880 and 1930, includes *modern* art and music, not to mention architecture and interior design in the same period. In the modernist commitment to get below the surface of things (including minds, institutions), the term also describes the psychoanalytic movement, as exemplified by Sigmund Freud, and functionalist social theory, as exemplified by Émile Durkheim. Postmodernism emerged most clearly in architecture and literature in the 1960s and '70s, and made its belated, largely unacknowledged appearance in the social sciences in Anthony Giddens' post-functional social theory. Giddens counts himself late modern (as I do, in part influenced by Giddens' post-functionalist perspective).[12]

In the first instance, poststructuralism refers rather narrowly to a reaction against structuralism, associated most of all with Claude Levi-Strauss and ascendant in France in the 1960s (and not to be confused with structural-functionalism—the Anglo-American branch of functionalist social theory). Levi-Strauss's conception of structure as an ensemble of binary oppositions arising from some innate property of the mind inspired Jacques Derrida's claim that all such oppositions originated in language and could be 'deconstructed' to reveal their asymmetric effects on social relations (see later). Poststructuralism has acquired a broader reach than this characterization might suggest. Yet it is still associated with French thinkers of the 1960s

---

[11] William E. Connolly, 'Identity and difference in global politics', in ibid., p. 333.

[12] Anthony Giddens, *The Consequences of Modernity* (Stanford: Stanford University Press, 1990), Table 2, p. 150. Also see Chapter 12.

and '70s and their followers in the first instance in literature departments in universities in the United States.

A more inclusive term than *poststructuralist*, and one more widely used in the field today, is *postpositivist*. I use this term for myself without fear that it automatically makes me postmodern instead of late modern. Ontologically positivists put things before relations and looks for methods to pin down selected properties of things, thereby making inferences about relations more compelling. Historicists have always put large ensembles of relations first, and postpositivists doubt that things can ever be so easily severed from relations, including the relation between observed or inferred things and their observers. In this respect, poststructuralists are emphatic postpositivists.

Method/anti-method

If the editors by and large use *postmodern* and *poststructuralist* interchangeably, they do suggest, rather in passing, a binary opposition between the two terms when they identify a number of 'tectonic shifts' shaking the world at that very time—'changes … in which objective reality is displaced by textuality'. These changes constitute 'the historical rupture' or 'postmodern moment that imbues and "justifies" this book'.[13] The implied opposition between (poststructural) observer and (postmodern) world reproduces a central assumption of Enlightenment thought, which of course postmodern/ poststructural thinkers have sought to dismantle.

Before accusing the editors of a careless slip, we need to ask how poststructuralists 'see' the world. Broadly speaking, this is a methodological question, but one that shades into an epistemological stance (no wonder scholars so often use the term *epistemology* when *methodology* would do). First, poststructuralists apply themselves to texts. Second, they construe the world's contents as texts. Third, texts are not objectively fixed features of the world but always have human authors. Fourth, every reader is an author, every reading alters every text. Fifth, since every text has many authors, texts have stable meanings only to the extent that authors offer converging interpretations, or readings; such is truth. Sixth, there are therefore no observers standing apart from the world; 'seeing' is a bad choice of metaphors.

On this account, it would seem then that the binary opposition of observer and world, as an Enlightenment conceit and methodological postulate, simply collapses. The world is postmodern if we read it that way; a poststructuralist scholar will do just this but a modern scholar will not. It would also seem that the poststructural method absolves the editors from any charge of having constructed a binary opposition between observer and world, there being

---

[13] Der Derian and Shapiro, *International/Intertextual Relations*, p. x.

187

only a 'world-text',[14] which is at the same time an 'intertext' or 'a multi-dimensional space in which a variety of writings, none of them original, blend and clash'.[15] There is, however, a lingering inconsistency. Even if the world is changing in some dramatic fashion, it cannot be a shift from 'objective reality' to 'textuality' because, on the poststructuralist account (at least as I read it), the world has never been objectively real. It has always been and will always be a changing text.

I interpret what you have just read as an application of the poststructural method to show that a claim about the world—formed as a before (modern) and after (postmodern) opposition—is unsustainable. The editors might respond that 'objective reality' is merely a shorthand description of the way most people read texts, thereby making the modern world-text seem like an objective reality to them, but that increasingly (in 1989) people were making textuality their working reality, which was changing the world-text in a variety of legible ways. I would retort that this reading was at odds with my reading at the time and remains so today, despite many more, highly legible changes in the world-text. If this kind of fruitless exchange is all we get when we attempt, in good faith, to use the poststructural method, then it hardly seems worth the trouble.

There is perhaps an escape from this impasse. As we have seen, the 'deconstructive process ... dismantles fixed oppositions and hierarchies'.[16] 'Antimethod' by virtue of a 'commitment to limn', not 'delimit', and therefore the antithesis to 'methodologism', the deconstructive process is better thought of as an 'organizing strategy'.[17] The term *strategy* suggests that the method of dismantling oppositions is not simply applied willy-nilly to the world-text, but is instead directed at selected oppositions in order to achieve an end beyond intellectual one-upmanship. For poststructuralists, that end is political.

Even if every opposition is, on careful reading, a hierarchy that grants, or at least codifies, an asymmetric distribution of values, some hierarchies are more pernicious and therefore more deserving of attention on strategic grounds. Der Derian lists fact/fiction, male/female, self/other. I do not doubt that any poststructuralist would include these three conspicuous examples on a short list. So would I.

---

[14] James Der Derian, 'The boundaries of knowledge and power in international relations', in ibid., p. 6 (with the hyphen); Michael J. Shapiro, Textualizing global politics', also ibid., p. 13 (without).

[15] Der Derian, 'The boundaries of knowledge and power in international relations', p. 6, quoting Barthes.

[16] Ibid., p. 4.

[17] Ibid., pp. 7, 4. Is 'method or antimethod' another opposition in need of dismantling?

A poststructuralist might also say that my deconstruction of the modern/ postmodern opposition serves no purpose beyond my own intellectual satisfaction or regrettable need to show how clever I am. Here I am not so sure. In the years since *International/Intertextual Relations* appeared, the modern–postmodern opposition has acquired a political cachet. Consider, for example, Michael Hardt and Antonio Negri's *Empire*, which endeavours to reframe the modern–postmodern opposition in such a way as to put 'postmodernism' on the wrong side of the political fence.[18] Given my own political sympathies, I side with the poststructuralists. But I am also prompted to ask if the opposition between what is political and what is not needs deconstruction. Demolish one opposition, and yet another takes its place. From the perils of infinite regress, political strategy offers only the illusion of escape.

Theory/metatheory

The most sustained consideration of the deconstructive process in *International/Intertextual Relations* is Ashley's. In his long, still riveting essay, 'Living on border lines', he puts this process in opposition to *logocentrism*.[19] Let me quote Ashley at some length, and not just to convey the distinctive flavour of his prose style.

> By logocentrism, Derrida means a practical orientation and a procedure that at once presupposes, invokes and effects a normalizing practical expectation. This is the expectation that all interpretation and practice must secure recognition and power by appeal to some identical consciousness, principle of interpretation, or necessary subjectivity having at least two qualities. First it is a central interpretive orientation—a coherent sovereign voice, if you will—that supplies a unified rational meaning and direction to the interpretation of the spatial and temporal diversity of history. Second, as a sovereign voice, this principle is itself regarded as a pure and originary presence— an unproblematic extrahistorical identity, in no need of critical accounting. ...
>
> The logocentric procedure is not difficult to understand. Its workings are most plainly seen in relation to familiar practical oppositions such

---

[18] Michael Hardt and Antonio Negri, *Empire* (Cambridge, MA: Harvard University Press, 2000), pp. 137–43.

[19] Richard K. Ashley, 'Living on border lines: Man, poststructuralism, and war', in Der Derian and Shapiro, *International/Intertextual Relations*, p. 261. *Logocentrism* is Derrida's term, to whom we also owe the term *deconstruction*.

as literal/figural, structure/superstructure, core/periphery, continuity/ change, nature/culture, serious/nonserious, individual/collective, real/ ideological, depth/surface, male/female, and domestic/international. Encountering these and other oppositions, the logocentric disposition inclines a participant in the regime of modernity to impose hierarchy. It inclines a participant to identify his voice of interpretation and practice with a subjective standpoint, … a higher reality, belonging to the domain of logos, or pure and indecomposable presence in need of no explanation. As for the other term in each pair, it is then defined, from the same interpretive standpoint, solely in relation to the first term, perhaps even as an inferior or derivative form. Privileging the one term, a logocentric discourse effects a hierarchy in which the other is rendered as a complication, a negation, a manifestation, an effect, a disruption, a parasitic (mis)representation, or a fall from the graceful presence of the first.[20]

One might easily conclude that 'doing theory' (Ashley's scare marks) epitomizes logocentric discourse, and doing theory is what poststructuralists must set themselves in opposition to. In Ashley's words, 'poststructuralism inverts the logocentric hierarchy that, in modern practice, privileges theory over historicity—according to the former, the status of sovereign voice of reasoning man … and marginalizing the latter as a problem that theory promises sooner or later to solve'.[21] I read this passage as an unambiguous indictment of doing theory.[22] By abstracting from history, how can any theory avoid turning some crucial pair of terms into a hierarchy?—just for example, historicity/history, theory/practice. Even for Ashley, doing theory is unavoidable.

The issue is not theory as such, but 'theoretical integrity and detachment', paradoxically affirmed when the poststructuralist is 'persistently, openly, blatantly politicizing in the theory she does'. Yet 'this does not mean wearing one's political causes on one's sleeve'; instead the poststructuralist 'must understand that theoretical practice is inescapably …a political practice'.[23] In my opinion, engaged detachment is an illusion, and the opposition between theory and practice is ignored rather than dismantled. Most scholars will associate theory with detachment and practice with engagement.

If detachment is the issue, political theory beckons as second-order theorizing about successive and competing political theories. Indeed much

---

[20] Ibid.
[21] Ibid., pp. 274, 272.
[22] As did Connolly, 'Identity and difference', pp. 336–7, in reference to similar passages.
[23] Ashley, 'Living on border lines', pp. 279–80.

of political theory is metatheory, which Der Derian usefully defines as 'theorizing about ... theories'.[24] If politicized theoretical practice depends on metatheory's extensive critical resources to keep it honest, there is a risk. Any turn to metatheory is likely to entrap the scholar in a discourse about foundations. Ashley advised abstention from metatheory (and its politics): 'poststructuralism eschews grand designs, transcendental grounds or universal projects of humankind'.[25]

Movement/moment

By renouncing metatheory, poststructuralists effectively disown the 'ism' in poststructuralism. The suffix *ism* suggests a movement, motivated by some large though not always explicit design or project, and eventuating in a school of thought. In keeping with poststructural ambivalence about theory, *International/Intertextual Relations*' editors forthrightly announced modest ambitions for their book. 'It should be clear from the outset ... that this book does not constitute a school of thought'.[26] Even though a number of scholars have made impressive, explicitly poststructuralist contributions to International Relations, there was no movement, and there is no school of thought by that name.

That said, quite a few poststructuralists have joined a much larger contingent of scholars in turning to ethics[27]—a trend easy enough to read as a movement. Or they aligned themselves with the postcolonial movement in social theory. To their credit, they have not joined forces with constructivists, even if others threw them together for metatheoretical convenience or by way of dismissal. Always receptive to the idea of doing theory, constructivists launched a movement. Constructivism's early metatheoretical texts took on iconic significance, a legion of acolytes answered the call to get empirical, deep fissures became apparent and camps formed, respectability beckoned, calcification set in. It is enough to make an old-time constructivist yearn for another 1989.

If *International/Intertextual Relations* did not spark a movement, it marked a moment to commemorate. That the moment has slipped into history does not mean, however, that the poststructuralists of 1989 have fallen silent or that their large claims have been refuted. Instead they have refined the art of identifying an indicative text and the method of dismantling its asymmetrical

---

[24] Der Derian, 'The boundaries of knowledge and power', p. 7.
[25] Ashley, 'Living on border lines', p. 284.
[26] Der Derian, 'The boundaries of knowledge and power', p. 8.
[27] For just one example, see David Campbell and Michael Shapiro, eds, *Moral Spaces: Rethinking Ethics and World Politics* (Minneapolis: University of Minnesota Press, 1999).

oppositions—practices I favour in my own work. They resist, as I cannot, the siren call of a grand narrative or general system in which to locate their texts on texts. If there is an exception, it is Walker's *After the Globe, Before the World* (2009).[28] As a magnificent exercise in metatheory and a sustained dismantling of innumerably linked 'dualisms', it systematically subverts the 'before and after' narrative signalled in the dualism of its title. In 20 years, I suggest, it will be remembered as a critical moment in the story it refuses to tell. Just as *International/Intertextual Relations* is today.

---

[28] R. B. J. Walker, *After the Globe, Before the World* (Abingdon: Routledge, 2009).

11

World-making, State-building
(2014)

The state is a historical artifact whose existence can be
reconstructed by observing semantic distinctions.

Oliver Kessler[1]

Blueprints

In the last 500 years, the state has emerged and then changed in significant
ways, and so has the vast complex of social relations we call the modern
world. Familiar periodizations of modernity assume that these parallel
developments coincide but that their doing so is no coincidence. To simplify a
superabundance of causal connections, we might say that states and the system
of states, here called international society, have continuously reconstituted
each other over the centuries, and that this process of co-constitution is
an integral feature of modernity as a constitutive whole. State-building
and world-making occur simultaneously on the basis of blueprints that are
periodically but not systematically updated. Anyone building a state today
must rely on incomplete, confusing, yet normatively controlling layers of
blueprints setting standards and limits on the properties that states must have
to function in the modern world—as societies and in international society.

Any effort to characterize social relations relies on metaphors, no matter
how conceptually aware the effort is. Speaking metaphorically (and we
always do), every concept—every representation of some state of affairs no
matter how abstract—was born a metaphor. While I defend this claim later

---

Oliver Kessler, 'Toward a sociology of the international? International relations between
   anarchy and world society', *International Political Sociology* 3, 1 (2009), pp. 87–108 (105).

in this essay, it will be noticed that I have already placed great emphasis on a familiar metaphor, *blueprint*. In the first instance, a blueprint is a visual representation of the plan for a building or some other thought-out object of use. By metaphorical extension, a blueprint is any system of linked metaphors, or self-defining semantic field, representing what *we* (some metaphorically identified collectivity: we moderns) think we know about our social arrangements—how they are put together, and how they work, at any given moment. We revise small sections of these blueprints of ours frequently, not always deliberately, in response to practical concerns. Along the way, we even change the way we draw our blueprints—the way that we draw semantic distinctions to represent the particulars of our social arrangements.

This process *looks* continuous and its effects *look like* incremental social change. Nevertheless, when we stand back, we can *see* (a revealing metaphor) that social practices and their metaphorical representation are subject to abrupt changes, and that we can make sense of these changes only retrospectively. To indicate this, I have already used another familiar metaphor. Successive blueprints sit one upon the other in *layers*. All of these metaphors suggest a visual representation of the past and a spatial framing of our relation to it.

Switching to a temporal metaphor (again, one that I have already introduced), each layer constitutes a period in the history of the modern world. With this metaphor in mind, I have adopted and extended the periodization of modernity informing Michel Foucault's archaeology of knowledge.[2] The term *archaeology* refers to a familiar practice in the modern world—metaphorically speaking, the practice of digging up the past. Instead of digging up, sorting and reconstructing material objects, an 'archaeology of knowledge' exposes the assumptions underpinning what we think we know about the world.

Foucault's idealist construction of epochal change is barely related to changes in material culture (mode of production, technological advances), if at all, and he was notably unwilling to generalize about causes. My own position is also idealist, but with qualifications: epochal changes are observers' constructions, dependent on selective interpretation of the historical record of innumerable changes, many of them material. With this qualification in mind, I have built on Foucault's scheme in order to examine the co-constitution of states and international society, always within the expanding limits, epoch by epoch, of what we can know.

In my scheme, there are six periods (epochs, ages: all interchangeable metaphors). Modernity begins with the Renaissance (roughly 1500–1650). The classical age (1650–1800), the modern age (1800–1900), modernism

---

[2]   Michel Foucault, *The Order of Things: An Archeology of the Human Sciences*, trans. A. M. Sheridan Smith (New York: Random House, 1970); Foucault, *The Archeology of Knowledge*, trans. A. M. Sheridan Smith (New York: Pantheon Books, 1972).

(1900–1970) and late modernity (1970–) follow. Whether late modernity is a provisional name for a transition to a postmodern age is an open question, to which I turn very briefly in my conclusion. I have added two periods—modernism and late modernity—to Foucault's scheme. In my view, they are implied in Foucault's later, genealogical work, when he turned his attention to the state in its modern incarnation. Time and space prevent me from attending to each period as fully as I would like, all the more because the transitions between periods (which I take to be roughly 50-year intervals: 1625–75, 1775–1825, 1880–1930, 1950–2000, 1970–2020), will detain me more than they did Foucault, for whom discontinuities were sharper breaks, and layers more self-contained, than I see them to have been.[3]

The point of this essay is to provide an overview of successive blueprints, each schematically representing a single epoch, each inscribed on a copy of the one before, each rendering the contents of earlier blueprints less legible. The layers thus documented have permeable boundaries. Nevertheless they demarcate great changes in world-making and state-building. These changes are registered in the characteristic metaphors we put to use during each period. Inscribed as they are on successive blueprints, they continue to dominate our ever more complex understanding of the state as ongoing construction project.

Metaphors

For methodological purposes, Foucault conceptualized periods as *discursive fields*, imagined in layers, each embedding texts to be excavated. Texts are linguistic artefacts; they present the archaeologist with evidence of what the people who produced them thought about and, by extension, how their societies worked. Foucault did not call this evidence metaphorical, perhaps because he associated a reliance on metaphors and other figures of speech quite specifically with Renaissance texts. That I do requires me to develop the claim (here, briefly) that concepts are always, ultimately metaphorical.[4] If they are, then so is knowledge as Foucault understood the term.

As a concept, *metaphor* traces back to Aristotle, who held that metaphors are names of things applied or extended to other things. If even all metaphors are names (named concepts), he did not claim that all names are metaphors, perhaps because he believed metaphors serve a different, meta-representational function: as figures of speech, they are used for expressive effect. There is, however, nothing in Aristotle's work that would have prevented him, or prevents us, from saying that metaphors are indistinguishable from concepts by reference to what we, as speakers, want them to *do* for us—we seek

---

[3] Also see Nicholas Greenwood Onuf, *The Mightie Frame: Epochal Change and the Modern World* (New York: Oxford University Press, 2018), pp. 37–50.

[4] Also see Chapter 4 and work cited therein.

to make our assertions, as representations of states of affairs, persuasive to others whenever we speak. In this respect metaphors are indistinguishable from similes, which open up and thus expedite the process of metaphorical extension. Even when, as rarely happens, a brand new concept gets a brand new name, the effect is the same: the name circulates, loses any sense of freshness or novelty (by which time, it is 'merely' a concept), and lends itself to metaphorical extension. Any distinction between metaphors and so-called literal concepts ignores or forgets how concepts get to be as we think of them.

Recent decades have seen a renewed interest in metaphors and, in particular, in the metaphors reflecting our bodily experience in the world.[5] I suggest that we can sort this inexhaustible supply of metaphors into four kinds. One kind reflects the experience of having to orient ourselves in space and time. A second kind reflects an awareness of our bodies. A third kind reflects our awareness of other bodies metaphorically identifiable as human being like ourselves. A fourth kind of metaphor places our embodied selves in relation to other embodied beings. (In earlier work I treated the last two kinds as one by virtue of their obviously social character.)

All four kinds of metaphors appear in modern texts devoted to the state, but never randomly. From epoch to epoch, writers emphasize one kind or another and link them in distinctive ways. Humanism's triumph over Scholasticism is a familiar trope and an easy way to for us to make sense of the Renaissance as the epoch. For Mediaeval Christianity, the Resurrection, and thus Christ's *body*, was a controlling metaphor, rendered palpably true by sacrament. Shifting focus from heaven to earth, and from the afterlife to life itself, Renaissance humanists gave the body a new frame of reference. Conceptions of political society as a *person, body* or *family* are most clearly inscribed on modernity's early blueprints during the transition from the Renaissance to the classical age.[6] The metaphorical association of the state with bodies and persons still affects the way we

---

[5]   Andrew Ortony, ed., *Metaphor and Thought* (Cambridge: Cambridge University Press, 1979); 2nd edn (1993); George Lakoff and Mark Johnson, *Metaphors We Live By* (Chicago: University of Chicago Press, 1980); George Lakoff and Mark Johnson, *Philosophy in the Flesh: The Embodied Mind and Its Challenge to Western Thought* (New York: Basic Books, 1999); Raymond W. Gibbs, *Embodiment and Cognitive Science* (Cambridge: Cambridge University Press, 2005); Raymond W. Gibbs, Jr., ed., *The Cambridge Handbook of Metaphor and Thought* (Cambridge: Cambridge University Press, 2008).

[6]   In this essay, I give no further consideration to the family as a metaphor for political society in general and the state in particular, or to paternal authority as a metaphor for internal sovereignty. The emblematic figure for this way of thinking in the classical age is Robert Filmer, whose *Patriarcha* served John Locke as a foil in the first of his *Two Treatises of Government* (1689). Nor do I consider the relation of families to their homes and thus their 'homelands'.

think, most obviously by making states into agents—active members of a society—and not just places.

Students of international relations generally believe that territorial sovereignty is the master principle defining the state as such and directing the development of international society. This point of view relies on a potent metaphor of the orientational kind, namely that the state is a *container*. The importance of container metaphors for the way we order what we take to be the given or natural contents of the world—make categories, classify things—is inestimable; the metaphor suits most people's conception of concept.[7] While I do not deny the importance of territory in state-building and world-making, I will try to show that it is a late product of Foucault's classical age and only becomes dominant in the modern age.

At the same time, container metaphors combine with body metaphors to form a metaphor of the fourth kind—an ensemble of bodies. International society and the states making it up have the metaphorical properties of a club of clubs, all of which have severely restricted membership criteria. The term *member* is itself revealing: *membrum* means limb or body part in Latin. Even if *club* is less familiar in this context than the other metaphors I have drawn attention to, it is so familiar in other contexts as to be latent in the way we think about states as separate members of a durable ensemble.

A different metaphorical complex marks the modernist period. Thinking of the state as a *building*, or functionally linked suite of containers, is a modernist innovation that continues to make sense to us. Late modern talk about the state has superimposed the metaphor of *network* on a blueprint where earlier metaphorical associations are still potent. This metaphor would seem to move bodies from rigid containers, such as the state, to more supple social arrangements with more flexible membership criteria.

Postmodern writers seek to strip the state of its multiple, imbricated metaphorical associations. To discredit these metaphors is to dispatch the state itself. Whether this is a plausible programme is another question. It can be conclusively answered only when, or if, the metaphorical conjunction of *post* and *modern* clearly identifies an epochal transformation in constitutive premises and processes.

Bodies and persons

Foucault's archaeology leaves open the possibility that what we know is constituted by the metaphors we use. I presume just this: all knowledge is an arrangement of metaphors. With Foucault, I hold that what we can know is subject to limits at any given moment, and that it is subject to abrupt

---

[7] Lakoff and Johnson, *Metaphors We Live By*, pp. 19–20.

shifts discernible in a succession of ages. According to Foucault, a culture's epistemic spaces are stable for long intervals; sudden shifts in the conditions of possibility for systematic thought have wrenching consequences for concepts, values and materially manifest practices, all of which are inscribed on what I am calling that culture's blueprint.

The Renaissance *episteme* starts with what the senses say about the world. Treating things that seem to be alike as indeed alike is the epistemic key, and one that favours an express reliance on metaphors to represent things and their relations. Knowledge is the accumulation of similarities, and the dissemination of knowledge depends on extension by analogy and affirmation by repetition. The *episteme* is its blueprint, and vice versa. With this blueprint, Renaissance humanists could see themselves in relation to the ancients, find an alternative to cyclical or apocalyptic interpretations of the past, and undermine the temporal unity and moral authority of mediaeval universalism.[8]

The classical age shifts attention from similarities to differences on the assumption that each thing possesses a fundamental nature uniquely its own. Because things are fundamentally different does not mean that they differ in every ascertainable property. For this reason, they can be sorted by the kinds of properties they have in common with some other things. Nature has an order that we cannot perceive directly but nevertheless can make sense of by ordering things. Order is itself to be understood in spatial terms, manifest, however schematically, in grids, tables and, needless to say, blueprints.

In a stern lecture, early in *Leviathan* (1651), Thomas Hobbes railed against 'the use of Metaphors, Tropes, and other rhetoricall figures, in stead of words proper'. Such absurdities stem from not beginning with definitions—'the Explications of names'—'which is a method that hath been used onely in Geometry, whose Conclusions have thereby been made indisputable'.[9] Adopting the geometric method, if only metaphorically, Hobbes firmly declared himself a classical thinker, not subject to the rhetorical excesses of his Renaissance predecessors.[10]

Nevertheless, Hobbes metaphorically applied the term *body* to immaterial aggregates of living bodies, as if such a body had material properties of its own. First defining 'SYSTEMES' in expressly metaphorical terms (they 'resemble the similar parts, or Muscles of a body naturall'), Hobbes held that

---

8 Constantin Fasolt, *The Limits of History* (Chicago: University of Chicago Press, 2004), pp. 16–22.
9 Thomas Hobbes, *Leviathan*, ed. Richard Tuck (Cambridge: Cambridge University Press, 1991), p. 34.
10 But see Quentin Skinner, *Reason and Rhetoric in the Philosophy of Hobbes* (Cambridge: Cambridge University Press, 1996), on Hobbes's eventual return to his humanist roots.

those bodies that people create by contract are either private or political—the latter 'otherwise Called *Bodies Politique*, and *Persons in Law*'. That bodies have heads (recall *Leviathan*'s famous Frontispiece) undoubtedly gives rise to the enduring metaphorical association of bodies with specifically political properties, such as sovereignty and representation. 'In Bodies Politique', Hobbes wrote, 'the power of the Representative is alwaies Limited: and that which prescribeth the Limits thereof, is the Power Soveraign'.[11]

It may seem surprising that a text as rigorously classical as *Leviathan* should so emphatically endorse primary metaphors centred on bodies. Hobbes's rhetorical strategy makes sense, however, in the context of his notoriously grim characterization of the state of nature, in which our bodies make us equally vulnerable to each other's best efforts to protect ourselves from each other. Hobbes's claim of equality applies to 'Naturall Persons', who proceed to constitute themselves, by contract, into an 'artificiall Person'.[12] Thus constituted, artificial persons are, at least for Hobbes *sui generis*—hardly equal in size, there is no reason to think them equal in kind.

Hobbes wrote at a time when natural law provided a template for nature's order. The great transitional figure to this time was Hugo Grotius. Never an advocate of natural equality of human beings, Grotius' enduring contribution—*De jure belli ac pacis* (1625)—was to make moral persons the proper subjects of natural law.[13] Following upon Hobbes, Samuel Pufendorf adopted the Grotian conception of moral persons in his great, systematizing treatise, *De jure naturæ et gentium* (1672): 'it follows as command of the law of nature, that every man should esteem and treat another as one who is naturally his equal ... '. Natural persons will come together as 'compound moral persons', but when they do so, they remain equal, as in nature, and obliged to esteem others.[14]

By implication, equality confers rights on all persons, natural and moral, as needed for them to play their part in nature's order. At the same time, equality imposes corresponding duties on all persons allowing them to exercise their rights. It would seem that Pufendorf was the first to draw this implication, which, of course, we take for granted today.[15] Pufendorf did not expressly argue that *all* persons are equal—natural persons would seem to be different in kind from compound persons, since the latter are, as

---

[11] Hobbes, *Leviathan*, p. 155, emphasis in original.

[12] Ibid., pp. 111–15.

[13] Hugo Grotius, *The Rights of War and Peace*, ed. Richard Tuck from Jean Barbeyrac's 1738 edn, trans. John Morrice (Indianapolis: Liberty Fund, 2005), 1, p. 138.

[14] Samuel Pufendorf, *Of the Law of Nature and Nations*, 4th edn, trans. Basil Kennett (Clark, NJ: Law Book Exchange, 2005), pp. 224, 7.

[15] Nicholas Onuf and Peter Onuf, *Nations, Markets and War: Modern History and the American Civil War* (Charlottesville: University of Virginia Press, 2006), pp. 69–74.

Hobbes emphasized, artificial. Yet Pufendorf's great treatise systematically discriminates between natural persons and nations, as its title, *De jure naturæ et gentium*, indicates. *Gentes*, or nations, are those compound persons that Hobbes called political bodies. As such, they constitute a distinctive *kind* of person for the reason that no one elsewhere has authority over them. Today we unhesitatingly say they are sovereign equals.

Sovereignty

Most discussions of sovereignty begin with Jean Bodin, Grotius and Hobbes, all of them important figures in the transition from the Renaissance to the classical age. Typically these discussions assume that sovereignty can only be understood as territorial. Were this not so, the familiar claim that sovereignty is indivisible would be difficult to sustain.[16] In my view, these writers never made any such assumption.

Consider this passage from Grotius' *Jus belli ac pacis*: 'Jurisdiction is commonly exercised on two Subjects, the one primary, *viz*. Persons, and that alone is sometimes sufficient, as in an Army of Men, Women, and Children, that are going in quest of some new Plantations; the other secundary, *viz*. the Place, which is called *Territory*.'[17] Sovereignty confers jurisdiction over natural persons in the first instance and then on places, which rather incidentally Grotius referred to as territory. Not only does this textual snippet reverse the now standard practice of giving priority to territorial jurisdiction, it suggests nothing at all about the sovereign, who is, as Grotius made abundantly clear, a moral person with the authority to exercise jurisdiction on behalf of 'a compleat Body of free Persons'—a *civitas*, and not a state, as most translations would have it (including the one I am using here), and a *body*, not a place.

Reading Grotius as an exponent of territorial sovereignty is anachronistic. There is, however, a different kind of text—the conjoined treaties of Münster and Onasbrück, adopted in 1648—which, we hear today, decisively linked sovereignty and territory and launched the so-called Westphalian system of international relations.[18] Detailed provisions itemize specific places. For example, § 73 of the Treaty of Münster names cities and villages that the Austrian Emperor was obliged to surrender to the French King. Most scholars

---

[16] See, for example, Jens Bartelson, 'On the indivisibility of sovereignty', *Republics of Letters: A Journal for the Study of Knowledge, Politics, and the Arts* 2, 2 (2011), available at: {https://arcade.stanford.edu/sites/default/files/article_pdfs/roflv02i02_Bartelson_060111_0.pdf} accessed 11 February 2022.

[17] Grotius, *Rights of War and Peace*, 2, p. 457, emphasis in translation.

[18] The two treaties are available in their original Latin and various translations from *Acta Pacis Westphalicae*, available at: {www.pax-westphalica.de/ipmipo/index.html} accessed 11 February 2022.

today hold that any such treaty text transfers sovereignty over the places named therein because the principle of sovereignty entails a clear notion of territorial integrity—places, for the most part adjacent, taken together as a whole. By referring to 'Vassals, Subjects, People, Towns, Boroughs, Castles, Houses, Fortresses, Woods, Coppices, Gold or Silver Mines, Minerals, Rivers, Brooks, Pastures', § 74 makes it clear that the places in question are features of a populated landscape and not abstractly conceived territories.

The treaties were written in Latin, a language in which there is no direct equivalent to the French term *souveraineté* or its English transliteration. Scattered in the Latin text of the two treaties are various forms of the terms *summa, superus, supremus*, all of which are orientational metaphors indicating status relations among kings and emperors, lords, vassals and subjects. On one occasion, the standard translation of the text offers a list of people and places similar to the one we saw in § 74, ending with the words 'and all other things belonging to the Sovereign Right of Territory' (§ 85, Treaty of Münster). The Latin text reads 'caeterisque omnibus et singulis ad sublime territorii ius', again suggesting that categories of people and places occupy vertically oriented status relations.

As quoted, the Latin text does not support the conclusion that territory is by itself a rightful or lawful whole. More generally, there is no persuasive evidence that the parties to the Westphalian settlement intended to reconceptualize authority as exclusive control over territory, much less launch a new European order based on any such idea. Nor is there persuasive evidence that anyone writing about sovereignty at the dawn of the classical age fully grasped the relation between state and territory that we now take for granted. As we would say today, they had worked out a conception of internal sovereignty, one that drew its power from the twinned metaphors of political society as a body of people, and its ruler as a moral person with jurisdictional powers over people and places.

Retrospectively, we can easily see that internal sovereignty in a world of sovereigns implies that all such sovereigns are equal. Writers in the classical age came to this conclusion only gradually, and only as status distinctions among rulers receded in importance. In 1758, Emer de Vattel could say: 'Nations being composed of men naturally free and independent, and who, before the establishment of civil societies, lived together in the state of nature,—nations or sovereign states are to be considered as so many free persons living together in the state of nature.'[19] And do so with no direct

---

[19] [Emer] de Vattel, *The Law of Nations, Or, Principles of the Law of Nature, Applied to the Conduct and Affairs of Nations and Sovereigns, with Three Early Essays on the Origin and Nature of Natural Law and on Luxury*, trans. Thomas Nugent (Indianapolis: Liberty Fund, 2008), p. 68.

reference to territory. His conception of external sovereignty does not presuppose a boundary between inside and outside or make the state into a container.

Vattel honoured the discursive heritage of Grotius, Hobbes and Pufendorf by calling states 'free persons'. States individually have legal personality, and collectively they are bound together by their rights and duties. Decades later, in the transition to the modern age, G. W. F. Hegel clearly distinguished between the internal and external aspects of sovereignty. Yet he too did so with no direct reference to territory. Indicatively, the state is 'an embodiment of spirit'—the body as primary metaphor now disembodied.[20]

Containers

We are left with a puzzle. In the classical age, writers were preoccupied with spatial order, classificatory systems and geometric representations of complex relations. We saw the 'construction of the globe itself as a geometrical object', but *not*, as Jens Bartelson has claimed, 'its division into distinct territorial portions'.[21] An archaeologist of the period cannot fail to notice the dominance of orientational metaphors. Prodigiously comprehensive texts contain an arrangement of containers, defended not as an author's contrivance but as nature's writ. Yet two centuries of writing about what we now call the state show a remarkable consistency in the deployment of the body as a metaphor, and a corresponding reticence about territory as a metaphorical container.

Classical discussions of sovereignty do make use of orientational metaphors. Vertical metaphors inform representations of internal sovereignty. While external sovereignty has no name, the principle of natural equality implies a horizontal orientation that we never see metaphorically developed. The state is a container only insofar as any body must be contained in order to maintain its internal coherence. States have people, land and laws, which together could have been homogenized or abstracted (different metaphors to the same effect) as territorial sovereignty. They were not—not consistently, and certainly not with the affective and normative resonance that we take for granted today.

The classical age created epistemic conditions under which people could think of sovereignty as territorial and therefore indivisible, or the state

---

[20] G. W. F. Hegel, *Elements of the Philosophy of Right* (1821), trans. H. B. Nisbet (Cambridge: Cambridge University Press, 1991), pp. 315, 359.

[21] Jens Bartelson, 'The social construction of globality', *International Political Sociology* 4, 3 (2010), pp. 219–25 (220).

as a container.[22] Indeed, the classical *episteme* made modern cartography possible; its 'geometric foundation ... implicitly encourages the use of lines and homogenous areas to differentiate space'. Yet sovereigns—'crowned heads'—did not make maps showing their realms as bounded, homogeneous territories until the Vienna settlement in 1815 compelled them to do so.[23] Of course, 18th-century sovereigns understood that status depended on the 'size' of their realms, acted strategically to absorb neighbours and prevent other sovereigns from doing so, and took advantage of the movement of resources from colonial possessions and across frontiers to increase their wealth. Retrospectively we take the preoccupation with size, power, conquest, marriage, taxes and tariffs as evidence that sovereigns could visualize their realms as clearly demarcated, bounded territories over which they exercised control. They did not—size meant many things (people, land, dynastic connections, fungible resources, perhaps even competence in the conduct of public affairs)—and not just because they had no need to. Without maps, they could not.

The modern age opened up new possibilities. Systematic map-making and related activities, such as taking censuses, require professionally staffed governments to mobilize and distribute resources for the express purpose of exercising continuous, effective control over resources. We associate this feature of the modern *episteme* with Max Weber, for whom rationalization was the key to the state's rapid rise to dominance. This development belatedly substantiates the classical emphasis on space and recourse to orientational metaphors: rationalized relations of super- and subordination depend on and fill up horizontally contained spaces. Territory displaces the realm, contains political society and grants moral personality a fixed jurisdictional field in which to operate.

How this development fits with Foucault's scheme is not obvious. In part this is because Foucault's account of the modern *episteme* is difficult to understand, in part because Foucault only told half the story. On his account, history replaces order as 'the fundamental mode of being of empiricities'. History is not simply 'the compilation of factual successions or sequences'; it *'gives place* to analogical organic structures, just as Order opened the way to *successive* identities and differences'. The modern *episteme* took metaphor out of the Renaissance world of appearances and deployed it in time. By invoking

---

[22] Readers may notice that I have ignored federation as a state-form in this essay. Suffice it to say here that the 'spatial logic' of federalism is eminently classical—containers are ordered in ascending levels. Nicholas Greenwood Onuf, *The Republican Legacy in International Thought* (Cambridge: Cambridge University Press, 1998), pp. 55–7. As an 18th-century development, federalism in practice has not fared well in the modern age.

[23] Jordan Branch, 'Mapping the sovereign state: Technology, authority, and systemic change', *International Organization* 65, 1 (2011), pp. 1–36 (20, 18).

INTERNATIONAL THEORY AT THE MARGINS

development, evolution and dialectical reasoning, modern thinkers could bring together 'totalities of elements without the slightest visible identity'.[24]

Weberian rationalization does not replace order so much as it takes 'the fundamental mode of being of empiricities' to precede order. The same may be said of history. Modern empiricities are stand-alone *things*, positivities—facts subject to isolation, verification, measurement, manipulation—in order to see how those things might be related. This is, of course, positivism, which mandates procedures (the scientific method) for disallowing consideration of most things on any given occasion.

Rationalization and utilitarian thinking inevitably follow from this way of thinking. Like positivist scientists, modern historians start with empiricities and concern themselves with questions of veracity, magnitude and relatedness. They differ from positivists because they organize those empiricities into 'analogical organic structures' (Foucault generalized from what he saw in modern biology to history). When historians do this, they are historicists, and this practice allows them to tell stories selectively based on a superabundance of ascertainable facts.

The one organic structure that modern historians have devoted themselves to most completely is the *nation*. As we hear so often, nations are imagined; they are a Foucauldian 'totality of elements' upon which identity has been imposed. Beginning with the term itself, the importance of body metaphors in the way we talk about the nation is well documented.[25] Insofar as the nation is a body in the first instance—a body of people loosely held together by common origin or shared traits—then the nation requires a container, which the state supplies. In turn, the nation supplies the state with the resources required for its rational administration. State and nation are co-constitutive, but only insofar as a demarcated, homogenized territory coincides with a specifically homogenized people. Matching state and nation is one of the great projects of the modern age. Notwithstanding the resources devoted to it, this project has succeeded only some of the time, and only then at great cost.

Clubs

The spatial orientation of the classical age made it conceivable to talk about political societies as if they were containers. The practical realization of this epistemic possibility only took place during the transition to the modern age, which in turn gave the state-as-container indispensable epistemic support. The spatial ordering of the classical age also brought forth the grand idea that

---

[24] Foucault, *The Order of Things*, pp. 219, 216, 265, emphases in translation.
[25] See, for example, Onuf and Onuf, *Nations, Markets and War*, ch. 5.

204

people are equals, imagined as such on the same level. Pufendorf's picture of human society implies two levels: the level in which people constitute themselves in political societies and the level in which these societies, as sovereign states, constitute themselves as a system or society.

Contemporary students of international relations routinely invoke the same two levels, second (international society) analogous to the first (domestic society), itself conceptualized as the liberal alternative to Hobbes's Leviathan. In my view, the causal dynamics run the other way.[26] First came a 'natural society' of rights-bearing nations (not to be confused with those modern nations I introduced in the previous section). Nations came to acknowledge their 'natural equality' and clarify their rights and duties only gradually. Over the better part of two centuries, natural law treatises documented, validated and expedited this process. If nations are naturally equal as sovereigns and routinely relate to each other by reference to their rights and duties, then by analogy natural persons are equal in their moral autonomy and should be able to relate to each other by reference to established rights and duties. In Britain's North American provinces and in France, violent assertions of popular sovereignty punctuated this more localized process, while in Britain, reformers eventually achieved similar results, often by reasserting historic rights. As a few political societies variously reconciled republican and liberal premises in the process of modernizing, the small, 'natural' society of nations—assured of their sovereign equality, now more often referred to as states—added members to the club.

In the English language, the metaphor of a social club, as a tightly bound group of people who are therefore like a physical club or weapon, goes back to the classical age. Clubs are defined as such by exclusionary membership rules. All members are equal; new members must be invited to join. Of course, clubs typically have many additional rules assigning status and offices to members, not to mention rules applicable both to relations of club members and to relations of the club and its members to the 'outside world'. Clubs routinely overlap each other in membership.

Clubs always have rules or procedures to select, screen and admit new members. When no officers have this duty, admission may result from a decentralized process in which some member (or members) treat some other person as a member of the club, thus making that person a member, but only in relation to the member so acting. In effect the member offering this invitation and the would-be member accepting it become a club whose membership of two persons overlaps the membership of the other club. If no one else in the first club joins the new club, it is likely to atrophy and

---

[26] Ibid., pp. 40–2; Nicholas Onuf, 'Recognition and the constitution of epochal change', *International Relations* 27, 2 (2013), pp. 121–40 (130–5).

disappear. If, instead, other members of the first club follow suit, then the two clubs will gradually merge into one. Indeed, we could say that the second club will swallow the first, but we are more likely to say that the first club has expanded its membership through successive acts of mutual recognition. In the instance of international society, formal rules for what we have come to call the recognition of states emerged in the transition to the modern epoch.

International society is a small club. Some members were club founders, though hardly in any formal way. Others underwent the process of progressive mutual recognition that I just described. Most recently, admission to membership in international organizations has augmented and gradually replaced pair-wise recognition. Only by virtue of being admitted to the club are states sovereign and therefore exclusive membership clubs in their own right. As such, states have developed ever more precise and restrictive membership rules of their own. Only because states as clubs constitute themselves as a club does international society exist in the enduring, familiar form that we now see it as having on our blueprints for state-building and world-making as co-constitutive processes. As I have said elsewhere, membership rules stitch states as societies and states in their own society tightly together as a constitutive whole.[27]

Buildings

The modern *episteme* developed a discontinuity in the last decades of the 19th century, one that deepened even after the century's turn. Not only did Foucault overlook this transformation (however much it is implied in his later work on governmentality), so too did Weber, whose account of modernity's development centres on our changing relation to the world or, more precisely, on our conscious awareness of our capacity to change the world by rationalizing its contents. And so did members of the Frankfurt School, itself a modernist development, in developing a critical stance towards modernity and its rationalizing tendencies.[28] Postmodernists are a conspicuous if ambiguous exception to the general tendency. In the very effort to replace modernism with something equally transformative, postmodernists have paid attention to what makes modernism an epistemic departure. Regrettably, even they too often use the terms *modern* and *modernist*, *modernity* and *modernism*, interchangeably. There is no great surprise in this: we all speak of modern art when obviously we are referring to work that exemplifies the modernist discontinuity in the way we represent the world.

---

[27] Onuf, 'Recognition and constitution'.
[28] Also see Chapter 6.

To simplify, perhaps unduly, modernism is a revolution in representation, a reaction against realism (here a synonym for accuracy) as the self-evident goal of representation.[29] Modern rationalization and positivism take realistic representation of the things of the world, by whatever medium, as a necessary ancillary to the discovery and manipulation of those things. Logical consistency, precise measurement and instrumental values follow in train. The modernist response to the requirements of realism arose first, or was at least first noticed, in literature and the arts, where representation was an end in itself and not just an instrument for storing and retrieving what we think we know about the world. In literature as in art and music, new ways of using words, actors on stage, pen, paint and chisel in hand, cameras, tonal registers and cultural artefacts took representation beneath the familiar surfaces of things, disrupted the conventional arrangement of those things, and reversed the relation between subject and object.

Modernism also spawned a new generation of human sciences: political science, sociology, psychology and anthropology. Sociologists came to call this process functional differentiation, which they observed everywhere in modern societies as a response to the scale and complexity of social activity.[30] Modernism is not simply about function. Nor is it simply about representation (a feature of modernity that Foucault assigned to the classical *episteme*). Following Émile Durkheim, the 'high modernist' of social theory, it asks us to represent function first (including the function of representation), and then relate functions to techniques on the one hand, and social arrangements on the other.

In my opinion, functional differentiation is boldly inscribed on the modernist blueprint for the state. Yet modernist texts in political and social theory leave a different impression. The simple explanation for this odd omission is not an indifference to functional differentiation, but a declared wish to stop talking about the state. Instead modernist political scientists and sociologists talked about political systems, always by reference to their structures, functions and processes—obviously, a highly abstracted set of metaphors. I see in this move a wholesale rejection of the body, person, container and club metaphors so integral to the centuries-long process of

---

[29] And see Chapter 4 for a fuller discussion.

[30] Some sociologists hold that functional differentiation is a mark of the modern age, while I see this process to have accelerated markedly with modernism. See, for example, Niklas Luhmann, *Theories of Distinction: Redescribing the Descriptions of Modernity* (Stanford: Stanford University Press, 2002), p. 111, emphasis in original: 'The breakdown of what we may call (following Otto Brunner) *old-European semantics* became inevitable when society changed its primary form of differentiation, when it shifted from the very elaborate order of hierarchical stratification, conceived of as "the order", to the primacy of functional differentiation.'

turning diverse political societies into those formally equal, functionally similar units that we now call states. This move was bound to fail.

Indeed it had already failed when systems were granted boundaries and subsystems were stipulated; systems are containers, and containers occupy levels. Soon enough we were exhorted to 'bring the state back in'. Rising to the occasion, institutionalists—some positivist and some historicist—tacitly granted functional differentiation its importance by conceptualizing the state as an institution composed of functionally related institutions. Inevitably, some states were identified as strong, others weak, and talk turned to building and strengthening the state.

More or less at the same time that systems metaphors prevailed among political scientists, international theorists espoused their own distinctive version of functionalism. Its origins reveal an affiliation with modernism in turn-of-the-century arts and letters.[31] The internationalist version of functionalism predicted that state agents would gladly surrender technical tasks to experts in international organizations. In the process, they would unknowingly divide sovereignty bit by bit until it would eventually be wholly gone. This theory developed only after governments created functionally delimited international institutions at the very beginning of the modernist age. This they did to accommodate the technical needs of advanced industrial societies (for example by standardizing weights and measures).

Even if functionalist theory duly contributed to the emergence of so-called supranational institutions in Europe after World War II, it failed utterly as theory. States did not dismantle themselves in the process of assigning technical tasks to international institutions. They were engaged in a much larger process of functionally differentiating themselves from within (as containers) and then institutionalizing functionally differentiated tasks in massive bureaucracies. State-building prompted institution-building among states as club members, and these institutions strengthened states, not weakened them.

Modernist architecture has left a lasting visual imprint on the modern world. Modernist office buildings house the functionally differentiated bureaucracies that no large organization—states, international institutions, corporations, even universities—can do without. City planners are modernists. Modernist architecture has even inspired governments to build brand new capital cities, such as Brasilia, to expedite the 'modernization' of the state. Rationalization and functional differentiation are necessary

---

[31] See, for example, L. S. Woolf, *International Government: Two Reports* (New York: Brentano's, 1916), 2nd report.

complements in this process, which can reinforce authoritarian tendencies in the effort to catch up with modernity.[32]

In practice, modernist architecture and city planning have spawned a metaphorical vocabulary we now take for granted. *Blueprint* is an indicative modernist metaphor. Once Marxists talked about superstructure; now we all talk about infrastructure. We visualize states as buildings, and we conceptualize state-building as an activity that depends on a large number of people with diverse technical skills collaborating on carefully laid-out plans that are nevertheless subject to adjustment as new problems and challenges arise. International institutions provide states with technical assistance, mostly by obtaining the services of technicians from other places. Consultants flourish, offering technical advice not just to governments, but to any institution willing to pay for it. There is much discussion of institutional design. Lawyers are everywhere, drafting metaphorical blueprints for metaphorical buildings.

Networks

The epistemic discontinuity that I have identified with modernism has been with us for at least a century, the modern age for two centuries. Each *episteme* opened new possibilities in the way we can talk about the world without foreclosing the space that earlier *epistemes* had opened our minds to. Much of what I have said would suggest that the continuing effects of the modern age and modernism on the way we talk about the state (and everything else) means that these two ages have not ended. Yet when I introduced my scheme for periodizing modernity, I dated the end of these two ages at 1900 and 1970 respectively. If this seems like a contradiction, then appearances are deceiving.

Epistemes do not successively displace their predecessors (as Foucault seems to have thought) but overlay each other (or so I have claimed). Each layer becomes progressively less legible as new layers are added. Each age has an extended afterglow, as we saw with the state as a container. The modern age is still easy to read but no longer strictly on its own terms. Everything we say about rationalization, for example, takes modernist differentiation for granted. The continuing, often complementary effects of rationalization and differentiation are so extensive in today's world that they may cast doubt on my claim that we are witnessing another epistemic break, the transition to which began around 1970, with another age ensuing, which I am not alone in calling late modernity.

---

[32] James C. Scott, *Seeing Like a State: How Certain Schemes to Improve the Human Condition Have Failed* (New Haven: Yale University Press, 1998), pp. 87–146.

The epistemic possibilities of a new age are difficult to recognize close at hand. Transitions are murky affairs. It should be no surprise that I am less confident that we are in the process of entering a new age than I am about the properties of the age preceding. Most observers who think they see an epistemic discontinuity in the making offer globalization as evidence. Often enough, these observers tell us that deterritorialization accompanies globalization—as consumerist culture, productive processes and financial markets globalize, sovereignty *erodes* (a frequent and evocative metaphor) and the modern state ceases to matter as a territorial configuration. I see in globalization something altogether different: striking evidence of functional differentiation wherever people are exposed to the complexities of modernity. This is evidence that modernism still defines the way we moderns talk about our world. It is a place, now global in scale, where functional differentiation within states has, on balance, increased the state's capacity to respond effectively to the *forces* (another evocative metaphor) that globalization has unleashed.

If, however, we look at the technical correlates of globalization, all of which I take to be integral to the modernist constitution of modernity, it is possible (a late modern possibility) to glean some evidence that we have indeed entered a transitional moment. The technology in question is overwhelmingly directed to the manipulation of and distribution of information; this is 'the information age'.[33] Thanks to late modern technology, we code, store and distribute information, which, by being limitless, weightless and infinitely divisible, does not resemble at all those things that positivists seek to manipulate—take apart and rearrange—with such difficulty and at such great cost. To describe the social implications of our ever easier access to information, Manuel Castells has used a metaphor— *network*—that is everywhere in use because we *see* networks everywhere. Marking late modernity is 'the rise of the network society'—one expansive society, and as many societies as there are networks.

Networks depend on flows of information. So-called traditional societies depend on dense networks loaded with locally available information, much of it created and distributed in face-to-face interactions. Yet even these societies have many networks, which, by definition occupy parallel planes in a fixed space: 'A network is a set of interconnected nodes. A node is the point at which a curve intersects itself.'[34] Because an intersecting set of

---

[33] Here I rely on Manuel Castells's *The Information Age*, 1, *The Rise of the Network Society*, 2nd edn (Oxford: Blackwell, 2000); also see Chapter 2 on the 'electronic revolution', and Nicholas Greenwood Onuf, *Making Sense, Making Worlds: Constructivism in Social Theory and International Relations* (Abingdon: Routledge, 2013), ch. 12.

[34] Castells, *The Rise of the Network Society*, p. 501.

curves must be located on the same plane, a curve that does not can only be located on a parallel plane (if the planes were not parallel, then they would themselves intersect).

Mapping any one network requires the identification of nodes on that plane and then the connecting lines of information flow. Each map resembles an elementary blueprint. Network maps lay one upon the other; layered networks stratify social space. More concretely (as Castells would have it), the nodes in a social network are agents, whether individual human beings or institutions formed by individual human beings. Each agent in a social network has a status by virtue of participating in that network. Participate in multiple networks, agents acquire a multiplicity of statuses.

Where do states fit in late modern network society? As clubs, states are contained network societies. Yet information is, as we learn daily, harder and harder to contain. Modern states exercise control over land, people, laws and a great variety of resources. Information was once one of those resources a state could hope to control, always at great cost. With the rise of the network society, information leaks, like any gas, from every container that is not perfectly tight. Wherever leaking information ends up defines the always provisional limits of the network society.

The stratification of networks also has implications for the state and its future. States will also experience a proliferation of status-defined networks that inexpensive machinery make readily available to almost everyone almost anywhere. In many of these networks, participants will adopt exclusionary criteria as a means of defining and protecting the status participation affords them, and they will secure resources to institutionalize their activities. In short, these networks will become clubs, in the process stratifying social space within states and beyond them.

With information come networks, with networks come clubs, with clubs comes stratification. Over the last two centuries, most modernizers thought that the whole point of modernity was to eradicate the suffocating old regime of privilege accorded by status, and to replace the old regime with a regime of responsible office-holders and rights-bearing individuals. Only the state, as legal person and container, could ensure that such a new regime could be instituted; modernizing the state itself was therefore always the first task. Late modernity now casts doubt on the state's capacity to protect the metaphorically rich legacy of epochal social change.

After modernity

Information floods the late modern world, perhaps to the point that we can no longer find and use the information we need to carry on in the world. If indeed a self-organized world of information effectively takes over our cognitive capacities and leaves us with no more than the trappings of agency, then we may have entered a time of epochal transition. Given the conditions of possibility granted us by successive *epistemes*, we cannot know until we have reached the other side of the transition. Insofar as modernist thought and the social sciences reaffirm 'the strange figure of knowledge called man', they remain within the confines of the modern *episteme*.[35] In my reconstruction, modernist thought and the social sciences add new blueprints to the growing pile of blueprints that tell us how modernity came to be the layered epistemic whole that it is. Inscribed on those blueprints is an ever stranger 'figure of knowledge' whom we call ourselves.

Clearly, then, the 'disappearance of man' would mark the appearance of an entirely new postmodern *episteme*.[36] That strange figure cannot be dissociated from five centuries of institutional support, of which none has been more central than the state. If the figure of man were to disappear, so would all of those many superimposed blueprints on which we constantly rely, in the first instance to tell ourselves who we are. And so would the state in all of its metaphorical richness. Successive *epistemes* have made it possible for states to be what they have become, or are capable of becoming, just as they make us what we are. Without a new set of postmodern blueprints, we cannot even begin to imagine what our figurative successors will have created for themselves.

---

[35] Foucault, *The Order of Things*, p. xxiv.
[36] Ibid., p. 386.

12

What We Do (2018)

In 1959, C. P. Snow announced that 'the whole of intellectual life in Western society is increasingly being split into two polar groups'. The members of the two groups have drifted so far apart that they can no longer understand each other. The context for Snow's lament was his own career as chemist, novelist, Cambridge Fellow and public servant; his targets were the 'literary intellectuals' and 'physical scientists' of his acquaintance. Snow generalized. Each group constitutes a culture unto itself—the cultures of art and science.[1]

Leading intellectuals in Snow's time overwhelmingly agreed that science and art are rival cultures. The two groups, so labelled, are centred in the arts and sciences in a few grand universities, the two cultures spreading out to the higher reaches of modern society. Snow neglected to point out that large universities and many specialized institutions of higher education devote a great deal of attention to the practical arts and applied science—law, medicine, pastoral service, business management, advertising, public administration, engineering, training in warfare. While he might have argued that these vocational activities are also subject to a cultural split, he simply ignored this possibility. In short, the art–science binary discounts a great deal of what goes on in 'the whole of intellectual life', and does so in a way that reeks of elitism and snobbery.

The field of International Relations offers a conspicuous instance of the cultural phenomenon to which Snow gave a name. The so-called great debate taking place in the 1960s effectively pitted art against science in terms that recall Snow's thesis and all its resonances.[2] Theory stands in for high culture, practice is shown off the stage. Would-be scholars (like me) immediately understood the status implications of choosing theory over practice, and science over art. No one talked about art, science or scholarship in any form

---

[1]   C. P. Snow, *The Two Cultures* (Cambridge: Cambridge University Press, 1993), pp. 3–4, 16.
[2]   Klaus Knorr and James N. Rosenau, eds, *Contending Approaches to International Politics* (Princeton: Princeton University Press, 1969).

as craft, or gave much attention to craft in any vocational practice—then or since.

Granting the term *culture* such affective and normative resonances is only possible because it has been emptied of content. When we do talk about culture, we make it residual, ephemeral, unaccountable, as such rarely applied to ourselves as scholars and to the field. Craft is more specific. It is skill in making, building, using, maintaining, adjusting, taking apart; it is about work, purpose, standards, tools. We talk about what we do, but only informally, or narrowly by reference to research methods. Such talk is never theoretically motivated or philosophically informed.

Craft, not culture, is the key to what we do as scholars. This essay offers a brief history of International Relations as a field of study so caught up in the art–science binary that we have lost sight of craft—not just our own, but the craft of those whose activities we study in the name of international relations. It then seeks to provide a philosophically informed account of craft in human relations on the belief that we cannot otherwise justify what we do as craftsmen and women. After assessing some of the social consequences of taking craft seriously, the essay concludes with a brief discussion of ethical and political implications.

History

The term *craft* has recently become fashionable in (if I may say) popular culture. The large reasons are obvious. In a time of mass-produced goods notable for their shoddy construction and short lives, people look for goods that are made by hand with care and pride, goods that are distinctive as well as durable, goods that are harder to find and cost more. Here again, the art–science binary asserts itself: science has helped to produce a mass culture of conformity and mediocrity; art and patronage of the arts save for some few of us the appearance of individuality, earned privilege and good taste. All such talk of craft is not about craft as such, but, yet again, about culture—in this case, contemporary popular culture, vacuously conceived and bathed in nostalgia.

There is a related fashion for talk about the professions. We hear that there are 'professional grade' cooktops, Christmas lights and 'cross-over vehicles'; we are led to believe that only professionals can make such mass-produced goods reliable, distinctive and desirable. Whether this is an elevation of the crafts and trades to a status previously denied them or a lowering of standards is an ideological question perhaps suited to the so-called cultural wars. It tells us nothing about what people do and how they become skilled in what they do. The professions are defined by certification. One must be certified in having acquired the requisite skills under the watchful eye of those who are already certified as possessing those skills.

The 'high professions'—law, theology and, with qualifications, medicine—have always been associated with 'higher education' as instruction in highly skilled practices. The grand universities had their origin as the site in which these skills were taught, and university training remains the *sine qua non* of certification in the high professions. That the line between the high professions and the other, lesser professions has progressively blurred as universities have broadened the range of their certifiable instructional activities underscores my critique of Snow's thesis, offsets the popular cultural sensibility that everyone who works is a professional by courtesy, and draws attention to the central relation between craft and training. There is, however, a complication, one that brings the art v. science binary back into consideration.

The complication is the *modern* university. For centuries the site of training and certification in the high professions (not to mention the certification of social standing), universities only became oriented to research—to the discovery, consolidation and diffusion of new knowledge—in the German-speaking world as a result of the Enlightenment. The German model of the research university arrived in the new world with the founding of Johns Hopkins University in 1876. Fifteen years earlier, Yale University had awarded its first PhD degree, and the first in the United States—a degree in philosophy, or knowledge for its own sake. Belatedly Cambridge and Oxford superimposed the German model on their still medieval colleges. Today the world over, the German model is held in high esteem. Whatever else goes on in the modern university, it is an institution dedicated to research.

Of course, other institutions also sponsor research. Yet few such institutions are committed to what we like to call basic research or sometimes even pure research—the creation of knowledge that has no necessary or immediate relevance to the work of other professionals. Those relatively few souls who undertake research for its own sake like to be called scholars, and most of them are denizens of modern research universities. They are organized into departments with substantial autonomy. In conducting research they simultaneously train their own kind. In effect, they certify themselves as members of specific disciplines.

The very term *discipline* has a double meaning: a craft that conforms to stringent standards and (therefore) a narrowly bounded body of knowledge. As new knowledge grows, new disciplines emerge. In due course, the arts and sciences clustered at Snow's two poles and the social or human sciences came to occupy an uncomfortable position between these contraries. Scholars in the arts and sciences created the modern research university within the shell of the medieval university, thus assuring their disciplines a place in this splendid invention. Scholars in the social sciences were obliged to carve out space for their disciplines, with overlapping boundaries and identity questions the inevitable result.

Better-established colleagues did not have to challenge the implicit claim of social scientists that their contributions to knowledge met credibly demanding standards, much less the standards prevailing in either the arts or the sciences. Self-doubt did the job. Had the needs of society, of the many other professions, not brought to the social sciences both students for its basic education and consumers for its scholarship, it seems unlikely these disciplines would have been able to sustain themselves. As it is, many universities across the world continue to subsume the social sciences in faculties given over to training in the high professions.

If the social sciences occupy an uncomfortable position in the modern research university, the situation is much aggravated in the case of International Relations. It is not even clear that International Relations deserves to be called a discipline. In the United States it is generally treated as a field of political science. Its subject is politics first and foremost; the title of Hans Morgenthau's legendary textbook, *Politics among Nations* (1948) says just this. International Relations is a latecomer among the social sciences, its emergence an affective and normative response to two world wars; hence Morgenthau's subtitle, *The Struggle for Power and Peace*. The scholars who insisted on autonomy from other social sciences quickly realized that they needed a theory making the subject matter called international relations (or international politics or world politics) uniquely their own. Once again, Morgenthau's textbook says it all: theory is set against practice, realism is declared a theory, six definitive principles of realism are pronounced.[3]

Claims on behalf of a theory specific to politics among nations—as we say, a theory of anarchy—are embedded in an origins-story. Members of every community always tell such stories; they are central to any community's identity. As told by self-styled realists, the story of International Relations favours the United States as the point of origin. To give the story even more drama, disagreements between liberal institutionalists dominant between the wars and the realists who came after World War II were dignified as a great debate over the future of International Relations—a debate that realists were widely judged to have won. The great debate elevated E. H. Carr to the founder's pantheon and appeased British scholars bridling over the origins-story as told in the United States. That self-styled realists prevailed over liberal institutionalists had dire consequences. Carr had characterized the latter as 'utopians', thus implying a lack of scholarly craft; the very term *realism* implies a refreshing freedom from the contrivances of craft.

---

[3] Hans J. Morgenthau, *Politics among Nations: The Struggle for Power and Peace* (New York: Alfred Knopf, 1948), chs 1–2.

Liberal institutionalists put great stock in international law, which required them to think like lawyers. The legal profession has a great respect for craft, practised for centuries, sharpened by contrasting tendencies in the Anglo-American common law and law based on the Napoleonic Code, and clarified through theoretical contestation, some of it prompted by theorizing in the social sciences.[4] Realists may have flirted with the idea that they were doing something daring and new, but they also evinced a great respect for history as practised by professional historians and for the ministerial archives, conference proceedings, treaty compilations, memoirs, and contemporaneous reports that are the stuff of history. Realists end up thinking like diplomats. Lawyers and diplomats are master craftsmen (sexism duly noted). Liberal institutionalists and realists are legal and diplomatic craftsmen by extension.

Neither lawyers nor diplomats put any great value on theory, certainly not for its own sake, and only when they see an immediate relevance to their practical concerns. Not only does the belated emergence of International Relations as a theory-oriented social science condemn it to irrelevance in the professional spheres of law and diplomacy, where it can only tell practitioners what their craft has already mandated for them, it condemns International Relations to neglect a great deal about its own origins—origins in training professionals for careers in the service of their nations (not to mention international institutions, banking and commerce, and their churches). The first professional schools of international affairs (Georgetown University's School of Foreign Service, 1919; Institut de hautes études internationales in Geneva, 1927; Fletcher School of Law and Diplomacy, 1933) made no pretence of carving out a discipline.

Many other such professional schools were founded in the aftermath of World War II, especially in the United States. Instruction was expressly interdisciplinary. Culturally distinctive regions were studied, and competence in local languages encouraged. Lawyers and diplomats taught law and diplomacy as substantive concerns. PhD programmes were an afterthought when they existed at all. To the extent that theory had a place in the curriculum, policy was its foremost concern, along with some rumblings about policy science. In effect, International Relations traded in its legacy of craft for the cult of theory subject to the methods of science. Conversely, professional schools of international affairs found little of value in International Relations' first great debate after World War II and even less in the battle of the 1960s over art and science.

---

4 Nicholas Greenwood Onuf, 'Global law-making and legal thought', in Onuf, ed., *Law-Making in the Global Community* (Durham: Carolina Academic Press, 1982), pp. 1–81.

Philosophy, first cut: human faculties

On the evidence of the so-called Third Debate of the 1980s, the second debate was an easy victory for science. More generally science bested art in the social sciences, and the losers turned to philosophy for a second attack on the citadel. Philosophers had already directed much of their attention to the rising hegemony of science, interminably quarrelling over the claims of science as a reliable source of knowledge. Whether critical of science or not, third debaters drew extensively on the history and philosophy of science; the claims of science set the terms of debate then and since.[5] As a consequence, we have lost sight of a philosophical legacy much older and grander than the science question, one that endorses craft as the indispensable engine for the development of modern science.

Here is the gist of that legacy: art, science and craft depend on the exercise of human faculties or powers—motor, sensory and cognitive. Aristotle talked at great length about these faculties, as did his mediaeval followers. Cartesian dualism may raise questions about their location without challenging the assumption that we are what we do. Among these faculties, those of the mind drew the most attention, for they are the one that would seem to be distinctively human. They are faculties that David Hume examined in *A Treatise of Human Nature* (1739–40) and Immanuel Kant in the *Critique of Pure Reason* (1781, 1787).

Hume, Kant and their Enlightenment contemporaries started with an individual human being whose cognition depends on sensory impressions and who is capable of speech. Three cognitive faculties dominate these discussions. First is imagination. Next is understanding, understood inclusively; neither the empiricist–rationalist binary nor the explanation–understanding binary is relevant. Third is judgement. While we might think that speech would be an obvious fourth power, it is also a social activity, as such a product of many people exercising their powers of mind. In revisiting the philosophical discussion of human faculties, we should not assume that the exercise of our cognitive faculties is unrelated to speech and thus from social experience. All of our faculties are inseparable from their public exercise.

A thorough consideration of the three faculties is beyond the scope of this essay. In ordinary language, we take imagination to be inventive or creative. We fabricate impressions from sensory experience or conjure them up from memory. Rather poetically, Hume said, 'I paint the universe in my

---

5   Patrick Thaddeus Jackson, *The Conduct of Inquiry in International Relations: Philosophy of Science and Its Implications for the Study of World Politics* (Abingdon: Routledge, 2011); Inanna Hamati-Ataya, 'IR theory and the question of science', in Ken Booth and Toni Erskine, eds, *International Relations Theory Today*, 2nd edn (Cambridge: Polity, 2016), pp. 69–84.

imagination'.[6] Kant's treatment of imagination in the *Critique of Pure Reason* is cryptic and unhelpful; it is not even clear that Kant considered imagination a primary faculty. Later, in the *Critique of the Power of Judgment*, he did say that imagination creates 'as it were, another nature'.[7] In the ordinary sense of the term, imagination produces art. We are *all* artists, *all* the time.

For Hume, the pervasiveness of imagination is hardly a blessing. 'Nothing is more dangerous to reason than the flights of the imagination', at least when we jump to conclusions about cause and effect. Moreover, 'understanding' is nothing more than 'the general and more established properties of the imagination'.[8] By treating the faculty of understanding as imagination codified in and by habit, Hume effectively reduced it to a secondary faculty. By contrast, Kant gave understanding far greater importance and discussed it at great length, in terms so complex and confusing (he held that understanding is spontaneous—a property we ordinarily associate with imagination) that we might better start where he stopped. Understanding is 'the *faculty of rules*'.[9]

Kant was thinking about natural laws, not social rules. Nevertheless, what is important for understanding is our ability to 'see' regularities, give them form and recognize their necessary or normative effects. The visual metaphor points to *representation* as a central concern of Kant's. Understanding takes place when representation trans*forms* stuff into objects by selecting properties for emphasis. Kant took this to be a process of abstraction, of categorization, of conceptualization—the process by which we replace impressions with symbols. As such, representation is collective and intrinsically social; through representation, visual or aural, we give each other some sense of what is on our minds. Undertaken expressly and in consideration of known rules, representation permits reasoning; collective representation produces science, here defined as systematic knowledge of the world as it appears to us by virtue of our variously enhanced sensory and cognitive faculties.

Now judgement. Hume is little help, since he took judgement to be a matter of inference from associated impressions. We jump to conclusions, often mistakenly. At some points, Kant also seems to have thought that judgement is connected to inference, or reasoning from particulars to the general. If so, judgement is not a faculty at all, but one way that we come to understand, by exercise of reason, why the world appears to us as it does.

---

6   David Hume, *A Treatise of Human Nature*, 2nd edn rev. P. H. Nidditch (Oxford: Clarendon Press, 1978), p. 108.

7   Immanuel Kant, *Critique of the Power of Judgment*, trans. Paul Guyer and Eric Matthews (Cambridge: Cambridge University Press, 2000), p. 192.

8   Hume, *A Treatise of Human Nature*, p. 267.

9   Immanuel Kant, *Critique of Pure Reason*, trans. Norman Kemp Smith (New York: St Martin's Press, 1965), p. 147; emphasis in translation.

At other points, Kant linked judgement to rules—not to *finding* rules (this is understanding), but to *following* rules. 'If understanding in general is to be viewed as the faculty of rules, judgement will be the faculty of subsuming under rules; that is, of distinguishing whether something does or does not stand under a given rule.' Moreover, logic offers 'no rules for judgment'. Thus 'judgment is a peculiar talent, which can be practiced only, and cannot be taught'.[10] Teaching judgement would require rules for employing rules, which would then require further rules *ad infinitum*.

Every rule offers a choice: follow the rule or not, with more-or-less predictable consequences following from one's choice. The exercise of judgement requires us to act on choices—to cause outcomes by guessing what they might be. When we do this repeatedly, in sequence, with an eye to relevant rules *and* an eventual or preferred outcome or goal, we engage in an iterated process of comparing states of affairs, or wholes. As Kant observed, 'the term "whole" is always only comparative'.[11]

Before-and-after comparisons depend on the faculty of memory, to which Hume attached so much importance. Side-by-side comparisons typically require an already available exemplar or model against which some state of affairs is compared. Unreliable as memory is, it offers us an inexhaustible supply of imaginatively reconfigured examples for the purposes of comparison. Judgement is goal oriented. Most of all, this is so when we make repeated choices to reach a preferred outcome. Each choice results in an adjustment in the relevant state of affairs and a renewed opportunity to choose yet another adjustment. Judgement implies purpose.

Any such formulation immediately brings Aristotle to mind. Aristotle pointed out that when we speak persuasively, we often use examples (*paradeigmata*) to make the point. If one example does not work, we choose another and then another. Kant also noticed the importance of examples in the exercise of judgement. They are 'the go-cart of judgment; and those who are lacking in ... natural talent can never dispense with them'.[12] Whatever the 'natural power of judgment', we all need 'adequate training' 'through examples and actual practice'.[13] And here Kant sounds very much like Aristotle when the latter discussed *technē* and *praxis* in the very first words of the *Nicomachean Ethics*. 'Every craft and every line of inquiry, and likewise every action and decision, seem to seek some good.'[14]

---

[10] Ibid., p. 177.

[11] Ibid., p. 435.

[12] Ibid., p. 178; also see *Critique of the Power of Judgment*, pp. 186–9.

[13] Kant, *Critique of Pure Reason*, p. 178.

[14] Aristotle, *Nicomachean Ethics*, 2nd edn, trans. Terence Irwin (Indianapolis: Hackett, 1991), p. 1.

Technē is the Greek term here translated as craft. *Methodos* is line of inquiry, *praxis* is action, *prohairesis* is decision and *agathos* is good as in reaching a goal. *Prohairesis* is a deliberate or premeditated choice. Action is a more inclusive term than activity, or *energeia*—a term which Aristotle also used in the very next sentence. *Methodos* conveys a contemporary, procedural sense of science. *Technē* is often translated as art. It always refers to a skilled activity and, of course, has given rise to such terms as *technique* and *technical*.[15]

In one sentence, Aristotle basically told us all we need to know about judgement, even though he seems never to have developed the concept expressly. He could have said that the exercise of judgement is indispensable to the construction and manipulation of objects for use in the world. To be exercised well, it requires craft or technique, which it also produces among its useful results. Indicatively, *technē* derives from the Greek word for carpenter. Through training and practice in using examples, craft *is* skilled activity. If art would seem to favour imagination and science to favour understanding, most artists and most scientists most of the time are concerned with the tools and immediate objects—models, prototypes, exemplars—of their *praxis*. Craft describes what they do in the name of art or science. And so it is in the social sciences, including International Relations.

Philosophy, second cut: working models

It is obvious even from this sketchiest of sketches (a term of art as craft) that the three faculties are inseparable in practice. Adult, competent human beings use all three (and many more) altogether all the time. Conspicuously missing from this sketch is apperception. Central to Kant's project, this faculty unifies the other faculties in relation to a conscious self, one that is oriented by *a priori* concepts of space and time. Aristotle had no need for such a faculty; *psuchē* suffices, *phusis* rules. Cartesian dualism demands a path, a link, between mind and world, which apperception provided to Kant's satisfaction (and mine), but not to most professional philosophers today. Developments in cognitive science and psychology have only enlivened disagreement over competing versions of realism (the mind in the world) and anti-realism (the world in the mind).

Many of these philosophers dismiss old-fashioned discussion of human faculties, remnants of which still make an appearance in late 19th-century pragmatism and early 20th-century phenomenology. Instead the claims of science and thus the science question have prompted an analytic philosophy preoccupied with formal conceptions of sense, meaning and truth. Even after the Third Debate had some scholars in International Relations talking

---

[15] See generally ibid., Glossary.

about epistemology and ontology, analytic philosophy and its concerns attracted little interest. Most of us are untroubled realists. Nevertheless, analytic philosophers do have something to teach us about craft.

Karl Popper is one. Perhaps better known among scholars in International Relations than any other analytic philosopher, his vision of science as a process of conjecture and refutation gets its due.[16]

Less familiar is Popper's 'pluralist' solution to the mind–body problem.[17]

> In this pluralist philosophy ..., there are three worlds; the first is the physical world or the world of physical states; the second is the mental world or the world of mental states; and the third is the world of intelligibles, or *of ideas in the objective sense*; it is the world of possible objects of thought: the world of theories in themselves, and their logical relations; of arguments in themselves; and of problem situations in themselves.[18]

From this description, one might think that Popper's world 3 is itself merely 'mental'. Calling ideas objective does not make them into objects—the physical objects constituting world 1. The Kantian formula of things-in-themselves does not help. Yet Popper definitely took the 'possible objects' of world 3 to reside outside the mind.

> By world 3 I mean the world of the products of the human mind, such as languages; tales and stories and religious myths; scientific conjectures or theories, and mathematical constructions; songs and symphonies; paintings and sculptures. But also aeroplanes and airports and other feats of engineering.[19]

Popper was a confirmed realist, indeed a hyper-realist, for whom the 'reality of the mental world 2—and with it, the reality of human suffering— ... is admitted by common sense'.[20] Human suffering is, of course, both a subjective experience (when I suffer) and an objective condition (when others suffer, including myself as an imagined other). Worlds 2 and 3 would seem to collapse into each other and then, by virtue of being real, fold into

---

[16] See, just for example, Jackson, *The Conduct of Inquiry in International Relations*, p. 1.

[17] Karl R. Popper, *Objective Knowledge: An Evolutionary Approach* (Oxford: Clarendon Press, 1972); Popper, 'Three worlds', The Tanner lecture on human values, University of Michigan, 1978, available at: {https://tannerlectures.utah.edu/_resources/documents/a-to-z/p/popper80.pdf} accessed 11 February 2022.

[18] Popper, *Objective Knowledge*, p. 154, emphasis in original.

[19] Popper, 'Three Worlds', p. 144.

[20] Ibid.

world 1. That world includes beings who act on mental states to produce physical artefacts for any number of reasons and leave those artefacts behind for other such beings to act upon. By stipulating a 'world of the products of the human mind' (in my view, the *only* world we know, the only world that we have access to), Popper clarified *what* we do—we *make* things, be they plans for lunch, theories or airplanes. Popper's scheme is less helpful in showing *why* we do it; the 'why' and thus 'the how' take place in the mind.

An anti-realist is better positioned to ask why and then how the mind produces the world we think we know. Among analytic philosophers, John McDowell has asked just these questions in a compelling way. Inspired by Wilfrid Sellars' demolition of 'The Myth of the Given' (the presumption that the world is somehow given to us as it is), McDowell adopted Sellars' notion of a 'logical space of reasons'.[21] This space is 'more extensive than the conceptual sphere, so that it can incorporate extra-conceptual impingements from the world'.[22] If the exercise of reason fills the space of concepts, the exercise of judgement fills the added space given over to reasons, which then include explanations and justifications for what we do. Reasons fall on both sides of the is–ought divide; indeed they show it no respect.

Imagining a space for reasons relieves us from having to shuttle back and forth ('oscillate') between a strict anti-realist stance and Popper's 'given' world.[23] Popper took the natural world to be a lawful place: 'Laws of nature are ... conjectural descriptions of the structural properties of nature—of our world itself.' This is, of course, the world that science purports to have given us, a world into which we probe ever more deeply.[24] For McDowell, there is, beyond the world of laws, a 'second nature', a nature readily seen in Aristotle's ethics.[25] Our nature is largely second nature, and our second nature is the way it is not just because of the potentialities we were born with, but also because of our upbringing, our *Bildung*. Given the notion of second nature, we can say that the way our lives are shaped by reason is natural, even while we deny that the structure of the space of reasons can be integrated into the realm of law.[26]

Popper and McDowell have presented us with complementary models of the human condition—models that link what, why, and how we do what we do. In briefest terms, what we do is make models. Both scholars indicate as

---

21 Willard Sellars, 'Empiricism and the philosophy of mind', *Minnesota Studies in the Philosophy of Science* 1, 19 (1956), pp. 253–329 (298–9); John McDowell, *Mind and World, with a New Introduction* (Cambridge, MA: Harvard University Press, 1996), pp. xiv–xx.

22 McDowell, *Mind and World*, p. 8.

23 Ibid., pp. 24, 40, 108.

24 Popper, *Objective Knowledge*, p. 196.

25 McDowell, *Mind and World*, pp. 78–85.

26 Ibid., pp. 87–8.

much by using the term *structure* as I have just quoted them to do. Structure is never a property of the world. It is something we say about the world, often enough in conjunction with the term *function*, or cause harnessed to purpose. David Hume's 'constant conjunctions' describe a simple, ancient model and a powerful reason to rely on habits, conventions and apparently stable kinds imputed to nature. All such models work by giving form without necessitating a belief in cause, whether material, proximate or final.

A model (body, case, exemplar, figure, frame, icon, layout, map, matrix, outline, pattern, plan, play, scheme, script, sketch, story, template, type—I could go on, and on) is an arrangement of objects and relations standing in for another such arrangement that seems to be a property of the world. Conventionally models are physical artefacts—scaled replicas of other physical artefacts. Yet this picture (or model) is incomplete because it leaves out cognitive processes linking the two sets of artefacts. Someone must have planned out how to build an airplane, which, once built, or even just planned, gives me a mental model that I can use to build a model airplane. Those mental models depend on other physical artefacts, which I am only capable of identifying as such because of the mental models I have at hand, and so on.[27]

Every model depends on mind-work. Nevertheless, the very idea of a mental model is relatively recent. It is attributed to Kenneth Craik, writing in the 1940s, and now in wide use. More helpful is Craik's conception of a 'working model'. He took working models to be physical artefacts or, more precisely, mechanical contrivances needing to be 'translated' through symbols into mental states assigning them the work they do.[28] In other words (though not his), working models must serve ends, or have a function, that we give to them. In his words, models do their work 'through a kind of artificial causation'.[29] Function is artificial causation—a property specific to one kind of models (we typically call them systems), and not external reality, where realists like Craik think proximate or efficient causes explain how the world is.

Models do different kinds of work, which we indicate by giving reasons for believing what we do, acting as we do. Framing models give us kinds, concepts, categories. They are standardized representations, naturalized metaphors, giving us places to put what we experience as the diverse contents of the world, and they do so for good reasons: so that we can find

---

[27] Nicholas Greenwood Onuf, *Making Sense, Making Worlds: Constructivism in Social Theory and International Relations* (Abingdon: Routledge, 2013), ch. 6.

[28] Kenneth Craik, *The Nature of Explanation* (Cambridge: Cambridge University Press, 1967), pp. 51–3, 81–3.

[29] Ibid., p. 63; also see p. 106.

them again, compare them, manipulate them. Theoretical models purport to explain what is going on between kinds. They give us proximate, yet still artificial or (conjectured) causes as additional reasons to believe that some sequences and regularities will take place within a stipulated frame.

Other models put forward a variety of artificial causes. Normative models ascribe force or obligation to regularities in conduct. Ethical models offer reasons to believe in the causal sufficiency of doing what feels good or right or honourable. Aesthetic models attach causal power to the experience of beauty, the sublime, ecstasy, madness. Models often framed as transcendental, spiritual or religious give us reasons to believe in what cannot be seen, predicted or explained; they find reason in first and final causes, in faith. All such models work without necessitating a belief in a lawful universe.

Sociology

People rely on models to express themselves. It cannot be otherwise and needs no special acknowledgement. Yet we, as scholars, are disposed to reflect on the requirements of our craft, not least when constituting a distinctive domain of knowledge—a field or discipline. This is an exercise in modelling and may well entail reflections on what we think we are doing in the name of theory. International Relations came to be seen as a field in the 1950s; one of its early theorists (and one of my teachers), George Liska, designated 1955–65 the heroic decade[30]—a judgement that stands to this day. As theory came to the fore, so did *model* as a term of art (or craft).

No one illustrates this development better than Morton Kaplan, one of the field's early heroes and forceful advocate of the turn to science. Kaplan examined 'six distinct international systems'. They 'are heuristic models'; only two—'the "balance of power" system and the loose bipolar system'—have 'historical referents', yet both models are simpler than those referents.[31] By implication, imagined models must be comparably simple. Also by implication, a single model of the international system, such as one premised on anarchy, is too simple for theoretical purposes, too generalized for any theory based on it to produce useful predictions.[32]

Another hero (and another of my teachers), Karl Deutsch, made his reliance on models explicit in terms reminiscent of Kaplan's. Models are to be judged on four criteria: empirical relevance, economy ('the model

---

[30] George Liska, 'The heroic decade and after: International relations as events, discipline, and profession', *SAIS Review* 10, 4 (1966), pp. 5–11.

[31] Morton A. Kaplan, *System and Process in International Politics* (New York: Wiley, 1957), pp. 21–2. Also see Chapter 1.

[32] See Morton A. Kaplan, 'Problems of theory building and theory confirmation in international politics', *World Politics* 14, 1 (1961), pp. 6–24 (7–9).

must be in some respect "simpler" than the situation modelled'), predictive performance, probability and originality (the last two being inversely related).[33] Like Kaplan, Deutsch linked generality and utility, not just for purposes of theoretical prediction, but for the comparison and evaluation of mental models. For both Kaplan and Deutsch, the only models of interest are theoretical because prediction is the *sine qua non* of modern science. Yet both concern themselves with models *before* theories are appended to them for purposes of comparison, evaluation and *choice* (Deutsch's term[34]), effectively conceding that these prior activities are integral to science.

Lastly, consider Kenneth Waltz's discussion of models.

> *Model* is used in two principal ways. In one sense a model represents a theory. In another sense a model pictures reality while simplifying it, say, through omission or through reduction of scale. If such a model departs too far from reality, it becomes useless. A model airplane should look like a real airplane. Explanatory power is gained by moving away from 'reality', not by staying close to it.[35]

One can quarrel with this characterization. Models do not represent theories, at least in the first instance; models are said to represent some aspect of the world, and theories purport to explain what is thereby represented. Waltz shares with Kaplan and Deutsch a tendency to conflate theories and the models upon which they depend; they might better have said 'theoretical model' when talking about theory. In the quoted passage, Waltz's segue from airplanes to explanations is a *non sequitur*. More intriguing is Waltz's unexamined realism (philosophical, not political), given his claim that explanatory power increases by moving away from 'reality'. His scare marks leave us to wonder what he thought reality really is.

Waltz's embrace of the market as a model upon which to base his general theory of international politics tells us more. Markets are models, 'not descriptive realities or concrete entities'; 'a market is not an institution or an agent in any concrete or palpable sense'. It is harder to say what a model *is*. Waltz's attempt sounds lame: 'The market is a cause interposed between the economic actors and the results they produce. It is not an agent in the sense of A being the agent that produces outcome X. Rather it is a structural cause.'[36] The term *result* clarifies nothing. Things result—things

---

[33] Karl W. Deutsch, *The Nerves of Government: Models of Political Communication and Control* (New York: Free Press, 1963), pp. 16–18.

[34] Ibid., p. 16.

[35] Kenneth N. Waltz, *Theory of International Politics* (Reading, MA: Addison-Wesley, 1979), p. 7, emphasis in original.

[36] Ibid., pp. 88–93, quoting pp. 89, 90.

recognized as such because they are models, whether physical artefacts or mental models. *Cause* points to the standard realism of workaday science. *Structural cause* is something else altogether—the artificial causation of models all the way down.

Waltz's language is loose and imprecise to the point of misleading the reader. These are the very words he applied to Kaplan in a twice-printed critique of Kaplan's system models.[37] Kaplan responded with a detailed counter-critique.[38] Among the many charges Waltz levied against Kaplan was a confusing conception of rules, as in 'the six essential rules' of the balance of power system.[39] Kaplan quite rightly retorted that these rules 'are neither descriptive nor prescriptive; they are analytical and theoretical'.[40] In other words, they are properties of the model, not the world, and they become prescriptive in practice only when agents act on the model.

Every model has rules—conditions and limits necessary to its ontological status. Kant emphasized the place of rules in judgement, itself a matter of comparing and evaluating wholes, cases, models. McDowell's *Bildung* involves learning an open-ended set of rules on how, when and where to do what we do, rules telling us what that 'what' is. We never stop learning. We constantly polish our skills, take care of our tools, and acquire new skills and tools, inevitably consulting the rules as we go along.

Where there are rules, we tend to assume there must be a rulebook or instruction manual. It is not that simple, even in the case of science, where one might think that a few methodological rules do the job. Conversely, art would seem to be a rule-less domain; no artist needs a rulebook. Implied here is the belief that the scientific method is the distillation of reason, while art gives free rein to imagination. This is, of course, an utterly impoverished way to view both art and science.

For science as craft, the rules of the scientific method are no doubt a good place to begin one's training. As Thomas Kuhn has emphasized, scientists also use 'concrete problem solutions' as examples in training, in the process turning them into 'exemplars'.[41] Conspicuously placed in textbooks, these exemplars guide choices in specified situations, just as rules always do. Yet methodological rules hardly scratch the surface. There are rules of personal

37 Kenneth N. Waltz, 'Theory of international relations', in F. I. Greenstein and Nelson W. Polsby, eds, *International Politics* (Reading, MA: Addison-Wesley, 1975), pp. 56–64; Waltz, *Theory of International Politics*, pp. 50–9.

38 Morton A. Kaplan, *Towards Professionalism in International Theory: Macrosystem Analysis* (New York: Free Press, 1979), pp. 1–81.

39 Kaplan, *System and Process in International Politics*, p. 23.

40 Kaplan, *Towards Professionalism in International Theory*, p. 67.

41 Thomas S. Kuhn, *The Structure of Scientific Revolutions*, 2nd edn (Chicago: University of Chicago Press, 1970), p. 187.

conduct and comportment, such as giving credit and showing respect. There are rules on the presentation of results, on what to do about mistakes, on the use and care of tools, on accounting for costs, on causing harm. Many of these rules are informal, and they vary in scope.

Every discipline has its own rules, and so does every laboratory, studio, salon, theatre, library, courtroom, clinic and battlefield. While artists need not concern themselves with the rules of the scientific method, they too rely on exemplars. Beyond the obvious 'how-to-do-it' rules, they also discover a thick mat of informal rules on personal conduct, presentation of work and so on. All such rules pertain to judgement and thus to craft. They do not pertain to art as the domain of imagination and science as the domain of reason.

A proper sociology of International Relations would devote a good deal of space, not available here, to the tools of our craft, and to the irrepressible tendency to think that tools are real because we can put our hands on them. It might begin with Martin Heidegger's phenomenological assessment of a world that is 'ready-to-hand'.[42] Such a world can only be (in my terms) a world of models. It might then proceed to a large literature on the function of tools in laboratory science, with needed digressions on Ian Hacking's striking claim that the experimental manipulation of electrons 'made me a realist'—'if you can spray them, then they are real'[43]—and on Bruno Latour's failure to see through the screen of his laborious materialism that causation in sociology refers only to what happens in models.[44] So it is in every laboratory, every studio, every place where someone is spraying electrons, paint, napalm, compliments or insults. Indeed, words are the most powerful tools we have—the tools that we are most dependent on, and skilled in using, to make models, comparisons and judgements. Whatever else we do, we are wordsmiths.

Conclusion

A proper sociology of International Relations must also devote itself to the profession. That we see it as a profession is nothing new. Liska held that the 'profession of international relations has the role of supplying the needs of the United States as a world power which lacks ... mid-level elites in the foreign policy process'.[45] While this stance may seem dated and parochial

---

[42] Martin Heidegger, *Being and Time*, trans. John Macquarrie and Edward Robinson (New York: Harper Row, 1962), pp. 95–122.

[43] Ian Hacking, *Representing and Intervening: Introductory Topics in the Philosophy of Natural Science* (Cambridge: Cambridge University Press, 1983), pp. 22–3.

[44] Bruno Latour, *Reassembling the Social: An Introduction to Actor-Network-Theory* (Oxford: Oxford University Press, 2005), pp. 99–106.

[45] Liska, 'The heroic decade', pp. 10–11.

(Liska was writing in the house organ of a professional school located in Washington), it is surely accepted today the world over, if not always acknowledged. When Waltz and Kaplan skirmished over models in the 1970s, Kaplan made a great point of the 'preprofessional' tone of Waltz's critique. Here professionalism is tied to rules of collegiality and comportment, all the more relevant in our time of public ridicule and internet vitriol, but rarely discussed in the field.

In the last few years discussion (in International Relations, mostly informal) has turned to professionalization, and not just as a matter of training. Instead professionalization is linked to formal standards of achievement. Everywhere, it seems, there is an obsession with citation counts, tenure and promotion files, and rankings—the ranking of journals, scholarly presses, departments, universities and, if only tacitly, disciplines. International Relations could hardly escape this obsession, and the field's late arrival and contestable boundaries are likely to have exacerbated it.

This is not the place for an extended discussion of professionalization as a global phenomenon, indeed a conspicuous feature of globalization. It might better be seen as a feature of modernization, but with a twist.[46] Half a century ago, modernization theory proclaimed a shift from ascription to achievement, from traditional status-ordering to modern societies founded on equal rights and rationalized offices. Professionalization masquerades as Weberian rationalization in the face of functional differentiation and specialization, but its effect is to instantiate a new status-order. Standards governing professional placement and standing are closely monitored and strictly enforced. Gate-keeping may be the source of much banter, but it is no joke.

Professionalization is an insidious form of politicization. There is no escaping politics by choosing to ply one's craft in small rooms almost anywhere on the planet (much as I personally would like it to be so). As scholars, we are citizens in a *civitas maxima*—the great republic of letters, in which the arts and sciences have always been indistinguishably valued. Citizenship confers extraordinary privilege and inescapable duties, most of which pertain to craft and its uses. The first duty is reflexivity. The second duty is to direct our activities, our skills, our craft, to what we take, on reflection and through talk, to be the common good.

---

[46] Nicholas Onuf, 'Late modern civil society', in Randall D. Germain and Michael Kenny, eds, *The Idea of Global Civil Society: Politics and Ethics in a Globalizing Era* (London: Routledge, 2005), pp. 47–63.

13

The Dinosaur Speaks! (2018)

When it comes to constructivism in International Relations, I am one of the dinosaurs. We dinosaurs are still in a reasonably good state of preservation, and still talking. When a dinosaur speaks, we generally expect the old fossil to talk like, well, a dinosaur. And so I shall.

There aren't very many of us—Alexander Wendt, Friedrich Kratochwil and I are usually put together in a museum display called 'IR in the 80s'.[1] John Ruggie should be added to this group, thanks chiefly to an early essay he wrote with Kratochwil (1986), as should Raymond (Bud) Duvall, mentor to Wendt and a number of other constructivists.[2] Nearby are feminists and a variety of self-styled 'posties'—postmodernists, poststructuralists and postcolonial thinkers—who are occasionally grouped with us as constructivists, despite resistance on both sides. No doubt the familiar dynamic of 'us' versus a stigmatized 'them' or 'other' helps to account for this inappropriate simplification. So does the socio-cultural context of the 1980s.

I will talk as if nothing much has happened since the dinosaurs came on the scene. I will talk about metatheory—the philosophical rationale behind constructivism—although the dinosaurs were pushed aside by a bunch of

---

[1]   Thanks to the following publications: Alexander E. Wendt, 'The agent-structure problem in international relations theory', *International Organization* 41, 3 (1987), pp. 335–70, and 'Anarchy is what states make of it: The social construction of power politics', *International Organization* 46, 2 (1992), pp. 391–425; Friedrich V. Kratochwil, *Rules, Norms, and Decisions: On the Conditions of Practical and Legal Reasoning in International Relations and Domestic Affairs* (Cambridge: Cambridge University Press, 1989); Nicholas Greenwood Onuf, *World of Our Making: Rules and Rule in Social Theory and International Relations* (Columbia: University of South Carolina Press, 1989).

[2]   Friedrich Kratochwil and John Gerard Ruggie, 'International organization: A state of the art on an art of the state', *International Organization* 40, 4 (1986), pp. 753–75. And see Alexander Wendt and Raymond Duvall, 'Institutions and international order', in Ernst-Otto Czempiel and James N. Rosenau, eds, *Global Changes and Theoretical Challenges: Approaches to World Politics for the 1990s* (Lexington, MA: Lexington Books, 1989), pp. 51–73.

furry little creatures with close-at-hand concerns. I will talk as if the issues animating philosophy (and especially the philosophy of science in the 1970s and '80s) have changed very little. And I could talk as if international theory lost its way once the dinosaurs had their say. But I won't—at least, not here.

Instead let me say this about the time of the dinosaurs. The end of the Cold War had nothing to do with constructivism's arrival on the scene, despite what I hear younger museum visitors saying to each other. I suspect Wendt is at least partly responsible for this vagrant belief. All those young visitors, not to mention their parents, read the following passage from his great book, *Social Theory of International Politics*: 'constructivist thinking about international politics was accelerated by the end of the Cold War, which caught scholars on all sides off guard but left orthodoxies particular exposed'.[3]

Wendt had already muddied the waters by claiming that 'a constructivist worldview underlies the classical international theories of Grotius, Kant and Hegel' and that many post-World War II writers advanced 'important constructivist approaches to international politics'.[4] If constructivist thinking had always been around, then it does make sense to say that it accelerated *after* 1989. Yet by exposing old orthodoxies, Wendt himself gave constructivism much of its initial momentum in 1987, *before* the Cold War ended.[5] This said, I don't have the slightest doubt that the end of the Cold War and the rise of identity politics gave constructivism an unexpected relevance to scholars in the field, prompted the emergence of a second generation of constructivists, and accounts for the empirical thrust (typically manifest in case studies) of so much scholarship undertaken in the name of constructivism.

In my view as a participant-observer, constructivism arose in the context of a 'culture war' conducted chiefly in research universities in the United States. This is how I would describe the uprising of scholars in the humanities chafing under the dramatic shift in resources from the liberal arts to the sciences, including the applied social sciences. Drawing inspiration from Continental social theory, humanists declared that the philosophical assumptions underlying modern science are untenable. Postmodernists, postpositivists, poststructuralists and postcolonial thinkers repudiated the 'Enlightenment project' of universal reason in favour of local, practical knowledge and multiple rationalities. We in the field are familiar with this development as the 'Third Debate'. As described by Yosef Lapid, the Third Debate reinforced the tendency, already evident in Robert Keohane's edited

---

[3]   Alexander Wendt, *Social Theory of International Politics* (Cambridge: Cambridge University Press, 1999), p. 4.

[4]   Ibid., p. 3.

[5]   For an example of Wendt's misguidance, see Milja Kurki, *Causation in International Relations: Reclaiming Causal Analysis* (Cambridge: Cambridge University Press, 2008), p. 277.

volume, *Neorealism and Its Critics*, to segregate positivists and postpositivists into hostile camps.[6] What Lapid, who had been Kratochwil's student, failed to make clear is how this ostensible debate relates to constructivism's early days.

There are, of course, many factors giving rise to constructivism. I have addressed them elsewhere as they affected me: feminist theory and the linguistic turn top the list.[7] Here, I want to emphasize a factor that I think motivated the three of us who are generally taken to represent constructivism's founding generation: Alex Wendt, Fritz Kratochwil and myself. This is the philosophy of science, which surged into prominence with the humanist campaign against science. Most conspicuously, Alex plumbed the literature on the philosophy of science even as a student. Fritz did so least conspicuously in the early days, though some of his later work constitutes a trenchant critique of misappropriated philosophy of science.[8] In my own case, I ransacked the literature to support a constructivism that went 'all the way down'. When I got there, even 'below' philosophy devoted specifically to science, I found myself with Wittgenstein's *Philosophical Investigations* and Nelson Goodman's *Ways of Worldmaking* for company.[9]

The question of foundations animated the 'post'-movement. In my view, then and now, this question must be addressed by anyone who could plausibly claim to be a constructivist. I don't mean to suggest that we must all become philosophers, or even that we should preface anything we say as scholars with pseudo-philosophical boilerplate. I do think *you* should be prepared to say, 'this is what I think about the so-called Third Debate,' and

---

[6] Yosef Lapid, 'The third debate: On the prospects of international theory in a post-positivist era', *International Studies Quarterly* 33, 3 (1989), pp. 235–54; Robert O. Keohane, ed., *Neorealism and Its Critics* (New York: Columbia University Press, 1986). Also see Chapter 11.

[7] Nicholas Onuf, 'Worlds of our making: The strange career of constructivism in International Relations', in Donald J. Puchala, ed., *Visions of International Relations: Assessing an Academic Field* (Columbia: University of South Carolina Press, 2002), pp. 119–41; Nicholas Onuf, 'Contradictions', in Naeem Inayatullah and Elizabeth Dauphinee, eds, *Narrative Global Politics: Theory, History and the Personal in International Relations* (Abingdon: Routledge, 2016), pp. 104–21.

[8] See especially Friedrich Kratochwil, 'Of false promises and good bets: A plea for a pragmatic approach to theory building (the Tartu Lecture)', *Journal of International Relations and Development* 10, 1 (2007), pp. 1–15; Friedrich Kratochwil, 'Of communities, gangs, historicity and the problem of Santa Claus: Replies to my critics', *Journal of International Relations and Development* 10, 1 (2007), pp. 57–78; Friedrich Kratochwil, 'Evidence, inference, and truth as problems of theory building in the social sciences', in Richard N. Lebow and Mark Irving Lichbach, eds, *Theory and Evidence in Comparative Politics and International Relations* (New York: Palgrave Macmillan, 2007), pp. 25–54.

[9] Ludwig Wittgenstein, *Philosophical Investigations*, 3rd edn, trans. G. E. M. Anscombe (Oxford: Basil Blackwell, 1968); Nelson Goodman, *Ways of Worldmaking* (Indianapolis: Hackett, 1978).

then actually have something to say if, against the odds, anyone—student or colleague—actually asks your opinion.

In all likelihood you will say, with ample precedent, that constructivism is the middle way—Emmanuel Adler's 'middle ground', Wendt's *via media*.[10] I myself suggested that constructivism functions as a four-way bridge between phenomenology, poststructuralism, rational choice and functionalism/structuralism[11]—cleverly worked out, perhaps, but ignored. So the question remains: Between what and what is it the middle way? Between positivism and postpositivism? Philosophical realism and philosophical idealism? Science and art? None of these formulations sounds right, I think because they ignore the metaphorical power of the term *foundation*. Foundations or their repudiation must come first, and not somewhere in the middle.

My own preference is for a Kantian frame of reference—that is to say, a philosophical idealism that takes Immanuel Kant's First Critique as a point of departure.[12] In that context, I have recently urged my colleagues in the field to consider constructivism as having a specific focus applicable to social relations in general. In short, we are best equipped to study the human disposition to fill the world with 'moderate-sized dry goods'. I have borrowed this expression from J. L. Austin and attempted to locate it in a Kantian framework.[13] Needless to say, my colleagues have paid me no mind whatsoever—something I attribute to their sense that philosophical idealism is no answer to the question of foundations.

Fair enough. If I nagged you all about foundations long enough, most of you would admit to being philosophical realists of one sort or another, and you'd probably prefer to have the dinosaur stand silent in its 1980s diorama. But the question remains: What is it about constructivism that makes it seem like the middle way?

Constructivism is much discussed and well practised in several disciplines. My question is specific to International Relations and its history as a field of study. Are constructivist scholars in the field temperamentally inclined to go for the 'middle' in most situations they find themselves in? Do zealous rat choice theorists and scorched-earth posties make us nervous? For that matter, do fundamentalists of any sort give us the willies? Are we disproportionately

---

[10] Emmanuel Adler, 'Seizing the middle ground: Constructivism in world politics', *European Journal of International Relations* 3, 3 (1997), pp. 319–63; Wendt, *Social Theory of International Politics*.

[11] Onuf, *World of Our Making*, pp. 57–60.

[12] Immanuel Kant, *Critique of Pure Reason*, trans. Norman Kemp Smith (New York: St Martin's Press, 1965).

[13] J. L. Austin, *Sense and Sensibilia* (Oxford: Clarendon Press, 1962); Nicholas Onuf, 'Constructivism at the crossroads; or, the problem of moderate-sized dry goods', *International Political Sociology* 10, 2 (2016), pp. 115–32.

centrist on matters of politics? Are we drawn to middle range theory as a practical goal? Do most of us think that talk about world-making is actually pretty pretentious?

I think the answer to these questions is *yes*. So let me return to the claim I made a moment ago—that we humans are disposed to fill the world with moderate-sized dry objects to which we assign value (and this is what makes them goods). And let me do so without the encumbrance of a Kantian framework. Instead I will rely on science for inspiration—the science of perception and its relation to cognition.

First, an observation about 'the world'. Here I am talking here about one's world—one's perceptual field, which each of us construe as an integrated whole, with one's perceiving self at its centre. (This is Kant's faculty of apperception, but never mind.) We see this world in three dimensions; as it changes we add time as a fourth dimension. *What* we see is a world, a perceptual field, full of things—things-in-themselves (oops, more Kant), things with discernible boundaries and determinate properties, things that change in strict relation to other things. I don't need to tell you that there is an enormous amount of a science dedicated to understanding how we 'resolve' the world out there into the things we know we see (and I acknowledge the visual bias in my remarks and indeed most of the relevant science).

The things we see most clearly are in the middle of our visual field. Things at the edges are relatively fuzzy; the retinal image is hyperbolic—if we bother to notice.[14] Most of the time we automatically re-scale things so that they have the same ascertainable properties wherever they are in the visual field.[15] As a cognitive operation, re-scaling constitutes a world of moderate-sized objects. Midway between the granular foreground and the gauzy backdrop, these objects are available for metrical comparison. Thanks to the instruments of modern science, we have been able to extend the range of re-scaled objects from the infinitesimal to the astronomic.

Furthermore, we moderns *may* perform these operations more 'naturally' than other people because we have replaced the hyperbolic visual field with a Euclidian field. In a 'carpentered world', as some psychologists have hypothesized, space and time have become metricized constants, such that we see objects in illusory geometric patterns. Whether the human mind always operates in what we often refer to as Kantian space-time, or this is a peculiar, deeply internalized feature of modern experience, is an open

---

[14] Patrick A. Heelan, *Sense Perception and the Philosophy of Science* (Berkeley: University of California Press, 1983).

[15] Psychologists call this 'size constancy scaling'; see Richard L. Gregory, *Eye and Brain: The Psychology of Seeing*, 5th edn (Princeton: Princeton University Press, 1997), chs 9–10.

question. Field researchers testing the hypothesis on non-Western subjects disagree on the interpretation of their tests.

What the relevant science does not say, but I will, is that re-scaling in Kantian space-time also applies to 'social facts'. We make these fuzzy, formless, fluid things into moderate-sized dry goods when we talk about them. I give you some obvious examples.

- Ideas are effectively formless until they are linguistically or symbolically represented. Even then they are too elusive to serve as social facts until they are endowed with additional properties.
- Norms are merely nebulous ideas until we give them the properties of rules.
- People are turned into moderate-sized objects by assigning them identities that they need not know themselves to possess.
- Agents have powers that they may take for granted, but that observers associate with the causal powers of some class of moderate-sized objects.
- Structures are arrangements of agents who have powers that observers see as having an effect on those agents and their jointly constructed world.
- States are social constructions *only* because we can visualize them as dry goods having more-or-less comparable properties.

Scholars resort to moderate-sized goods they call frameworks, approaches or theories to study complex phenomena such as international relations; they say they work within fields, such as International Relations, to locate themselves, as a familiar class of goods, in metaphorically contained, manageably scaled space.

The point should be clear. The way we make useful, moderate-sized social objects with material properties, the way we infuse them with value, the way we do it together through a myriad of cognitive and linguistic operations: this is exactly what seems to entrance constructivists. And only constructivists. Everyone else starts with goods already in place.

Afterword

When this book was in draft, an enthusiastic reviewer for Bristol University Press wondered what its 'through-line' might be. Faced with the question, I too began to wonder. *Theory* is the obvious candidate. This term shows up in the book's title, four times in its first paragraph, in every chapter, hundreds of times altogether. As I remarked in the Introduction, I call myself a theorist and always have; I use to teach 'theory courses' regularly.

Yet I do not propose theories, much less test hypotheses. In the Introduction, I declare, perhaps too grandly, that 'there is no theory to orient the study of international relations' and proceed to say that there is 'an abundance of theorizing at the margins. Theories are linked propositions about the world and its workings; theorizing is linguistically mediated activity falling somewhere, *anywhere*, between informed speculation and formal stipulation.' If theory is this book's through-line, then it does so as an absent centre, thus warranting Charlotte Epstein's judgement, quoted in the Introduction, that I am searching for an 'unconstructed universal posited beyond the social world that founds the possibility of theorizing it'.

In the Introduction, I dispute the charge of pursuing unconstructed universals even as I engage in a linguistically mediated activity that I call theorizing. I also argue that the social world itself makes it possible for us to theorize about that world, thereby making it what it is and us who we are. The social world is a self-constructed universal for each and every one of us, Derrida and Epstein not excepted; 'our world' is my world. In this light, the term *theory* functions in this volume as a periodic place marker and not as a through-line whose function is to assure thematic continuity.

If *theory* is a misleading term for what holds this collection of loosely related essays together, a looser term, such as *theorizing*, might be a better choice for the job. In the Introduction, after all, I say that theorizing is a vocation; the essays variously theorize 'the international' as modernity's absent centre. As linguistically mediated activity ranging from speculation to stipulation, the term is too loose. It offers insufficient guidance to function as a line, a red thread, running through a patchwork of essays attending to a number of themes.

Metatheory (also rendered *meta-theory*) is another possibility. One section of Chapter 10 is called 'Theory/metatheory'. There I second James Der Derian in defining metatheory as 'theorizing about … theories'. In Chapter 13, I equate metatheory with the 'philosophical rationale behind constructivism'. This is confusing, perhaps, because I introduced constructivism to my colleagues as 'a philosophical position', and not as a theoretical project.[1] Insofar as those same colleagues and their students have tended to see constructivism as a theory that comes with a philosophical rationale (usually, scientific realism, thanks chiefly to Alexander Wendt and Colin Wight[2]), it would make sense to define metatheory as the philosophical rationale behind theorizing in the social sciences—in what we routinely call 'social theory'. The philosophy of science played an important part in 'consciousness-raising' in the social sciences early in my career—Thomas Kuhn's *The Structure of Scientific Revolutions* (1962) in particular—and it continues to do so. I found the emphasis on science too limiting myself, looked further afield in philosophy, and took the so-called language turn when writing *World of Our Making* in the 1980s.

The first two essays in this volume precede publication of that book. While they theorize *about* extant theories (as Der Derian would have it), they are not self-consciously metatheoretical. The term itself was not then in wide use; I first encountered it in an edited volume called *Metatheory in Social Science*, published in 1986.[3] Wendt used it when he reviewed *World of Our Making* in 1991.[4] Concisely defining metatheory as 'second order or meta-theorizing',[5] he shifted attention from theory as a project (and therefore an

---

[1] Nicholas Greenwood Onuf, *World of Our Making: Rules and Rule in Social Theory and International Relations* (Columbia: University of South Carolina Press, 1989), p. 37.

[2] Alexander Wendt, *Social Theory of International Politics* (Cambridge: Cambridge University Press, 1999); Colin Wight, *Agents, Structures and International Relations: Politics as Ontology* (Cambridge: Cambridge University Press, 2006).

[3] Donald W. Fiske and Richard A. Shweder, eds, *Metatheory in Social Science: Pluralism and Subjectivities* (Chicago: University of Chicago Press, 1986). None of the book's contributors used the term.

[4] Alexander Wendt, 'Bridging the theory/meta-theory gap in International Relations', *Review of International Studies* 17, 4 (1991), pp. 383–92, also reviewing Martin Hollis and Steve Smith, *Explaining and Understanding International Relations* (Oxford: Clarendon Press, 1990). The field has since seen considerable discussion of metatheory. Some highlights: Fred Chernoff, *Theory and Metatheory in International Relations* (Basingstoke: Palgrave, 2008); John G. Gunnell, 'Social scientific inquiry and meta-theoretical fantasy: The case of International Relations', *Review of International Studies* 37, 4 (2011), pp. 1447–69; Lucas G. Freire, 'The potential and the pitfalls of metatheory in IR', *Estudos Internacionais* 1, 2 (2013), pp. 271–302; Scott Hamilton, 'A genealogy of metatheory in IR: How "ontology" emerged from the inter-paradigm debate', *International Theory* 9, 1 (2017), pp. 136–70.

[5] Wendt, 'Bridging the theory/meta-theory gap', p. 383, emphasis added.

object) to theorizing as an activity. Metatheory is shorthand for theorizing *about* theorizing.

For Wendt, the point of metatheory is to 'free up first order theorists' so that they can get on with 'the task of constructing substantive arguments *about* world politics'.[6] Second-order theorizing is a secondary task. Metatheory stands on the wrong side of theory—twice divorced from practice. This is a frequent charge in the literature just cited: theory's measure is its relevance to policy; metatheory becomes an end in itself. By implication, scholars who theorize about theorizing are self-indulgent and expendable.

Any such argument assumes that theory in its bare bones, as an object, is assuredly *about* the world. It presupposes the world's immediate, objective thereness. In this volume, I raise doubts about any such assumption, thereby confirming the charge of airy-fairy self-indulgence. By implication, anyone whose concern is international relations, or the condition and trajectory of the modern world, should, *must*, address the challenges of a world gone awry. I can hardly deny that disaster looms, that my left-republican politics entail a duty to contribute to the common good, that my privileged position in today's world amplifies my voice. In Chapter 2, I forecast disaster for the modern world; for decades, literally thousands of students heard me say what I say there, passionately, sorrowfully. In Chapter 8, I sort through ethical systems with a steady eye on relevance for a troubled world; I have done so many times all over the world. In this volume's final two chapters, I set out guidelines for good scholarship garnered from long experience and directed to those who want their work to make a difference; I believe that doing so makes a difference.

My own work has long been dedicated to the proposition that everyone is involved in the collective enterprise of world-making. I am not equipped to contribute directly to the management of global challenges. I resist raising my voice about those challenges precisely because I might be credited with expertise that I do not possess. No op-eds, blogs, consultancies, 15-second sound bites.

I am better suited to the world of theory, even if I do not propose theories, even if I disavow the convention of divorcing theory and practice. I cannot subscribe to the view that the world *is* what it is, whoever happens to be looking at it. As I said in the Introduction, context always matters. That theories do not depend on context for their validity or power is, of course, the conventional metatheoretical stance of most scientists who think that their minimalist theories 'work'—that their theories explain how the world works.

Over the last half-century, the philosophy of science and social theory tells a different story. No theory is context free; every theory is embedded

---

6   Ibid., p. 392.

in a story open to many ways of being told. Scattershot theories *about* world politics—theories that barely work at all—beg for second-order theorizing. Insofar as theorists of 'the international' fail to theorize an absent centre (anarchy, anyone?), people like me find a place in the scholarly division of labour. Insofar as frustrated scholars abandon or repudiate theorizing altogether, they have mistaken craft for vocation, part for whole.

As the contents of this volume attest, I do metatheory, and I do it by telling stories—diversely situated, loosely linked, and populated by a large cast of scholars theorizing about many unrelated theories. Wendt complained that *World of Our Making* 'is not reader-friendly'; its 'elliptical style' is distracting.[7] He is hardly alone in these sentiments. Readers may come to the same conclusion after reading this volume. I suggest that theorizing about theorizing will always depend on the explication of difficult texts, that making connections among texts is necessarily elliptical, and that the language required will inevitably puzzle, even baffle, many readers. I also believe that I am a good storyteller—considering the demands of the stories I insist on telling.

To illustrate my expository practices, I quote a passage from Roland Barthes' volume of metatheoretical essays called *Mythologies* (1957):

> The oppressed is nothing, he has only one language, that of his emancipation; the oppressor is everything, his language is rich, multiform, supple, with all the possible degrees of dignity at its disposal: he has an exclusive right to meta-language [méta-langage]. The oppressed makes the world, he has only an active, transitive (political) language; the oppressor conserves it, his language is plenary, intransitive, gestural, theatrical: it is Myth.[8]

Barthes' frame of reference is mythmaking. In consecutive essays, he linked the use of language to politics on the left and right. His political commitments are clear enough: on the left are the oppressed, whose language is simple, direct, active; on the right are the oppressors, whose language is 'rich, multiform, supple, with all the possible degrees of dignity'. I like to think that my language is rich and supple. If Barthes got things right, I am obliged

---

7 Ibid., pp. 385–6.

8 Roland Barthes, *Mythologies*, trans. Annette Lavers (New York: Noonday Press, 1972), p. 150. Speaking in 1956, Roman Jakobson gave credit to the logician Alfred Tarski for introducing the term *metalanguage* in the 1930s; Jakobson called it one of 'six basic aspects of language'. 'Metalanguage as a linguistic problem', in Roman Jakobson, *Selected Writings, Volume VII: Contributions to Comparative Mythology*, ed. Stephen Rudy (Berlin: Mouton, 1985), pp. 113–21 (116–17, 113).

to concede that I am one of the oppressors (as was Barthes himself), whatever I might say about my politics.

I do think that Barthes got it right. My use of the English language reveals extraordinary privilege. It is no wonder that those who are less privileged than I find my use of language somehow smug and austere at the same time, inaccessible and oppressive. Reinforcing this judgement is my theatrical use of the grammatical first person, ever insisting that *my* world is the only world there is, always making myself the 'hero' of my own story.[9] This is mythmaking. So is my claim to occupy the margins of international theory—margins that I have made for myself and expect others to adopt, in the process putting me at the top margin (in chapter headings) and the bottom (in footnotes).

In the passage I quoted, Barthes seems to be saying that the oppressed *make* (*fait*, italicized in the French text) the world, while people like me merely seek to conserve what others have made. A few pages earlier, he held that 'primary language' ('the real language of the woodcutter') '*speaks things*' ('parle *les* choses') while 'second-order language' ('un langage second, un méta-langage') '*speaks of things*' ('parle *des* choses'). Yes, speaking directly is active world-making, as such materially grounded. When I speak *of* trees, yes, I am talking *about* the world—a world made up of trees and many other 'things'. What I say is no less shaped by experience, sharpened with practice, subject to endorsement, emulation and resistance. Speaking *is* doing; what we talk about *always* matters.

Exoticizing plain-speaking woodcutters to make a political point (much as Rousseau did), Barthes held that the woodcutter can only tell a simple story of oppression and emancipation. This is simply wrong. Everyone tells stories about all sorts of things. They do it all the time—often with consummate skill.

Stories empower; they confer power. They constitute (substantiate, rationalize, normalize, legitimate) the 'web of human relationships'.[10] Children hear stories from their earliest days. Once they learn the syntactical niceties of storytelling, they do it too. Every society is saturated in stories telling us who we are, how to act, when to speak, what to say, what is real, what is true. We tell stories to change the way things are, to repair the world or to restore it, to keep it as it is—thereby making the world what it is, margins and all.

---

[9] The ironic scare marks acknowledge Hannah Arendt's compelling story about 'enacted stories': *The Human Condition*, 2nd edn (Chicago: University of Chicago Press, 1998), pp. 181–8.

[10] Arendt, *The Human Condition*, p. 184; also see p. 204, on 'the web of human affairs and relationships and the stories engendered by them'.

Storytelling is mythmaking, and mythmaking is world-making. Many of the stories we tell about ourselves are evasive and exasperating. Myths work as wholes to give meaning to worlds. World-making is complicated, open ended and readily misconstrued. Often enough, the language we use to tell our stories is discomforting and disorienting—even more when we tell stories about the stories we tell, the myths we believe, the intricacies of world-making. All such language about language makes oppressive demands on those who want the world to be a good and simple place, who yearn for justice, who believe that good, simple theories solve all problems, who live within the margins, who love sentimental stories with happy endings. I cannot say this more plainly.

Instead of metatheory, metalanguage might seem to be an intriguing possibility for this volume's through-line. I first encountered the term (and Barthes' use of it) in Halvard Leira and Benjamin de Carvalho's contribution to the *SAGE Handbook of the History, Philosophy and Sociology of International Relations* (2018), when Andreas Gofas, Inanna Hamati-Ataya and I were editing this large text (53 contributors, 600 double-columned pages, devoted, as we say in our Acknowledgements, to the field's 'meta-theoretical landscape').[11] In addition to metalanguage and metatheory (usually hyphenated), various contributors sprinkled the volume with meta-this and that: meta-analysis, meta-consciousness, meta-discourse, meta-narrative, meta-practice. In our introductory essay, my colleagues and I described the use to which scholars in the field put history, philosophy and sociology as 'meta-discourses'.

Like metatheory and metalanguage, meta-discourse points to an object that results from an activity such as theorizing, storytelling, or more generally talking in accordance with established practice. We end up with count nouns (as linguists call them)—theories, stories, talks, texts, practices. Andreas, Inanna and I were never entirely happy with the title we chose for our handbook. Possibilities that we did not consider: *SAGE Handbook of History, Philosophy and Sociology as Disciplined Modes of Theorizing about Disciplined Theorizing about International Relations*. Too cumbersome. *Theorizing 'the International': A SAGE Handbook*. Too cute. Nothing works. Language fails.

Or does it? Cascading night thoughts. Gerunds. Theorizing about theorizing is an activity, a craft, a vocation, a through-line. *This* is what

---

[11] Halvard Leira and Benjamin de Carvalho, 'The function of myths in International Relations: Discipline and identity', in Andreas Gofas, Inanna Hamati-Ataya, and Nicholas Onuf, eds, *SAGE Handbook of the History, Philosophy and Sociology of International Relations* (London: SAGE Publications, 2018), pp. 222–35 (224). Chapter 12 in this volume reprints my contribution to the *Handbook*.

I do—high modernist theorizing, complete with fancy language, in late modern circumstances. Storytelling. Margin-making. Mythmaking. World-making.

13 February 2022

References

Abbott, Andrew (1988) *The System of Professions: An Essay on the Division of Expert Labor* (Chicago: University of Chicago Press).

Adair, Douglass (1957) '"That politics may be reduced to a science": David Hume, James Madison, and the Tenth *Federalist*', *Huntington Library Quarterly* 20, 4, pp. 343–60.

Adler, Emmanuel (1997) 'Seizing the middle ground: Constructivism in world politics', *European Journal of International Relations* 3, 3, pp. 319–63.

Albert, Mathias, Barry Buzan, and Michael Zürn, eds (2013) *Bringing Sociology to International Relations: World Politics as Differentiation Theory* (Cambridge: Cambridge University Press).

Almond, G. A. (1956) 'Comparative political systems', *Journal of Politics* 18, 3, pp. 391–409.

Almond, G. A. (1970) *Political Development* (Boston: Little, Brown).

Appadurai, Arjun (1996) *Modernity at Large: Cultural Dimensions of Globalization* (Minneapolis: University of Minnesota Press).

Arendt, Hannah (1964) *Eichmann in Jerusalem: A Report on the Banality of Evil* (New York: Viking Press).

Arendt, Hannah (1998) *The Human Condition*, 2nd edn (Chicago: University of Chicago Press).

Aristotle (1984) 'On the soul', in Jonathan Barnes, ed., *The Complete Works of Aristotle*, 1 (Princeton: Princeton University Press), pp. 641–92.

Aristotle (1991) *Nicomachean Ethics*, 2nd edn, trans. Terence Irwin (Indianapolis: Hackett).

Ashley, Richard K. (1989) 'Living on border lines: Man, poststructuralism, and war', in James Der Derian and Michael J. Shapiro, eds, *International/ Intertextual Relations: Postmodern Readings of World Politics* (Lexington, MA: Lexington Books), pp. 259–321.

Austin, J. L. (1962) *Sense and Sensibilia* (Oxford: Clarendon Press).

Baker, Gideon (2010) 'The "double law" of hospitality: Rethinking cosmopolitan ethics in humanitarian intervention', *International Relations* 24, 1, pp. 87–103.

Baker, Gideon (2011) *Politicizing Ethics in International Relations: Cosmopolitanism as Hospitality* (Abingdon: Routledge).

Barnes, Jonathan, ed. (1984) *The Complete Works of Aristotle*, Revised Oxford Translation, 2 (Princeton: Princeton University Press).

Barnett, Michael (2012) 'International paternalism and humanitarian governance', *Global Constitutionalism* 1, 3, pp. 485–521.

Bartelson, Jens (2010) 'The social construction of globality', *International Political Sociology* 4, 3, pp. 219–25.

Bartelson, Jens (2011) 'On the indivisibility of sovereignty', *Republics of Letters: A Journal for the Study of Knowledge, Politics, and the Arts* 2, 2, available at: {https://arcade.stanford.edu/sites/default/files/article_pdfs/roflv02i02_Bartelson_060111_0.pdf}

Barthes, Roland (1957) *Mythologies* (Paris: Éditions du Seuil).

Barthes, Roland (1972) *Mythologies*, trans. Annette Lavers (New York: Noonday Press).

Bell, Daniel (1973) *The Coming Post-Industrial Society: A Venture in Social Forecasting* (New York: Basic Books).

Bell, Daniel (1976) *The Cultural Contradictions of Capitalism* (New York: Basic Books).

Bellamy Foster, John (1982) 'Marxian economics and the state', *Science & Society* 46, 3, pp. 257–83.

Benhabib, Seyla (1986) *Critique, Norm, and Utopia: A Study of the Normative Foundations of Critical Theory* (New York: Columbia University Press).

Benhabib, Seyla (1989–1990) 'Critical theory and postmodernism: On the interplay of ethics, aesthetics, and utopia in critical theory', *Cardozo Law Review* 11, 5–6, pp. 1435–49.

Benhabib, Seyla (1992) *Situating the Self: Gender, Community and Postmodernism in Contemporary Ethics* (New York: Routledge).

Benhabib, Seyla (1996) *The Reluctant Modernism of Hannah Arendt* (Thousand Oaks, CA: Sage).

Benhabib, Seyla (2006) *Another Cosmopolitanism* (Oxford: Oxford University Press).

Bourdieu, Pierre (1977) *Outline of a Theory of Practice*, trans. Richard Price (Cambridge: Cambridge University Press).

Bozeman, Adda B. (1960) *Politics and Culture International History* (Princeton: Princeton University Press).

Branch, Jordan (2011) 'Mapping the sovereign state: Technology, authority, and systemic change', *International Organization* 65, 1, pp. 1–36.

Brecht, Arnold (1959) *Political Theory: The Foundations of Twentieth-Century Political Thought* (Princeton: Princeton University Press).

Bresnan, Joan, and Tatiana Nikitina (2010) 'The gradience of the dative alternation', in Linda Ann Uyechi and Lian-Hee Wee, eds, *Reality Exploration and Discovery: Pattern Interaction in Language and Life* (Stanford: CSLI Publications), pp. 161–84.

Brown, Chris (1994) '"Turtles all the way down": Anti-foundationalism, critical theory and international relations', *Millennium* 23, 1, pp. 213–36.

Bukovansky, Mlada, Ian Clark, Robyn Eckersley, Richard Price, Christian Reus-Smit, and Nicholas J. Wheeler (2012) *Special Responsibilities: Global Problems and American Power* (Cambridge: Cambridge University Press).

Buller, David (2005) *Adapting Minds: Evolutionary Psychology and the Persistent Quest for Human Nature* (Cambridge, MA: MIT Press).

Buss, David M. (2003) *The Evolution of Desire: Strategies of Human Mating*, rev. edn (New York: Basic Books).

Campbell, A. (1988) 'International law and primitive law', *Oxford Journal of Legal Studies* 8, 2, pp. 169–96.

Campbell, David, and Michael Shapiro, eds (1999) *Moral Spaces: Rethinking Ethics and World Politics* (Minneapolis: University of Minnesota Press).

Carr, Edward Hallett (1946) *The Twenty Years' Crisis 1919–1939*, 2nd edn (London: Macmillan).

Castells, Manuel (2000) *The Information Age*, 1, *The Rise of the Network Society*, 2nd edn (Oxford: Blackwell).

Catechism of the Catholic Church (2003) (New York: Doubleday).

Cavallar, Georg (2008) 'Vitoria, Grotius, Pufendorf, Wolff and Vattel: Accomplices of European colonialism and exploitation or true cosmopolitans?' *Journal of the History of International Law* 10, 2, pp. 181–209.

Chernoff, Fred (2008) *Theory and Metatheory in International Relations* (Basingstoke: Palgrave).

Chitty, Naren (2017) 'Introduction', in Chitty, Naren, Li Ji, Gary D. Rawnsley, and Craig Hayden, eds, *The Routledge Handbook of Soft Power* (Abingdon: Routledge).

Chomsky, Noam (1980) *Rules and Representations* (New York: Columbia University Press).

Cicero (1991) *On Duties*, trans. Margaret Atkins (Cambridge: Cambridge University Press).

Connolly, William E. (1989) 'Identity and difference in global politics', in James Der Derian and Michael Shapiro, eds, *International/Intertextual Relations* (Lexington, MA: Lexington Books), pp. 323–42.

Craik, Kenneth (1967) *The Nature of Explanation* (Cambridge: Cambridge University Press).

Crelinsten, Ronald D., and Alex P. Schmid, eds (1995) *The Politics of Pain: Torturers and Their Masters* (Boulder, CO: Westview Press).

Delbeke, Jos (1981) 'Recent long-wave theories: A critical survey', *Futures* 13, 4, pp. 246–57.

Der Derian, James (1987) 'Mediating estrangement: A theory for diplomacy', *Review of International Studies* 13, 2, pp. 91–110.

Der Derian, James (1987) *On Diplomacy: A Genealogy of Western Estrangement* (Oxford: Basil Blackwell).

Der Derian, James (1989) 'The boundaries of knowledge and power in international relations', in James Der Derian and Michael J. Shapiro, eds, *International/Intertextual Relations: Postmodern Readings of World Politics* (Lexington, MA: Lexington Books), pp. 3–10.

Der Derian, James, and Michael J. Shapiro, eds (1989) *International/ Intertextual Relations: Postmodern Readings of World Politics* (Lexington, MA: Lexington Books).

Derrida, Jacques (1972) *Marges de la philosophie* (Paris: Les Éditions de Minuit).

Derrida, Jacques (1974) *Of Grammatology*, trans. Gayatri Chakravorty Spivak (Baltimore: Johns Hopkins University Press).

Derrida, Jacques (1978) *Writing and Difference*, trans. Richard Macksey and Alan Bass (Chicago: University of Chicago Press).

Derrida, Jacques (1982) *Margins of Philosophy*, trans. Alan Bass (Chicago: University of Chicago Press).

Derrida, Jacques (1992) *Given Time, 1, Counterfeit Money*, trans. Peggy Kamuf (Chicago: University of Chicago Press).

Derrida, Jacques (1999) *Adieu: To Emmanuel Levinas*, trans. Pascale-Anne Brault and Michael Nass (Stanford: Stanford University Press).

Derrida, Jacques (2000) *Of Hospitality*, trans. Rachel Bowlby (Stanford: Stanford University Press).

Derrida, Jacques (2005) 'The principle of hospitality', *Parallax* 11, 1, pp. 6–9.

Deutsch, Karl W. (1963) *The Nerves of Government: Models of Political Communication and Control* (New York: Free Press).

de Vattel, [Emer] (2008) *The Law of Nations, Or, Principles of the Law of Nature, Applied to the Conduct and Affairs of Nations and Sovereigns, with Three Early Essays on the Origin and Nature of Natural Law and on Luxury*, trans. Thomas Nugent (Indianapolis: Liberty Fund).

Donnelly, Jack (2012) 'The elements of the structures of international systems', *International Organization* 66, 4, pp. 609–43.

Drinkwater, Derek (2005) *Sir Harold Nicolson and International Relations: The Practitioner as Theorist* (Oxford: Oxford University Press).

Easton, David (1953) *The Political System* (New York: Alfred Knopf).

Easton, David (1957) 'An approach to the analysis of political systems', *World Politics* 9, 3, pp. 383–400.

Easton, David (1959) 'Political anthropology', in Bernard J. Siegel, ed., *Biennial Review of Anthropology, 1959* (Stanford: Stanford University Press), pp. 210–62.

Elias, Norbert (1982) *Power and Civility: The Civilizing Process, 2*, trans. Edmund Jephcott (New York: Pantheon).

Enloe, Cynthia (1990) *Bananas, Beaches and Bases: Making Feminist Sense of International Politics* (Berkeley: University of California Press).

Epstein, Charlotte (2103) 'Constructivism or the eternal return of universals in International Relations: Why returning to language is vital to prolonging the owl's flight', *European Journal of International Relations* 19, 3, pp. 499–519.

Fasolt, Constantin (2004) *The Limits of History* (Chicago: University of Chicago Press).

Fei Xiaotong (1992) *From the Soil: The Foundations of Chinese Society*, trans. Gary Hamilton and Wang Zheng (Berkeley: University of California Press).

Fiske, Alan Page (1991) *Structures of Social Life: The Four Elementary Forms of Human Relations* (New York: Free Press).

Fiske, Donald W., and Richard A. Shweder, eds (1986) *Metatheory in Social Science: Pluralism and Subjectivities* (Chicago: University of Chicago Press).

Fodor, Jerry (1983) *The Modularity of Mind: An Essay on Faculty Psychology* (Cambridge, MA: MIT Press).

Forrester, Jay W. (1981) 'Innovation and economic change', *Futures* 13, 4, pp. 323–31.

Foucault, Michel (1971) *The Order of Things: An Archeology of the Human Sciences*, trans. A. M. Sheridan Smith (New York: Pantheon Books).

Foucault, Michel (1972) *The Archeology of Knowledge*, trans. A. M. Sheridan Smith (New York: Pantheon Books).

Foucault, Michel (1978) *Security, Territory, Population: Lectures at the Collège de France, 1977–1978*, trans. Graham Burchill (Basingstoke: Palgrave Macmillan).

Foucault, Michel (1979) *Discipline and Punish: The Birth of the Prison*, trans. A. M. Sheridan Smith (New York: Vintage Books).

Freire, Lucas G. (2013) 'The potential and the pitfalls of metatheory in IR', *Estudos Internacionais* 1, 2, pp. 271–302.

Fried, Morton H. (1967) *The Evolution of Political Society: An Essay in Political Anthropology* (New York: McGraw Hill).

Fromm, Erich (1941) *Escape from Freedom* (New York: Rinehart and Winston).

Fukuyama, Francis (1989) 'The end of history', *The National Interest*, 16, pp. 3–18.

Gallie, W. B. (1955–6) 'Essentially contested concepts', *Proceedings of the Aristotelian Society,* new series, 56, pp. 167–98.

Galtung, Johan (1964) 'A structural theory of aggression', *Journal of Peace Research* 1, 2, pp. 95–119.

Galtung, Johan (1969) 'Violence, peace and peace research', *Journal of Peace Research* 6, 3, pp. 167–91.

Galtung, Johan (1970) 'Feudal systems, structural violence, and the structural theory of revolutions', *Proceedings of the International Peace Research Association Third General Conference*, 1 (Assen: Van Gorcum), pp. 110–88.

Galtung, Johan (1971) 'A structural theory of imperialism', *Journal of Peace Research* 8, 2, pp. 81–117.

Galtung, Johan (1980) '"A structural theory of imperialism"—Ten years later', *Millennium: Journal of International Studies* 9, 3, pp. 181–96.

Galtung, Johan (1990) 'Cultural violence', *Journal of Peace Research* 27, 3, pp. 291–305.

Galtung, Johan (1996) *Peace by Peaceful Means: Peace and Conflict, Development and Civilization* (London: Sage).

Geertz, Clifford (1966) *Agricultural Involution: The Processes of Ecological Change in Indonesia* (Berkeley: University of California Press).

Giarini, Orio (1980) *Dialogue on Wealth and Welfare: An Alternative View of World Capital Formation* (Elmsford: Pergamon Press).

Giarini, Orio, and Henri Loubergé (1978) *The Diminishing Returns of Technology: An Essay on the Crisis in Economic Growth* (Elmsford: Pergamon Press).

Gibbs, Raymond W., Jr (2005) *Embodiment and Cognitive Science* (Cambridge: Cambridge University Press).

Gibbs, Raymond W., Jr, ed. (2008) *The Cambridge Handbook of Metaphor and Thought* (Cambridge: Cambridge University Press).

Giddens, Anthony (1990) *The Consequences of Modernity* (Stanford: Stanford University Press).

Gilpin, Robert G. (1986) 'The richness of the tradition of political realism', in Robert O. Keohane, ed., *Neorealism and Its Critics* (New York: Columbia University Press), pp. 301–32.

Gofas, Andreas, Inanna Hamati-Ataya, and Nicholas Onuf, eds (2018) *SAGE Handbook of the History, Philosophy and Sociology of International Relations* (London: Sage).

Goodman, Nelson (1978) *Ways of Worldmaking* (Indianapolis: Hackett).

Gopnik, Alison (2009) *The Philosophical Baby: What Children's Minds Tell Us about Truth, Love, and the Meaning of Life* (New York: Farrar, Strauss and Giroux).

Gopnik, Alison, and Andrew N. Meltzoff (1997) *Words, Thought, and Theories* (Cambridge, MA: MIT Press).

Gopnik, Alison, and Henry M. Wellman (1994) 'The theory theory', in Lawrence A. Hirschfeld and Susan A. Gelman, eds, *Mapping the Mind: Domain Specificity in Cognition and Culture* (Cambridge: Cambridge University Press), pp. 119–48.

Gordon, David M. (1980) 'Stages of accumulation and long economic cycles', in Terence K. Hopkins and Immanuel Wallerstein, eds, *Processes of the World System* (Beverly Hills, CA: Sage), pp. 9–45.

Gore-Booth, Paul Henry, ed. (1979) *Satow's Guide to Diplomatic Practice*, 5th edn (London: Longman).

Gouldner, Alvin W. (1970) *The Coming Crisis of Western Sociology* (New York: Basic Books).

Graham, Alan K., and Peter M. Senge (1980) 'A long-wave hypothesis of innovation', *Technological Forecasting and Social Change* 17, 4, pp. 283–311.

Gregory, Richard L. (1997) *Eye and Brain: The Psychology of Seeing*, 5th edn (Princeton: Princeton University Press).

Griffin, Roger (2007) *Modernism and Fascism: The Sense of a Beginning under Mussolini and Hitler* (Basingstoke: Palgrave Macmillan).

Gross, Bertram (1980) *Friendly Fascism: The New Face of American Power* (New York: M. Evans).

Grotius, Hugo (2005) *The Rights of War and Peace*, ed. Richard Tuck from Jean Barbeyrac's 1738 edn, trans. John Morrice, 1 (Indianapolis: Liberty Fund).

Gunnell, John G. (2011) 'Social scientific inquiry and meta-theoretical fantasy: The case of International Relations', *Review of International Studies* 37, 4, pp. 1447–69.

Gutmann, Matthew C. (1996) *The Meanings of Macho: Being a Man in Mexico City* (Berkeley: University of California Press).

Haas, Michael (1970) 'International subsystems: Stability and polarity', *American Political Science Review* 64, 1, pp. 98–123.

Habermas, Jürgen (1984) *The Theory of Communicative Action*, 1, *Reason and the Rationalization of Society*, trans. Thomas McCarthy (Boston: Beacon Press).

Habermas, Jürgen (1987) *The Theory of Communicative Action*, 2, *Lifeworld and System: A Critique of Functionalist Reason*, trans. Thomas McCarthy (Boston: Beacon Press).

Hacking, Ian (1983) *Representing and Intervening: Introductory Topics in the Philosophy of Natural Science* (Cambridge: Cambridge University Press).

Hamati-Ataya, Inanna (2016) 'IR theory and the question of science', in Ken Booth and Toni Erskine, eds, *International Relations Theory Today*, 2nd edn (Cambridge: Polity), pp. 69–84.

Hamilton, Scott (2017) 'A genealogy of metatheory in IR: How "ontology" emerged from the inter-paradigm debate', *International Theory*, 9, 1, pp. 136–70.

Hardt, Michael, and Antonio Negri (2000) *Empire* (Cambridge, MA: Harvard University Press).

Haritos-Fatouros, Mika (2003) *The Psychological Origins of Institutionalized Torture* (London: Routledge).

Harrington, Michael (1976) *The Twilight of Capitalism* (New York: Simon and Schuster).

Harris, Marvin (1968) *The Rise of Anthropological Theory: A History of Theory of Cultures* (New York: Crowell).

Harris, Marvin (1977) *Cannibals and Kings: The Origins of Cultures* (New York: Random House).

Harris, Marvin (1979) *Cultural Materialism: The Struggle for a Science of Culture* (New York: Random House).

Harris, Paul L. (1994) 'Thinking by children and scientists: False analogies and neglected similarities', in Lawrence A. Hirschfeld and Susan A. Gelman, eds, *Mapping the Mind: Domain Specificity in Cognition and Culture* (Cambridge: Cambridge University Press), pp. 294–315.

Hart, H. L. A. (1960) *The Concept of Law* (Oxford: Clarendon Press).

Hayek, Friedrich A. (1944) *The Road to Serfdom* (Chicago: University of Chicago Press).

Heelan, Patrick A. (1983) *Sense Perception and the Philosophy of Science* (Berkeley: University of California Press).

Hegel, G. W. F. (1991) *Elements of the Philosophy of Right*, trans. H. B. Nisbet (Cambridge: Cambridge University Press).

Heidegger, Martin (1962) *Being and Time*, trans. John Macquarrie and Edward Robinson (New York: Harper Row).

Heinz, Wolfgang S. (1995) 'The military, torture, and human rights: Experiences from Argentina, Brazil, Chile and Uruguay', in Ronald D. Crelinsten and Alex P. Schmid, eds, *The Politics of Pain: Torturers and Their Masters* (Boulder, CO: Westview Press), pp. 65–98.

Henrich, Joseph (2020) *The WEIRDest People in the World: How the West Became Psychologically Peculiar and Particularly Prosperous* (New York: Farrar, Straus and Giroux).

Hirschman, Albert O. (1977) *The Passions and the Interests: Political Arguments for Capitalism before Its Triumph* (Princeton: Princeton University Press).

Hobbes, Thomas (1991) *Leviathan*, ed. Richard Tuck (Cambridge: Cambridge University Press).

Hoffman, Donald D. (2020) *The Case against Reality: How Evolution Hid the Truth from Our Eyes* (London: Penguin Books).

Hoffmann, Stanley (1959) 'International relations: The long road to theory', *World Politics* 11, 3, pp. 315–62.

Hoffmann, Stanley (1961) 'International systems and international law', *World Politics* 14, 1, pp. 205–37.

Hoffmann, Stanley (1977) 'An American social science: International Relations', *Daedalus* 106, 3, pp. 41–60.

Hoffmann, Stanley (1978) *Primacy or World Order: American Foreign Policy since the Cold War* (New York: McGraw Hill).

Hollis, Martin, and Steve Smith (1990) *Explaining and Understanding International Relations* (Oxford: Clarendon Press).

Holt, Robert T., and John E. Turner (1975) 'Crises and sequences in collective theory development', *American Political Science Review* 69, 3, pp. 979–94.

Huggins, Martha, Mika Haritos-Fatouros, and Philip Zimbardo (2002) *Violence Workers: Police Torturers and Murderers Reconstruct Brazilian Atrocities* (Berkeley: University of California Press).

Hume, David (1963) 'Idea of a perfect commonwealth', in *Essays: Moral, Political, Literary* (Oxford: Oxford University Press), pp. 512–29.

Hume, David (1963) 'Of the Origin of Government', in *Essays: Moral, Political, Literary* (Oxford: Oxford University Press), pp. 37–41.

Hume, David (1978) *A Treatise of Human Nature*, 2nd edn rev. P. H. Nidditch (Oxford: Clarendon Press).

Hume, David (1999) *An Enquiry concerning Human Understanding*, ed. Peter Millican (Oxford: Oxford University Press).

Iovino, Serenella (2017) *Ecocriticism and Italy: Ecology, Resistance, and Liberation* (London: Bloomsbury).

Jackson, Patrick Thaddeus (2011) *The Conduct of Inquiry in International Relations: Philosophy of Science and Its Implications for the Study of World Politics* (Abingdon: Routledge).

Jackson, Robert H. (1990) *Quasi-States: Sovereignty, International Relations and the Third World* (Cambridge: Cambridge University Press).

Jakobson, Roman (1985) *Selected Writings, Volume VII: Contributions to Comparative Mythology*, ed. Stephen Rudy (Berlin: Mouton), pp. 113–21.

Jefferson, Thomas, letter to John Adams, 28 October 1813, in Lester J. Cappon, ed., *The Adams-Jefferson Letters* (Chapel Hill: University of North Carolina Press, 1959), pp. 387–92.

Jönnson, Christer, and Martin Hall (2005) *Essence of Diplomacy* (Basingstoke: Palgrave Macmillan).

Joseph, Jonathan (2010) 'Is Waltz a realist?' *International Relations* 24, 4, pp. 478–93.

Joseph, Jonathan (2017) 'The hegemony of governmentality: Towards a research agenda', *All Azimuth* 6, 2, pp. 5–18.

Kahn, Herman (1982) *The Coming Boom: Economic, Social and Political* (New York: Simon and Schuster).

Kahn, Herman, William Brown, and Leon Martel (1976) *The Next Two Hundred Years: A Scenario for America and the World* (New York: William Morrow).

Kahn, Herman, and John B. Phelps (1979) 'The economic present and future', *The Futurist* 13, 3, pp. 202–22.

Kang, David C. (2010) *East Asia before the West: Five Centuries of Trade and Tribute* (New York: Columbia University Press).

Kant, Immanuel (1965) *Critique of Pure Reason*, trans. Norman Kemp Smith (New York: St Martin's Press).

Kant, Immanuel (1991) 'Perpetual peace: A philosophical sketch', in Hans Reiss, ed., *Kant: Political Writings*, 2nd edn (Cambridge: Cambridge University Press), pp. 93–130.

Kant, Immanuel (1997) *Critique of Practical Reason*, trans. Mary Gregor (Cambridge: Cambridge University Press).

Kant, Immanuel (2000) *Critique of the Power of Judgment*, trans. Paul Guyer and Eric Matthews (Cambridge: Cambridge University Press).

Kaplan, Morton A. (1957) *System and Process in International Politics* (New York: Wiley).

Kaplan, Morton A. (1961) 'Problems of theory building and theory confirmation in international politics', *World Politics* 14, 1, pp. 6–24.

Kaplan, Morton A. (1979) *Towards Professionalism in International Theory: Macrosystem Analysis* (New York: Free Press).

Kaplan, Morton A., and Nicholas de B. Katzenbach (1961) *The Political Foundations of International Law* (New York: Wiley).

Keens-Soper, H. M. A., and Karl W. Schweizer, eds (1983) *The Art of Diplomacy: François de Callières* (New York: Holmes & Meier).

Kelsen, Hans (1961) *General Theory of Law and State* (New York: Russell & Russell).

Kelsen, Hans (1967) *Principles of International Law*, 2d edn, rev. Robert W. Tucker (New York: Holt, Rinehart and Winston).

Kennedy, David (2005) *The Dark Side of Virtue* (Princeton: Princeton University Press).

Keohane, Robert O., ed. (1986) *Neorealism and Its Critics* (New York: Columbia University Press).

Keohane, Robert O., and Joseph S. Nye, Jr, eds (1972) *Transnational Relations and World Politics* (Cambridge, MA: Harvard University Press).

Kershnar, Stephen (2001) *Desert, Retribution, and Torture* (Lanham, MD: University Press of America).

Kessler, Oliver (2009) 'Toward a sociology of the international? International relations between anarchy and world society', *International Political Sociology* 3, 1, pp. 87–108.

Knorr, Klaus, and James N. Rosenau, eds (1969) *Contending Approaches to International Politics* (Princeton: Princeton University Press).

Kondratiev, N. D. (1979) 'The long waves in economic life', *Review* 2, 4, pp. 519–62.

Kratochwil, Friedrich V. (1989) *Rules, Norms, and Decisions: On the Conditions of Practical and Legal Reasoning in International Relations and Domestic Affairs* (Cambridge: Cambridge University Press).

Kratochwil, Friedrich V. (2007) 'Evidence, inference, and truth as problems of theory building in the social sciences', in Richard N. Lebow and Mark Irving Lichbach, eds, *Theory and Evidence in Comparative Politics and International Relations* (New York: Palgrave Macmillan), pp. 25–54.

Kratochwil, Friedrich V. (2007) 'Of communities, gangs, historicity and the problem of Santa Claus: Replies to my critics', *Journal of International Relations and Development* 10, 1, pp. 57–78.

Kratochwil, Friedrich V. (2007) 'Of false promises and good bets: A plea for a pragmatic approach to theory building (the Tartu Lecture)', *Journal of International Relations and Development* 10, 1, pp. 1–15.

Kratochwil, Friedrich V. (2014) *The Status of Law in World Society: Meditations on the Role and Rule of Law* (Cambridge: Cambridge University Press).

Kratochwil, Friedrich V., and John Gerard Ruggie (1986) International organization: A state of the art on an art of the state', *International Organization* 40, 4, pp. 753–75.

Kuhn, Thomas S. (1970) *The Structure of Scientific Revolutions*, 2nd edn (Chicago: University of Chicago Press).

Kurki, Milja (2008) *Causation in International Relations: Reclaiming Causal Analysis* (Cambridge: Cambridge University Press).

Lakoff, George, and Mark Johnson (1980) *Metaphors We Live By* (Chicago: University of Chicago Press).

Lakoff, George, and Mark Johnson (1999) *Philosophy in the Flesh: The Embodied Mind and Its Challenge to Western Thought* (New York: Basic Books).

Lang, Jr, Anthony F., Nicholas Rengger, and William Walker (2006) 'The role(s) of rules: Some conceptual clarifications', *International Relations* 20, 3, pp. 274–94.

Langbein, John H. (1977) *Torture and the Law of Proof: Europe and England in the Ancien Régime* (Chicago: University of Chicago Press).

Lapid, Yosef (1989) 'The third debate: On the prospects of international theory in a post-positivist era', *International Studies Quarterly* 33, 3, pp. 235–54.

Latour, Bruno (2005) *Reassembling the Social: An Introduction to Actor-Network-Theory* (Oxford: Oxford University Press).

Lea, Henry C. (1968) *Superstition and Force: Essays on the Wager of Law—The Wager of Battle—The Ordeal—Torture*, 2nd edn (New York: Greenwood Press).

Lebow, Richard N. (2010) *Forbidden Fruit: Counterfactuals and International Relations* (Princeton: Princeton University Press).

Leira, Halvard, and Benjamin de Carvalho (2018) 'The function of myths in International Relations: Discipline and identity', in Andreas Gofas, Inanna Hamati-Ataya, and Nicholas Onuf (eds), *SAGE Handbook of the History, Philosophy and Sociology of International Relations* (London: Sage), pp. 222–35.

Lenin, V. I. (1939) *Imperialism, The Highest Stage of Capitalism* (New York: International Publishers).

Lenski, Gerhard E. (1966) *Power and Privilege: A Theory of Social Stratification* (Chapel Hill: University of North Carolina Press).

Leslie, Alan M. (1987) 'Pretense and representation: The origins of "Theory of mind"', *Psychological Review* 94, 4, pp. 412–26.

Leslie, Alan M. (1994) 'ToMM, ToBy, and agency: Core architecture and domain specificity', in Lawrence A. Hirschfeld and Susan A. Gelman, eds, *Mapping the Mind: Domain Specificity in Cognition and Culture* (Cambridge: Cambridge University Press), pp. 119–48.

Levin, Michael (1990) 'Torture and other extreme measures taken for the general good: Further reflections on a philosophical problem', in Peter Suedfeld, ed., *Psychology and Torture* (New York: Hemisphere Publishing), pp. 89–100.

Lewis, W. Arthur (1978) *The Evolution of the International Economic Order* (Princeton: Princeton University Press).

Lindblom, Charles E. (1977) *Politics and Markets: The World's Political-Economic Systems* (New York: Basic Books).

Liska, George (1966) 'The heroic decade and after: International relations as events, discipline, and profession', *SAIS Review* 10, 4, pp. 5–11.

Luard, Evan (1976) *Types of International Society* (New York: Free Press).

Luhmann, Niklas (2002) *Theories of Distinction: Redescribing the Descriptions of Modernity* (Stanford: Stanford University Press).

Lukács, Georg (1972) *History and Class Consciousness: Studies in Marxist Dialectics* (Cambridge, MA: MIT Press).

Lyotard, Jean-François (1984) *The Postmodern Condition: A Report on Knowledge*, trans. Geoff Bennington and Brian Massumi (Minneapolis: University of Minnesota Press).

Mach, Ernst (1914) *The Analysis of Sensations and the Relation of the Physical to the Psychical*, rev. Sydney Waterlow, trans. C. M. Williams (Chicago: Open Court).

Machiavelli, Niccolò (1961) *Il Principe* (Turin: Einaudi).

Machiavelli, Niccolò (1998) *The Prince*, trans. Harvey C. Mansfield, 2nd edn (Chicago: University of Chicago Press).

Mandel, Ernest (1978) *Late Capitalism* (London: Verso).

Mandel, Ernest (1980) *Long Waves of Capitalist Development* (Cambridge: Cambridge University Press).

Mandel, Ernest (1981) 'Explaining long waves of capitalist development', *Futures* 13, 4, pp. 332–8.

Mannheim, Karl (1940) *Man and Society in an Age of Reconstruction: Studies in Modern Social Structure* (London: Kegan Paul).

Mansfield, Edwin (1968) *The Economics of Technological Change* (New York: Norton).

Marx, Karl (1965) *Pre-Capitalist Economic Formations*, trans. Jack Cohen (New York: International Publishers).

Marx, Karl, and Friedrich Engels (1970) *The German Ideology*, 3rd edn (Moscow: Progress Publishers).

Mattingly, Garrett (1964) *Renaissance Diplomacy* (Baltimore: Penguin).

Mauss, Marcel (1967) *The Gift: Forms and Functions of Exchange in Archaic Societies*, trans. Ian Cunnison (New York: Norton).

McClelland, Charles A. (1961) 'The acute international crisis', *World Politics* 14, 1, pp. 182–204.

McClelland, Charles A. (1965) *Theory and the International System* (New York: Macmillan).

McDougal, Myres S., and Harold Lasswell (1959) 'The identification and appraisal of diverse systems of public order', *American Journal of International Law* 53, 1, pp. 1–29.

McDowell, John (1996) *Mind and World, with a New Introduction* (Cambridge, MA: Harvard University Press).

Mead, Walter Russell (2004) 'America's sticky power', *Foreign Policy* 141, pp. 46–53.

Meadows, Donella H., Dennis L. Meadows, Jørgen Randers, and William W. Behrens III (1972) *Limits to Growth: A Report for the Club of Rome's Project on the Predicament of Mankind* (New York: Universe Books).

Mehta, Uday S. (1990) 'Liberal strategies of exclusion', *Politics & Society* 18, 4, pp. 427–54.

Mensch, Gerhard (1979) *Stalemate in Technology: Innovations Overcome the Depression* (Cambridge: Ballinger).

Milgram, Stanley (1974) *Obedience to Authority: An Experimental View* (New York: Harper & Row).

Miller, Martin (2007) "'24" gets a lesson in torture from the experts', *Los Angeles Times* (13 February), pp. E1, 14.

Mitrany, David (1966) *A Working Peace System* (Chicago: Quadrangle Books).

Modelski, George (1961) 'Agraria and Industria: Two models of the international system', *World Politics* 14, 1, pp. 118–43.

Morgenthau, Hans J. (1946) *Scientific Man vs. Power Politics* (Chicago: University of Chicago Press).

Morgenthau, Hans J. (1948) *Politics among Nations: The Struggle for Power and Peace* (New York: Alfred Knopf).

Morgenthau, Hans J. (1960) *Politics among Nations: The Struggle for Power and Peace*, 3rd edn (New York: Alfred Knopf).

Morgenthau, Hans J. (1967) *Politics among Nations: The Struggle for Power and Peace*, 4th edn (New York: Alfred Knopf).

Morse, Edward L. (1976) *Modernization and the Transformation of International Relations* (New York: Free Press).

Moseley, K. P., and Immanuel Wallerstein (1978) 'Precapitalist social structures', *Annual Review of Sociology* 4, pp. 259–90.

Nagel, Jack H. (1975) *The Descriptive Analysis of Power* (New Haven: Yale University Press).

Newton, Isaac (1729) *The Mathematical Principles of Natural Philosophy*, trans. Andrew Motte, 1 (London: printed for Benjamin Motte).

Nicolson, Harold (1939) *Diplomacy* (New York: Harcourt Brace).

Nicolson, Harold (1954) *The Evolution of the Diplomatic Method* (London: Cassell).

Nicolson, Harold (1955) *Good Behaviour: Being a Study of Certain Types of Civility* (London: Constable).

Nye, Jr, Joseph S. (1965) *Pan-Africanism and East African Integration* (Cambridge, MA: Harvard University Press).

Nye, Jr, Joseph S. (1971) *Peace in Parts: Integration and Conflict in Regional Organizations* (Boston: Little, Brown).

Nye, Jr, Joseph S. (1990) *Bound to Lead: The Changing Nature of American Power* (New York: Basic Books).

Nye, Jr, Joseph S. (1990) 'Soft power', *Foreign Policy* 80, pp. 153–71.

Nye, Jr, Joseph S. (2004) *Soft Power: The Means to Success in World Politics* (New York: Public Affairs).

Nye, Jr, Joseph S. (2008) 'Public diplomacy and soft power', *Annals of the American Academy of Political and Social Science* 616, 1, pp. 94–109.

Nye, Jr, Joseph S. (2011) *The Future of Power* (New York: Public Affairs).

Olson, Mancur (1982) *The Rise and Decline of Nations: Economic Growth, Stagflation, and Social Rigidities* (New Haven, Yale University Press).

Onuf, Nicholas Greenwood (1982) 'Global law-making and legal thought', in Nicholas Greenwood Onuf, ed., *Law-Making in the Global Community* (Durham: Carolina Academic Press), pp. 1–81.

Onuf, Nicholas Greenwood (1983) 'Reports to the Club of Rome', *World Politics* 36, 1, pp. 121–46.

Onuf, Nicholas Greenwood (1989) *World of Our Making: Rules and Rule in Social Theory and International Relations* (Columbia: University of South Carolina Press).

Onuf, Nicholas (1995) 'Levels', *European Journal of International Relations* 1, 1, pp. 35–58.

Onuf, Nicholas (1998) 'Everyday ethics in international relations', *Millennium: Journal of International Studies* 27, 3, pp. 669–93.

Onuf, Nicholas Greenwood (1998) *The Republican Legacy in International Thought* (Cambridge: Cambridge University Press).

Onuf, Nicholas (2002) 'Worlds of our making: The strange career of constructivism in International Relations', in Donald J. Puchala, ed., *Visions of International Relations: Assessing an Academic Field* (Columbia: University of South Carolina Press), pp. 119–41.

Onuf, Nicholas (2005) 'Late modern civil society', in Randall D. Germain and Michael Kenny, eds, *The Idea of Global Civil Society: Politics and Ethics in a Globalizing Era* (London: Routledge), pp. 47–63.

Onuf, Nicholas (2008) *International Legal Theory: Essays and Engagements, 1966–2006* (Abingdon: Routledge-Cavendish).

Onuf, Nicholas Greenwood (2010) 'Fitting metaphors: The case of the European Union', *Perspectives: Review of International Affairs* 18, 1, pp. 63–76.

Onuf, Nicholas (2010) 'Old mistakes: Bourdieu, Derrida, and the "force of law"', *International Political Sociology* 3, 4, pp. 315–18.

Onuf, Nicholas Greenwood (2013) *Making Sense, Making Worlds: Constructivism in Social Theory and International Relations* (Abingdon: Routledge).

Onuf, Nicholas (2013) 'Organizing for good: Republican theory in a changing world', *The Global Community: Yearbook of International Law and Jurisprudence 2013*, pp. 507–33.

Onuf, Nicholas (2013) 'Recognition and the constitution of epochal change', *International Relations* 27, 2, pp. 121–40.

Onuf, Nicholas (2016) 'Constructivism at the crossroads; or, the problem of moderate-sized dry goods', *International Political Sociology* 10, 1, pp. 115–32.

Onuf, Nicholas (2016) 'Contradictions', in Naeem Inayatullah and Elizabeth Dauphinee, eds, *Narrative Global Politics: Theory, History and the Personal in International Relations* (Abingdon: Routledge), pp. 104–21.

Onuf, Nicholas Greenwood (2018) *The Mightie Frame: Epochal Change and the Modern World* (New York: Oxford University Press).

Onuf, Nicholas, and Peter Onuf (2006) *Nations, Markets and War: Modern History and the American Civil War* (Charlottesville: University of Virginia Press).

Organization of American States (1985) 'Inter-American Convention to Prevent and Punish Torture', 9 December 1985.

Ortony, Andrew, ed. (1979) *Metaphor and Thought* (Cambridge: Cambridge University Press).

Ortony, Andrew, ed. (1993) *Metaphor and Thought*, 2nd edn (Cambridge: Cambridge University Press).

Parry, John T. (2006) 'Escalation and necessity: Defining torture at home and abroad', in Sanford Levinson, ed., *Torture: A Collection*, revised edn (Oxford: Oxford University Press), pp. 145–64.

Parsons, Talcott (1951) *The Social System* (New York: Free Press).

Peters, Edward (1996) *Torture*, expanded edn (Philadelphia: University of Pennsylvania Press).

Pettit, Philip (1997) *Republicanism: A Theory of Freedom and Government* (Oxford: Oxford University Press).

Piatier, Andre (1981) 'Innovation, information and long-term growth', *Futures* 13, 5, pp. 371–82.

Pinker, Stephen (2002) *The Blank Slate: The Modern Denial of Human Nature* (New York: Penguin Books).

Pinker, Stephen (2007) *The Stuff of Thought: Language as a Window into Human Nature* (New York: Viking).

Polanyi, Karl (1944) *The Great Transformation: The Political and Economic Origins of Our Time* (New York: Farrar & Rinehart).

Popper, Karl R. (1957) *The Poverty of Historicism* (London: Routledge & Kegan Paul).

Popper, Karl R. (1972) *Objective Knowledge: An Evolutionary Approach* (Oxford: Clarendon Press).

Popper, Karl R. (1978) 'Three worlds', The Tanner lecture on human values, University of Michigan, available at: {https://tannerlectures.utah.edu/_resources/documents/a-to-z/p/popper80.pdf}

Premack, David (1990) 'The infant's theory of self-propelled objects', *Cognition* 36, 1, pp. 1–16.

Premack, David, and Ann Premack (2003) *Original Intelligence: Unlocking the Mysteries of Who We Are* (New York: McGraw-Hill).

Preston, John, ed. (2021) *Interpreting Mach: Critical Essays* (Cambridge: Cambridge University Press).

Pufendorf, Samuel (2005) *Of the Law of Nature and Nations*, 4th edn, trans. Basil Kennett (Clark, NJ: Law Book Exchange).

Pynchon, Thomas (2013) *Bleeding Edge* (New York: Penguin).

Rappaport Hovav, Malka, and Beth Levin (2008) 'The English dative alternation: The case for verb sensitivity', *Journal of Linguistics* 44, 1, pp. 129–67.

Reich, Robert B. (1991) *The Work of Nations: Preparing Ourselves for 21st Century Capitalism* (New York: Alfred Knopf).

Reich, Simon, and Richard N. Lebow (2014) *Good-Bye Hegemony! Power and Influence in the Global System* (Princeton: Princeton University Press).

Reich, Simon, and Richard N. Lebow (2017) 'Influence and hegemony: Shifting patterns of material and social power in world politics', *All Azimuth* 6, 1, pp. 17–47.

Rejali, Darius M. (1994) *Modernity and Torture: Self, Society, and State in Modern Iran* (Boulder, CO: Westview Press).

Rescher, Nicholas (1978) *Scientific Progress: A Philosophical Essay on the Economics of Research in Natural Science* (Pittsburgh: University of Pittsburgh Press).

Richter, Daniel K. (1992) *The Ordeal of the Longhouse: The Peoples of the Iroquois League in the Era of European Colonization* (Chapel Hill: University of North Carolina Press).

Riggs, Fred W. (1961) 'International relations as a prismatic system', *World Politics* 14, 1, pp. 144–81.

Rochester, J. Martin (1974) *International Institutions and World Order: The International System as a Prismatic Polity* (Beverly Hills, CA: Sage).

Rosecrance, Richard N. (1963) *Action and Reaction in World Politics: International Systems in Perspective* (Boston: Little, Brown).

Rosenau, James N., ed. (1969) *International Politics and Foreign Policy*, 2nd edn (New York: Free Press).

Rosenau, James N. (1972) *The Dramas of Political Systems: An Introduction to the Problems of Governance* (North Scituate, MA: Duxbury Press).

Rosenau, James N. (1974) *Citizenship between Elections: An Inquiry into the Mobilizable American* (New York: Free Press).

Rosenau, James N. (1980) *The Scientific Study of Foreign Policy*, rev. edn (London: Frances Pinter).

Rosenau, James N. (1986) 'Before cooperation: Hegemons, regimes, and habit-driven actors in world politics', *International Organization* 40, 4, pp. 849–94.

Rosenau, James N. (1989) 'The scholar as an adaptive system', in Joseph Kruzel and James N. Rosenau, eds, *Journeys through World Politics: Autobiographical Reflections of Thirty-four Academic Travelers* (Lexington, MA: Lexington Books), pp. 53–67.

Rosenau, James N. (1990) *Turbulence in World Politics: A Theory of Change and Continuity* (Princeton: Princeton University Press).

Rosenau, James N., ed. (1993) *Global Voices: Dialogues in International Relations* (Boulder, CO: Westview Press).

Rosenau, James N. (1997) *Along the Domestic-Foreign Frontier: Exploring Governance in a Turbulent World* (Cambridge: Cambridge University Press).

Rosenau, James N., and Mary Durfee (1995) *Thinking Theory Thoroughly: Coherent Approaches to an Incoherent World* (Boulder, CO: Westview Press).

Rossi, Christopher R. (2021) *Remoteness Reconsidered: The Atacama Desert and International Law* (Ann Arbor: University of Michigan Press).

Ruggie, John Gerard (1983) 'Continuity and transformation in the world polity: Toward a neorealist synthesis', *World Politics* 35, 2, pp. 261–85.

Ruggie, John Gerard (1998) *Constructing the World Polity: Essays on International Institutionalization* (London: Routledge).

Ruthven, Malise (1978) *Torture: The Grand Conspiracy* (London: Weidenfeld & Nicolson).

Said, Edward (1993) *Culture and Imperialism* (New York: Alfred Knopf).

Scarry, Elaine (1985) *The Body in Pain: The Making and Unmaking of the World* (New York: Oxford University Press).

Schmitter, Philippe C. (1974) 'Still the century of corporatism?' *Review of Politics* 36, 1, pp. 84–128.

Schumpeter, Joseph A. (1939) *Business Cycles*, 1 (New York: McGraw-Hill).

Schumpeter, Joseph A. (1942) *Capitalism, Socialism and Democracy* (New York: Harper).

Scott, George Ryley (2003) *The History of Torture throughout the Ages* (London: Kegan Paul).

Scott, James C. (1998) *Seeing Like a State: How Certain Schemes to Improve the Human Condition Have Failed* (New Haven: Yale University Press).

Searle, John R. (2010) *Making the Social World: The Structure of Human Civilization* (Oxford: Oxford University Press).

Sellars, Willard (1956) 'Empiricism and the philosophy of mind', *Minnesota Studies in the Philosophy of Science* 1, 19, pp. 253–329.

Service, Elman R. (1975) *Origins of the State and Civilization: The Process of Cultural Evolution* (New York: Norton).

Shapiro, Michael J. (1989) 'Textualizing global politics', in James Der Derian and Michael J. Shapiro, eds, *International/Intertextual Relations: Postmodern Readings of World Politics* (Lexington, MA: Lexington Books), pp. 11–22.

Sharp, Paul, and Geoffrey Wiseman, eds (2007) *The Diplomatic Corps as an Institution in International Society* (New York: Palgrave Macmillan).

Shue, Henry (2006) 'Torture', reprinted with elisions in Sanford Levinson, ed., *Torture: A Collection*, revised edn (Oxford: Oxford University Press), pp. 47–59.

Simon, Herbert A. (1957) *Models of Man: Social and Rational* (New York: Wiley).

Simon, Julian L. (1981) *The Ultimate Resource* (Princeton: Princeton University Press).

Skinner, Quentin, ed. (1985) *The Return of Grand Theory in the Social Sciences* (Cambridge: Cambridge University Press).

Skinner, Quentin (1996) *Reason and Rhetoric in the Philosophy of Hobbes* (Cambridge: Cambridge University Press).

Skinner, Quentin (1998) *Liberty before Liberalism* (Cambridge: Cambridge University Press).

Smith, Adam (1984) *The Theory of Moral Sentiments* (Indianapolis: Liberty Fund).

Snow, C. P. (1993) *The Two Cultures* (Cambridge: Cambridge University Press).

Stinchcombe, Arthur L. (1968) *Constructing Social Theories* (New York: Harcourt, Brace & World).

Sunstein, Cass R. (2014) *Why Nudge? The Politics of Libertarian Paternalism* (New Haven: Yale University Press).

Sweezy, Paul M., and Charles Bettelheim (1971) *The Transition to Socialism* (New York: Monthly Review Press).

Tomasello, Michael (2003) *Constructing a Language: A Usage-Based Theory of Language Acquisition* (Cambridge, MA: Harvard University Press).

Treaties of Münster and Onasbrück, 24 October 1648, in *Acta Pacis Westphalicae*, available at: {http://www.pax-westphalica.de/ipmipo/index.html}

United Nations, 'Convention against Torture and Other Cruel, Inhuman or Degrading Treatment or Punishment', 10 December 1984.

United Nations, 'Declaration on Environment and Development', Conference on Environment and Development, 3–14 June 1992, A/CONF.151/26, 1, Annex 1.

United Nations, '2005 World Summit Outcome', General Assembly Resolution 60/1, 16 September 2005.

van Ham, Peter (2010) *Social Power in International Politics* (Abingdon: Routledge).

Walker, R. B. J. (1993) *Inside/Outside: International Relations as Political Theory* (Cambridge: Cambridge University Press).

Walker, R. B. J. (2009) *After the Globe, Before the World* (Abingdon: Routledge).

Wallerstein, Immanuel (1974) *The Modern World-System: Capitalist Agriculture and the Origins of the European World-Economy in the Sixteenth Century* (New York: Academic Press).

Wallerstein, Immanuel (1974) 'The rise and future demise of the world capitalist system: Concepts for comparative analysis', *Comparative Studies in Society and History* 16, 4, pp. 387–415.

Waltz, Kenneth N. (1975) 'Theory of international relations', in F. I. Greenstein and Nelson W. Polsby, eds, *International Politics* (Reading, MA: Addison-Wesley), pp. 1–85.

Waltz, Kenneth N. (1979) *Theory of International Politics* (Reading, MA: Addison-Wesley).

Wanninski, Jude (1978) 'Taxes, revenues and the "Laffer curve"', *Public Interest* 50, pp. 3–16.

Weber, Max (1930) *The Protestant Ethic and the Spirit of Capitalism*, trans. Talcott Parsons (New York: Scribner's).

Weltman, John J. (1973) *Systems Theory in International Relations* (Lexington, MA: Lexington Books).

Wendt, Alexander E. (1987) 'The agent-structure problem in international relations theory', *International Organization* 41, 3, pp. 335–70.

Wendt, Alexander (1991) 'Bridging the theory/meta-theory gap in International Relations', *Review of International Studies* 17, 4, pp. 383–92.

Wendt, Alexander (1992) 'Anarchy is what states make of it: The social construction of power politics', *International Organization* 46, 2, pp. 391–425.

Wendt, Alexander (1999) *Social Theory of International Politics* (Cambridge: Cambridge University Press).

Wendt, Alexander, and Raymond Duvall (1989) 'Institutions and international order', in Ernst-Otto Czempiel and James N. Rosenau, eds, *Global Changes and Theoretical Challenges: Approaches to World Politics for the 1990s* (Lexington, MA: Lexington Books), pp. 51–73.

Wesson, Robert G. (1978) *State Systems: International Pluralism, Politics, and Culture* (New York: Free Press).

Wight, Colin (2006) *Agents, Structures and International Relations: Politics as Ontology* (Cambridge: Cambridge University Press).

Wight, Martin (1960) 'Why is there no international theory?', *International Relations* 2, 1, pp. 35–48.

Wight, Martin (1968) 'Why is there no international theory?', in Herbert Butterfield and Martin Wight, eds, *Diplomatic Investigations: Essays in the Theory of International Politics* (Cambridge, MA: Harvard University Press), pp. 17–34.

Wight, Martin (1977) *Systems of States*, ed. Hedley Bull (Leicester: Leicester University Press).

Wittgenstein, Ludwig (1968) *Philosophical Investigations*, 3rd edn, trans. G. E. M. Anscombe (Oxford: Basil Blackwell).

Woolf, L. S. (1916) *International Government: Two Reports* (New York: Brentano's).

Young, Margaret A. (2012) *Regime Interaction in International Law* (Cambridge: Cambridge University Press).

Young, Oran R. (1968) *A Systemic Approach to International Politics*, Research Monograph No. 33, Center of International Studies, Princeton University.

Young, Oran R. (1968) *Systems of Political Science* (Englewood Cliffs, NJ: Prentice-Hall, 1968).

Young, Oran R. (1972) 'The actors in world politics', in James N. Rosenau, Vincent Davis, and Maurice A. East, eds, *The Analysis of International Politics: Essays in Honor of Harold and Margaret Sprout* (New York: Free Press), pp. 125–44.

Zimmerling, Ruth (2005) *Influence and Power: Variations on a Messy Theme* (Dordrecht: Springer).

Zinnes, Dina A. (1980) 'Prerequisites to the study of system transformation', in Ole R. Holsti, Randolph M. Siverson, and Alexander L. George, eds, *Change in the International System* (Boulder, CO: Westview Press), pp. 3–21.

Index of Names

Index of Concepts

Concepts constitute theories; theorists must decide on which concepts to start with and where to take them; theorizing inevitably affects chosen concepts. For a volume laced with a great many concepts, constructing an index specifically and exclusively devoted to them is a Sisyphean task—all the more when those concepts make repeated appearances, reveal multiple meanings, and refer to each other in complex, recurrent patterns. In constructing *this* index myself, I could not hope to situate the many concepts that I have put to use either topically or theoretically, much less identify shifts in tone and thrust or map a profusion of links and levels. Instead, this index marks the occasions in which discussion introduces, turns on, or develops the concepts listed below.

Printed in the USA
CPSIA information can be obtained
at www.ICGtesting.com
JSHW061919010324
58416JS00004B/38